Money in
American Politics

ALSO BY RICHARD LAWRENCE MILLER

Lincoln and His World:
Volume 4, The Path to the Presidency, 1854–1860
(McFarland, 2012)

Lincoln and His World:
Volume 3, The Rise to National Prominence, 1843–1853
(McFarland, 2011)

Money in American Politics

The First 200 Years

Richard Lawrence Miller

McFarland & Company, Inc., Publishers
Jefferson, North Carolina

ISBN (print) 978-1-4766-8408-6
ISBN (ebook) 978-1-4766-4180-5

Library of Congress and British Library
cataloguing data are available

Library of Congress Control Number 2021007004

Printed in the United States of America

McFarland & Company, Inc., Publishers
Box 611, Jefferson, North Carolina 28640
www.mcfarlandpub.com

To Nancy,
with thanks

Table of Contents

Preface

Do you care about money? Has it ever influenced your desires or job performance? If so, you're in distinguished company. Over the years, persons who ran our government were affected by money just as the rest of us were. Michael Blumenthal (Carter Treasury) was crass but perceptive when he declared, "Nothing works if you don't make money."[1] Building the transcontinental railroad, winning World War II, and landing humans on the moon involved ingenuity, sacrifice, and spirituality. But without money no manufacturer would deliver locomotives to Union Pacific. In World War II great corporations made airplanes and battleships for money, not from patriotism. Project Apollo was started by money, not by politicians and engineers.

Assorted White House officials have worried about meeting mortgage payments, holding off creditors, and avoiding bankruptcy. Others made fortunes by devoting much time to supervising their business interests while running the government. Yet some business interests of Presidents and cabinet members are hidden from the public.

In school, students are taught about governmental principles underlying political controversies. Instructors seldom talk about money that Presidents and cabinet members stood to gain or lose, depending on who prevailed in a political dispute. Perhaps this book will help fill gaps in that knowledge. To ignore the business activities of our leaders is to ignore most of their adult lives. Having such awareness allows us to see motivations in government decisions that may otherwise be obscure.

This book shows the profit motive at work in American history. Our story concentrates on Presidents and cabinet members, demonstrating how they and their associates gained and lost wealth, and how this affected our nation's well-being.

Where do Presidents and their cabinets come from? George Washington and Jimmy Carter didn't just emerge from the woodwork in response to their country's call. They had close ties to top businessmen who ran the economies of America and even the world. Sometimes Presidents and cabinet members were themselves powerful members of the business community. They didn't achieve such a position by ignoring financial consequences of their decisions. Our leaders were well aware of who stood to make or lose money when the White House spoke.

Such attentiveness doesn't make our leaders crooks and robbers. Government policies that aid our leaders' private prosperity may also be good for our country and the rest of the world. Yet there is danger that leaders can be led astray by self-interest. Has that ever happened to you? Have you ever lied to yourself about why you wanted to do something? Have results ever been bad?

Rich people run America. This is the pre-eminent fact of American government. Yes, a poor orphan may grow up to be President but, likely, first he or she must grow rich. We often hear of financial sacrifices endured by our leaders, implying they became poor in our service. This book will prove such stories largely incorrect. Asking whether our leaders might be affected by the same things that influence everyone else may be impolite. But answers to such queries are necessary if the people are to control our government.

This book surveys presidencies stretching from George Washington to Jimmy Carter. Subsequent presidencies certainly merit examination, but stopping at Carter may reduce the likelihood that this book might be misconstrued as a polemic in current political fights rather than a historical work. The author of this book is a historian, not an investigative reporter.

Officials of various administrations are identified thusly: (FDR AG), meaning the person served as President Franklin Roosevelt's attorney general. Involvement of an official in a business operation may precede or follow service in government; for example, a law case handled by a cabinet officer may demonstrate something about the person even though the case occurred decades before the individual held a public position. To help understand the impact of dollar amounts with which officials were dealing, the approximate 2019 buying power of the original amount may be given in parentheses. The Historical Currency Conversions web site *https://futureboy.us/fsp/dollar.fsp* was invaluable for that information.

Chapter 1

Colonial Antecedents

England viewed its American colonies as a business proposition. Most colonies were founded to make money for either an individual (such as Maryland, New York, New Jersey, and the Carolinas) or a corporation (such as Virginia and Massachusetts). The English government treated the colonists as other businessmen and employees were treated. This was fine as long as colonists viewed themselves as a business operation subservient to the English government. For a century and a half, however, the colonies had access to great wealth and received little interference from the British government. A gradual but radical change occurred. Influential colonial entrepreneurs began to think that the government was holding down profits while boosting taxes. Some Americans even suspected that the colonies didn't need the British government anyway, that these thirteen real estate operations had grown so strong that they could declare themselves autonomous sovereign states and make the world concede the point. Until then no one imagined that a business company could become an independent country.

Among the commercial enterprises which contributed to that development was the Ohio Company, organized ca. 1747 by English financiers and elite Virginians to obtain Indian trade and 500,000 acres on the Ohio River. Royal land grants to Lord Baltimore and William Penn seemed to conflict with the Ohio Company plans, but the company said it could put British settlers into the area, which would confound French ambitions for that region. The British government told the Ohio Company to go ahead.

To the London government this seemed like a sensible geopolitical action. Moreover, the move would use a private business company as a front to further government policy; if things got sticky the English government could always deny involvement.

Philadelphia fur merchants, however, were sputtering in anger. The king had given William Penn a monopoly to operate in the Ohio country, and now the British government was unilaterally canceling that business contract. Philadelphia fur merchants gave hardly a thought to sending out agents to rile up Ohio country Indians, turning the native population against the Virginia real estate operators. The fur merchants succeeded too well, creating an atmosphere where French operatives could encourage the Indians to attack Virginians in the Ohio region.

George Washington's brother was president of the Ohio Company. The Washington family, Lord Halifax (who owned much of Virginia), and Virginia governor Robert Dinwiddie had an informal alliance in business and government. Taking note of Frenchmen moving into the Ohio country, Dinwiddie urged the Virginia legislature to provide funds for frontier defense in the name of freedom and Protestantism. The legislature patriotically complied, and Dinwiddie and the other Ohio Company partners breathed easier. If the French got a strong foothold in the Ohio country, the company would fail. All the money invested in it might never come back.

Personal finances of Virginia's leaders weren't a publicized factor in recruiting soldiers to confront the French. Poor people who comprise an army may have great respect for His Excellency, but might grow unruly if they realized they were dying to protect his pocketbook. The facts, however, were well known among leadership circles in Williamsburg, Philadelphia, London, and Paris. Governor Dinwiddie knew that the Philadelphians had riled up the Indians in the first place, and that the native population might listen if the Philadelphians changed their story. Perhaps the Philadelphia fur traders were now a bit uneasy themselves; in a firefight the French-allied Indians might not distinguish between Pennsylvanians and Virginians. William Trent, business partner of Philadelphia's and America's most famous citizen Benjamin Franklin, agreed to go into the Ohio country for Governor Dinwiddie. Trent's mission was to contact the French and politely ask them to leave the Ohio region so the Ohio Company could operate freely. Trent aborted the mission when he learned the Frenchmen were in no mood to receive such a message. Dinwiddie then sent a man with a large personal stake in the outcome (which helps any mission succeed). Dinwiddie sent Major George Washington.

Washington went all the way to Fort LeBoef and confronted the French in their stronghold. One can imagine the scene. A mass of grizzled French woodsmen and Indian allies, fingering guns and knives, surround a 22-year-old kid who explains that a piece of paper in London says his brother owns all this land, so would you squatters leave now. Please.

The mission failed. Dinwiddie then appointed Trent as a captain and authorized him to immediately enlist 100 fellow traders and frontiersmen. Maj. George Washington was promoted to lieutenant colonel and told to recruit another 100 men. The Virginians had tried approaching the Frenchmen with a smile. Now the Virginians came back with a smile and a gun, a combination the French found much more persuasive. When the guns and tomahawks finished their work, the Virginians and the Ohio Company had won a great military victory. They had also started the French and Indian War. This was the first global war.

England came close to losing. Although England won in the end, leaders both in the British Isles and the American colonies were left outraged. London was angry that businessmen in Philadelphia and Williamsburg had bumbled into a war with France. England had to spend a lot of money to fight the war, and at the conflict's end still had to find another £130,000,000 (over $23 billion in 2019 buying power) somewhere to finish paying war contractors. London decided if the colonists started the war, they could at least pay part of the tab. Americans, however, looked at the vast territory that England got from France in the peace treaty (everything east of the Mississippi River, from the North Pole to the Gulf of Mexico, except New Orleans) and felt London should be satisfied. And there was more.

London tended to view the colonies as one entity, America Inc. The colonies shared no such feeling of unification, and instead thought of themselves as thirteen independent operations. New Yorkers were angered about being taxed for a war provoked by Virginians, but resentment was directed toward London, rather than Virginia, because London was presenting the bill.

Britain was in no mood to fight another war on the American frontier. England felt this geopolitical interest for peace required friendly relations with Indians. Since settlers moving into Indian lands upset the native residents, England banned settlers west of the Appalachians. This decree ignored an important fact. British (including colonial) soldiers who fought the French and Indian War had been promised land as an enlistment bonus. Acting as the veterans' claims agent, George Washington got London to set aside 200,000 acres for the enlistment bonus. The land came from the Walpole Grant, a ruined scheme of Benjamin Franklin. Once again a Virginian was profiting at a Philadelphian's expense. The land that Washington chose for the veterans was lush, beautiful to behold, and west of the Appalachian mountains. Veterans were delighted until England's geopolitical decree came down. Technically the British government had complied with the contract it had made with war recruits, but the performance smacked of double-cross. In addition, veterans had to pay taxes on the land. Since the vets couldn't settle on the property and make it productive, they had to sell out to avoid debtor prison. And since no one could use the property, the price had to be cheap, and the buyer would be a wealthy speculator. Perhaps no veteran thought to ask whether Colonel Washington's excellent sources of information within the Virginian and British governments might have tipped him off to the decree before it was publicly announced. It is uncontested that the real estate Washington got for the veterans was in an area he himself coveted. He personally surveyed the area and thereby learned where the choice acreage was. After the settler ban decree was issued, Washington furtively acquired tens of thousands of acres from veterans. Since he made other large real estate purchases openly, one wonders why he took pains to act secretly in acquiring the veterans' land.[2]

By 1763, at the end of the French and Indian War, provoked by the Washington family's business interests, the Americans and the British were disgusted with each other's behavior. Disputes involved impairment of contracts, taxation, representation in the national legislature, and uses of land. These matters would be among the first that the future United States government would deal with.

George Washington remained interested in frontier land. His activities violated British law and eventually almost started a war between Virginia and Pennsylvania.[3] In concert with British cabinet member Thomas Cummings, who moved in the same circles as Lord Shelburne (a key member of the British Board of Trade which was the government division in charge of colonial affairs), Washington and associates tried to acquire all of Illinois and parts of what became Minnesota, Wisconsin, Iowa, Missouri, Tennessee, Indiana, and Arkansas. Washington worked on this gigantic land scheme up to 1772 but had to give up—foiled by the British government. He did acquire other tracts west of the Appalachians, tracts whose titles (ownership papers) and value were limited by the British ban on settlers. Washington thereby stood to profit if the Revolution succeeded. This was known at the time.

In 1764, the year after England forbade settlers west of the Appalachians, Parliament passed the Sugar Act which added a new tax and hindered the colonial marine industry. This was bad for Washington's relative Isaac Roosevelt, whose great great grandson would be President Franklin Roosevelt. The Sugar Act also confounded marine traders such as the father of Henry Knox (Washington War), the father-in-law of Timothy Pickering (Washington War and State), the brother of Washington's relative Robert Smith (Jefferson Navy), Washington's relative Benjamin Crowinshield (Madison and Monroe Navy), and Washington's relative Elbridge Gerry (Madison VP). Gerry's large marine operation would secretly funnel Spanish government aid to the Revolution.

Soon after passage of the Sugar Act, England began to extend and strictly enforce the Navigation Acts. These were a series of laws that began over a century earlier. London regarded the Acts as mutually beneficial for colonists and the home island. In particular the Acts granted colonists a monopoly within the empire for a long list of goods and also in their trans-Atlantic transportation. This monopoly benefited colonial businessmen. Many, however, found the monopoly irksome because it practically forbade direct trade with other countries. For example, in theory a Georgia businessman in the West Indies trade might have to ship goods from Cuba all the way to England, pay customs duty there, and then send the goods across the stormy Atlantic again in order to get to Georgia. As years passed, fewer and fewer colonial businessmen bothered with this roundabout method, and instead shipped direct from Cuba to Georgia. Americans viewed this practice as common sense. London viewed this as ingrates turning to smuggling.

Tobacco was one product that Americans could export to England and nowhere else, limiting business opportunities of planters such as George Washington, the father of his relative James Madison, Washington's relative Thomas Jefferson, and Patrick Henry's relative John Breckinridge (Jefferson AG). Paper was another listed item, affecting booksellers such as Henry Knox (Washington War), who also sold wallpaper and stationery, and did printing and binding. The Navigation Acts also included sugar, tea, rice, molasses, naval stores, hemp, indigo, glass, paint, lead, copper ore, pig iron, beaver pelts, deerskins, and enough other items to affect every businessman in America.

Another aspect of the Navigation Acts eventually ruined Thomas Jefferson. The Acts were intended to prevent British specie from flowing to America through trade. Even importing British specie or minting colonial money was illegal. To conduct trade in such circumstances, American businessmen devised an elaborate system of IOUs. British commercial houses habitually refused such American IOUs as payment of American debts. Jefferson's father-in-law owed probably over £3,700 to William Jones of Bristol, England (his firm was later called Farrell & Jones). The father-in-law's death stuck Jefferson with this debt. How this responsibility for payment became Jefferson's obligation is unclear, as bankruptcy laws existed. Perhaps Jefferson cosigned notes. Whatever the reason Jefferson became liable. He tried to extinguish the obligation through big sales of his land. Purchasers gave Jefferson IOUs, which was standard business practice in America. Jefferson offered the IOUs to Farrell & Jones, but the firm refused to accept them. So Jefferson was now without the land but still stuck with all the debt. Because he lost the land, after the Revolution he had no way of paying the debt, which was still binding. Interest charges had increased the responsibility to over £4,500 in 1794 ($634,000 in 2019 buying power), plus £2,000 owed to Henderson, McCaul & Co. Jefferson was obsessed by all this debt while he was a member of Washington's cabinet and was still trying to pay it off in 1800, the year he was elected President.

As mentioned above, London was peeved by American colonists who traded directly with foreign countries without first shipping the goods to

England. London called this smuggling, which indeed it was, since customs officers were bypassed (partly to avoid tariffs, but partly because customs officers would of course turn in the American merchants as criminals for taking the transit shortcut). Top colonial businessmen didn't like being called criminals (which they were), but weren't about to abide by laws that would hinder their business. When lawlessness becomes common among a society's leaders, a drastic change of government is in the making. London was blind to this, however. Its officials invented "writs of assistance." These let customs officers have "no knock" entry into buildings without having to name any witness of criminality to justify such entries. This enraged the American business community, and is a reason why the U.S. Constitution requires search warrants. Civil liberties protect businesses.

Boston was a big marine trade town with many warehouses. In 1770 resentments spilled into the streets, with angry colonists confronting a detachment of British army soldiers who tried to suppress the riot. History calls the confrontation the Boston Massacre. Several troops who fired on the crowd were indicted for following their captain's orders, and he was charged with murder. Washington's relative John Adams agreed to defend the British soldiers in court. He was a top "Establishment" lawyer—attorney for Plymouth Company, which sponsored the first settlement in Massachusetts, and he eventually handled the colony's richest clients. He was a natural choice for the soldiers to use. Adams leaped at the chance to advertise his lawyer skills and thereby pick up more clients. Another reason he defended the troops was because his relative Samuel Adams asked him to. Sam had helped fire up the mob that provoked the shooting, and he wanted to be sure the soldiers' lawyer could be trusted to play down that aspect of the killings. John was sympathetic to the rebels, and skillful enough at law to represent the interests of both Sam (secretly) and the soldiers (publicly) without betraying either of them. The captain was found innocent, and two troopers received mild punishment for manslaughter.

Sam later organized the Boston Tea Party. This event provoked London to close the port of Boston (enraging the colony's top businessmen) and force homeowners to let British troops live in the homes (enraging wealthy families so much that the U.S. Constitution forbade the practice). Other colonies wondered when some incident would cause London to do the same, or worse, to them. London officials and American businessmen lost patience with each other, and the Revolutionary War broke out.

Revolution

The Revolution wasn't forced on the American people by businessmen promoting selfish interests. Businessmen, however, provided leadership.

This is one reason the American Revolution took a path different from the French Revolution or Russian Revolution.

In wars, as in anything else, some ways of making money are legitimate, and some are unsavory.

In the marine industry one approach was privateering, distinguished from piracy by a piece of paper. George Washington tried to get into Revolutionary privateering, and Henry Knox (Washington War) succeeded. Timothy Pickering's (Washington State) brother-in-law was partner in the Revolutionary privateers *Black Prince*, *Pickering*, and *Lion*. Washington's relatives Robert Smith (Jefferson Navy) and Elbridge Gerry (Madison VP) were each involved in Revolutionary privateering. Gerry's marine trade provided valuable aid to the Revolution. He would send to Spain ships loaded with fish, and returning vessels would be full of war materiel. Part of the cargo would be from the Spanish government, and thus already the property of the American Continental government. Part would be war goods that Gerry bought in Spain for resale to the Revolutionary Army at a profit. At times materiel already belonging to the Continental government seems to have gotten mixed in with items Gerry was selling. During the Revolution, the father of Washington's relative Benjamin Crowinshield (Madison Navy) was part owner of a ship that supplied the British in the West Indies.

Timothy Pickering (Washington State) was the Revolutionary Army's quartermaster general, a job which he probably expected to help his Philadelphia commission merchant business after the war. Jeremiah Wadsworth was commissary general for all Continental forces. He made a lot of money from commissions. In 1779 he resigned and set up a secret private business arrangement with Henry Knox's (Washington War) friend Commissary General Nathaniel Greene. The brother of Robert Smith (Jefferson Navy) was a Continental Navy purchasing agent who sold to France some wheat and flour desired by Continental troops. The grandfather of Gideon Welles (Lincoln Navy) also supplied the French, but Wadsworth and Alexander Hamilton's (Washington Treasury) close associate John Church were the big suppliers to French land forces. Church used the alias "Carter" in this arrangement and may have been involved in corrupting the French army commissary. In addition to Continental Army supply contracts, one of the partners' subcontractors was also seeking British army supply contracts. Hamilton's relative William Duer (Washington Asst Treasury) wrote Church a letter of introduction to Hamilton's father-in-law Gen. Phillip Schuyler. In October 1780 Church told Wadsworth to have Schuyler kill a plan that would reduce the partners' profits. Schuyler's response is unknown, but the plan died. Continental Army quartermaster general Timothy Pickering (Washington State) worked closely with Wadsworth in all this.

In 1782 Washington's relative Robert Morris gave Wadsworth and Church a contract to supply Continental forces around West Point, in addition to the French business. Alexander Hamilton's relative John R. Livingston was also involved. The scale of Church's operation is illustrated by his dealings on just one day, March 5, 1783. On that day Church made over 100 percent profit on sales to Daniel Parker, Church's biggest flour subcontractor. The same day Church also got half the profits from Robert Morris on an operation involving bills of exchange for 73,000 livres. Years later Church loaned Morris money which Morris was unable to repay. Church had his business agent Alexander Hamilton (Washington Treasury) start legal action that helped send Morris to debtor prison, a miserable end for someone who served his country as Superintendent of Finance under the Articles of Confederation.

Hamilton's father-in-law Philip Schuyler was an Albany, NY, businessman who, after becoming a major general, sold supplies to Continental forces, while influencing purchases of the Northern Department. Robert Morris, who worked informally as a de facto Secretary of the Treasury before that office was created, was peeved that Schuyler's commission charges were twice the normal rate. Schuyler also assisted the family of Edward Livingston (Jackson State) in many business deals and gave army contract business to William Duer (Washington Asst Treasury). Duer's massive military contracts sometimes involved the Livingstons. During the Revolution, the father of James K. Paulding (Van Buren Navy) was commissary for the New York militia. Toward the war's end Benjamin Franklin's relative Alexander Dallas (Madison Treasury) shared a Philadelphia boarding house with a commissioner who was closing out the affairs of the Continental Army's commissary and quartermaster departments, putting Dallas in an excellent position to make business deals based on insider information. Duer, Robert Morris, and Schuyler were business allies of French general Lafayette.

Frontier Real Estate

When the Revolutionary War ended, so did the British ban on settlers west of the Appalachians. What was later known as the American Upper Midwest was called the Northwest Territory. Congress immediately expedited purchases of Northwest Territory frontier land by wealthy speculators. A new Ohio Company was organized. Despite the same name, this new Ohio Company was completely different from the Washington family company that provoked the French and Indian War. Although President George Washington had no financial interest in the new company, his actions affected it. For instance in 1792 Congress authorized him to grant over 1,000,000 acres to the Ohio Company. Alexander Hamilton (Washington Treasury) owned a small part of the company—5½ shares entitling him to between 690 and 1,230 acres. As Secretary of the Treasury, Hamilton was supposed to decide the validity of some Ohio Company western grants. He declined due to his involvement in the company, and asked the Attorney General to decide. Nonetheless Hamilton stood to profit from settling the frontier. His relative William Duer (Washington Asst Treasury) stood to gain far more, as he got 100,000 acres from Ohio Company in return for giving the company a share of the profits from sales of that acreage to Europeans. Duer helped found Scioto Company to handle sales even though it owned no land. The company specialized in marketing tracts to Europeans "sight unseen." The two companies quarreled, leaving many settlers without a title to their land, making them squatters even though they had paid Scioto Company. Duer and Henry Knox (Washington War) shared big real estate interests in Maine, and Duer offered to sell some of this property to persons who had been cheated by his Scioto Company. Knox was a friend of Theophile Casenove, president of the Holland Land Company which ruled much of New York state. Casenove was on the fringes of the Scioto Company, and Knox may have secretly been a key figure in Scioto. Negotiations between Scioto and the national government were handled by the Board of Treasury, whose three members were Hamilton's relative Walter Livingston, Washington's relative Arthur Lee, and Samuel Osgood (Washington PG). Osgood, who had real estate dealings with Duer, was fully aware of the company's plans.

Another Northwest Territory real estate operation belonged to Albert Gallatin (Jefferson Treasury) and a partner. They bought 120,000 acres on the Ohio River, opened a store and land office, and by selling only a fraction of the property quickly recovered three-fourths of the purchase price. The partners planned to give away 24,000 acres to settlers in order to increase the remainder's value. Their project was near George Washington's Ohio country lands, and he discovered Gallatin during a foray against settlers squatting on Washington's land. Impressed with the young man, Washington invited him to be the general's land agent in the area. Gallatin declined, since his own project was a full-time job. During Washington's presidency Gallatin sold much of his land to Washington's relative Robert Morris who assigned the land to Thomas Willing, president of the Bank of the United States. Morris went broke before paying Gallatin for the land, causing Gallatin to lose both the payment and the land itself. As Secretary of the Treasury Gallatin still owned land in Northwest Territory and promoted settlement of the area. In the end, however, he described his decades of Western activity as troublesome and unprofitable.

President Washington promised to give a Northwest Territory patronage job to his relative William Henry Harrison but left office before a suitable vacancy occurred. When Washington's relative John Adams succeeded the general as President, Adams made good on the promise of his predecessor and appointed Harrison secretary of Northwest Territory. He later became governor and eventually President of the United States. As governor Harrison was involved in various land deals, particularly in a settlement started by Daniel Boone's brother. For years Harrison's business associate John Findlay headed the Cincinnati federal land office, where collecting mandatory fees on land transactions was virtually a license to mint money. Harrison's father-in-law John Cleves Symmes was one of the Northwest Territory's biggest real estate operators. He may have helped Harrison get land illegally.[4] As a member of the U.S. House of Representatives Committee on Public Lands, Harrison dealt with legalities of Symmes's land claims and refused to begin legal actions against him despite the territorial legislature's instructions to do so.

As the topic of "instructions" has arisen, let us momentarily digress about that topic which is important but little-known today. In the 1800s legislatures or public meetings could call upon elected officials to do something. By custom the official had to obey the instruction or resign. This gave the population substantial control over elected officials. If the custom still existed, government policy might be very different than it is now.

Constitution

The Northwest Territory was organized when the national government operated under the Articles of Confederation. They worked fine for disposing of frontier real estate. Frontiersmen and rural aristocrats were quite satisfied with the Articles. Although the United States is often portrayed as in chaotic condition under the Articles, just about the only persons who noticed chaos were businessmen involved in non-agricultural interstate trade. One such businessman was George Washington.

In the 1770s Washington urged his relative Thomas Johnson, governor of Maryland, to help form a public company to aid navigation on the Potomac River. Baltimore interests feared the project and stymied it. Washington then turned to private enterprise. He and another person were trying to raise £30,000 to start the project when the Revolution intervened. Afterward Thomas Jefferson and James Madison urged their relative Washington to head Potomac River development. In 1785 Maryland and Virginia authorized formation of Potomac Company. Washington's relative John Marshall (Adams State) joined the unanimous vote in the Virginia legislature.

Eminent domain was granted to the company along with perpetual tolls authority. All profits and property were owned by company shareholders, a group Marshall soon joined. This helped form the future Chief Justice's ideas on relations between corporations and government. In Maryland former governor Thomas Johnson led the measure through the legislature. He became a company director, and Washington later appointed him to the U.S. Supreme Court. Washington was Potomac Company president. He invested $10,000 (worth $253,000 in 2019 buying power) in twenty-four shares of stock but refused a salary or bonus stock as company president. The Virginia legislature later gave him another fifty shares. The company's work boosted the value of Western lands owned by Washington and by Thomas Johnson. Johnson planned to buy land where the Great Falls canal would have to go through, but his relative "Light Horse" Harry Lee beat him to it. Lee bought the 500 acres in 1788 for £4,000. He invited Robert Morris and James Madison to be partners. Madison joined at Washington's urging. Madison's money was already tied up with Mohawk Valley land speculation in New York state, so as his contribution to the Potomac operation he wrote publicity for Lee's enterprise instead of contributing money. Two years later, however, Lee needed funds from Madison to help pay £3,000 of old Virginia currency still owed to George William Fairfax on the deal. Having no money to invest, Madison withdrew from the partnership.

Potomac Company offered above average pay to workers clearing away Shenandoah Falls, but laborers felt the sum was inadequate. Washington presided over a hearing into the matter. When employees threatened a strike, all free laborers were fired. Slave labor exclusively was used from then on.

Potomac Company was an interstate corporation working under the jurisdiction of Virginia and Maryland. Occasional divergence of views between the two governments was enhanced by the emphasis the Articles of Confederation put on states' rights. Lack of executive and judicial branches in the national government further hindered interstate commerce, making debt collections difficult across state boundaries. State tariffs and diverse currencies complicated matters still more. Running America's first big interstate corporation, the juggling required to satisfy both Virginia and Maryland vexed Washington. Even Pennsylvania could get involved, and it had a history of antagonism with Washington. He decided something had to be done and invited a few interested persons for a chat at Mount Vernon.

The chat's outcome was a convention of businessmen from around the country who met at Annapolis, Maryland, in 1786. They shared experiences and formed an overall picture of the national business scene. Annapolis delegates were the sort of persons who knew how to get things done—men such as Alexander Hamilton (Washington Treasury), Edmund Randolph

(Washington State), and Stephen Higginson (who saved Timothy Pickering (Washington State) from real estate disaster and who was in contact with John Adams (Wash VP) regarding the convention). They decided a still bigger meeting was needed and called for a grand convention to meet at Philadelphia in May 1787 to discuss commerce and "other matters" pertaining to national government. The delegates in Philadelphia the next summer formed a definite plan to improve the country's business climate, and presented the plan as a document called the Constitution of the United States.

Predominance and influence of businessmen in the federal government ever since is thus in accord with the hopes of the Founding Fathers. Quite possibly these hopes weren't shared by many Americans in the 1700s. Property ownership qualifications and religious affiliation requirements limited suffrage. In 1790 New York City had a population of 30,000. Of that population 3,900 were qualified to vote for state representative and 1,200 for state senator. Ca. 1840 only twenty percent of the Illinois population could vote. Voter turnout is often under 100%, and elected candidates generally lack a unanimous vote, so state governments represented a distinct minority of the population. In Virginia white male citizens could vote in each county where they owned 100 acres or more, and in Virginia and elsewhere elections lasted several days. Thus a wealthy person could vote several times. In addition there was no secret ballot. Voters had to declare their choice out loud in front of candidates, sheriff, and assembled multitude. Thus small freeholders could be intimidated; it was to their benefit to publicly support their local aristocrat. In Maryland bribery of voters was legal, and indirect bribery such as free liquor was common everywhere. Even with the odds so firmly in favor of the propertied class, various state conventions called to ratify the Constitution often experienced acrimonious debate. Rural aristocrats realized the Constitution was designed to favor commerce and manufacturing, a bias that would drastically alter the nation's character. Urban interests prevailed, however, and the Constitution went into operation. Thirty-nine delegates in Philadelphia had signed the document. Thirty immediately entered the new federal government.

Chapter 2

Banks

Bankers have dominated our highest positions in government. Only railroads, real estate, and law come close to the prevalence of banking as a business background for Presidents and cabinet members. Since our governmental leaders have been top capitalists, naturally they were intimately involved with creation of capital.

George Washington was irked by America's lack of money lending institutions; he was always short of cash despite ample security for loans. As President he resolved to do something about it, not only from self-interest but because he shared Alexander Hamilton's (Washington Treasury) vision of an industrial economy rather than Thomas Jefferson's (Washington State) vision of an economy anchored in pastoral life. Washington knew America would need more money if industry were to grow, and he understood Hamilton's method of creating money from thin air. Jefferson and other Virginians clasped their gold coins ever tighter and scuttered about with dark murmurings about the Devil New Yorker. Washington just sat calmly with hands folded, and smiled.

For many years people believed that money had to be extracted from the ground in the form of precious metal. Consequently there was never enough money. The historic problem of money supply in this country has been scarcity and deflation, not inflation. Alexander Hamilton had the stunning insight that gold and silver were only symbols for money, that real money was a mental belief, not a tangible object. Therefore, Hamilton reasoned, money could be created out of thin air. Here is how he did it. First, he made sure the United States government always paid its debts. Then the government could safely go slightly into debt, as creditors knew the promise of payment was "as good as gold." Those promises were substituted for gold in big commercial transactions, with the equivalent of promissory notes passing from hand to hand. The promises were bills owed by the government. Readers of this book may have such bills, in various dollar denominations, residing in their wallets. The promises were used as money, and in fact *were* money. When more currency is needed the Treasury Department doesn't run the presses to produce more dollar bills. Instead the national debt is increased.

Hamilton kick-started the creation of money when he announced that the federal government would pay all debt owed by state governments for Revolutionary War expenses. Certificates of state debt were popular speculative items in the early Washington administration. They were worth pennies on the dollar until Hamilton made his announcement. Hamilton's relative Edward Livingston (Jackson State) bought Rhode Island debt certificates around the 1780s. Hamilton's relative Elbridge Gerry put over $49,000 into state and national securities during the Revolution. He also took such securities in payment for war supplies. Gerry supported Hamilton's full redemption policy. Around the 1780s Benjamin Stoddert (Adams Navy) jointly with another man owned at least $90,000 of depreciated securities. In 1790 Harvard University had over $100,000 of depreciated securities.

Insiders such as Hamilton's relative William Duer (Washington Asst Treasury), Hamilton's father-in-law Phillip Schuyler, and Washington's relative Robert Morris were able to make big financial killings by buying up state debt certificates after (or even before) Hamilton announced his decision to have the federal government redeem them in full. Hamilton himself conducted speculations as an agent for his relative John Church. "Big" killings refer to operations able to acquire $1,000,000 of certificates for $20,000, operations that involved express coaches and fast ships loaded with money, operations that required cooperation from Dutch bankers in raising the venture capital.

In 1788 (before the Constitution took effect) Robert Morris, William Duer, Daniel Parker, Henry Knox (Washington War), and Samuel Osgood (Washington PG) planned to buy up some of the U.S. debt to France. Osgood was then a member of the Treasury Board under the Articles of Confederation, and thus had excellent insider connections. Jean Pierre Brissot de Warville was the French connection. U.S. ambassador to France Thomas Jefferson sent warnings to the U.S. government that European speculation on the American national debt was underway. Top American officials were already aware of this speculation, of course, since they had organized it.

Banks, insurance companies, and the stock market create and destroy money. Banks produce money by giving out loans, or more precisely a bank's loan customers create money by taking on debt. The sum of a bank's loans should exceed the total deposits, and the amount of excess is the amount of money created. This is similar to the way government creates money by going into debt. Yet many persons who tremble over the federal deficit freely deposit their money in banks without a second thought.

In addition to creating money by exploiting the national debt, Hamilton was also interested in increasing the money supply through banking. He examined the experience of the Bank of England, Bank of North America, and Bank of New York.

For years President Washington and his wife collected dividends from her Bank of England stock. This is one reason Washington was more aware of banking than some of his Virginia colleagues were. He even had the sophistication to realize the role of British banks in financing English military operations in the Revolution. Washington's London merchants Robert Carey & Co. collected interest on the stock during the Revolution. Possibly they held the stock itself as a lien against £1,400 Washington owed them.

The second bank Hamilton studied was the Bank of North America. During the Revolution Washington's relative Robert Morris (the U.S. government's Superintendent of Finance, and business associate of Adams State) recommended that Congress establish a national bank, to be called the Bank of North America. Congress authorized Morris to issue stock and have bank directors elected, but then Congress decided it lacked proper authority and refused to incorporate the institution. Congress told Washington's relative Edmund Randolph (Washington AG) to explain the situation to Morris, whose reputation was at stake. Morris said Congress committed itself with the original authorization. To stop now would allow stockholders to withdraw their investments. That was a crucial point; money can overcome scruples, and with an uneasy conscience Randolph himself drew up the incorporation papers, and Congress approved the measure. By special federal law this was the only national bank not required to use the word "national" in its name.

Morris sold $50,000 (just over $1,000,000 in 2019 buying power) of stock to Dutch capitalists in 1782. Bank of New York president Jeremiah Wadsworth (Hamilton relative) had $41,000 ($955,000 in 2019 buying power) of stock the next year. Wadsworth's business partner John Church held a good-sized amount of stock. Church's and Duer's (Washington Asst Treasury and Hamilton relative) associate Daniel Parker also owned Bank of North America stock. Morris asked Hamilton's father-in-law to invest in the bank money that the government owed the father-in-law from flour sales. Ca. 1784 Bank of North America stock was making fourteen percent a year.

Morris was a Bank of North America director. Among other operations associated with this organization, Morris deposited $254,000 of national government money. Part of that was then loaned back to the government. Other early directors included Thomas Fitzsimons (real estate associate of Morris), the son-in-law of Benjamin Franklin (Ben himself was a stockholder and lived just a block from the bank), several Constitutional Convention delegates, future U.S. Supreme Court Justice James Wilson, Samuel Osgood (Wash PG), and William Bingham (father-in-law to one of the Baring brothers who ran the gigantic British Baring Brothers bank).

Ca. 1788 Washington's first Treasury Secretary Hamilton promised Bank of North America president Thomas Willing (father-in-law of William Bingham) "that in the conduct of the business of my Department it will always give me pleasure to promote that institution over which you preside." Like Washington's second Treasury Secretary Oliver Wolcott, Willing was a leader in the fund drive to pay debts of Hamilton's estate.

The bank operated for decades, attracting attention from assorted Presidents and cabinet members. In the 1790s Andrew Jackson had credit there. In 1854 Louis McLane (Jackson Treasury and State) had 100 shares, worth $14,000 ($413,000 in 2019 buying power). McLane got an annual income of $15 per share. The bank was a client of William Seward's (Lincoln State) law firm. Washington's relative Elihu Root (TR State) was a lawyer for the bank, and Root's father-in-law was a director. The firm of Root's law partner Henry Stimson (Taft War, Hoover State, FDR & Truman War) handled many cases for the bank, being joined in at least one by the Dulles (Eisenhower State) law firm.

The third bank Hamilton studied was the Bank of New York. His study was easy because he was an organizer, director, and attorney of the bank. For seven years this was a private bank until Hamilton finally got a charter through the state legislature. The original board of directors had four Tories; at least one had sold supplies to the British during the Revolution. Apparently the Bank of New York was capitalized with 1,000 shares selling for $500 apiece in gold or silver. In 1784 there were 227 shareholders having 536 shares among them. In 1791 there were 193 shareholders with 723 shares among them. This was an early example of more and more capital tending to accumulate among fewer and fewer persons.

Hamilton owned one share from ca. 1784. He got $321 in dividends on his share from November 1790 to May 1792 ($8,400 in 2019 buying power). The Bank of New York allowed Hamilton to overdraw his account, a traditional way of lending money to favored persons without requiring them to go through the process of getting a loan. Hamilton's relative John Church and Church's business partner Jeremiah Wadsworth were both directors. Wadsworth became the bank's president. George Washington's relatives Isaac Roosevelt (FDR's great great grandfather) and James Roosevelt (FDR's great grandfather) each also served as Bank of New York president.

John Church wanted to acquire control of the institution, but its charter allowed a maximum of seven votes by any one shareholder no matter how many shares the investor owned. Hamilton got the charter amended to allow one vote for every five shares above ten. Other stockholders included Hamilton's patron Nicholas Cruger and Hamilton's business competitor Aaron Burr (Jeff VP).

The brother of Edward Livingston (Jackson State) sought to charter a land bank. Such a bank used mortgages on land for capital instead of using promissory notes, bills of lading, and commercial paper. Such a bank therefore catered to rural interests and to debtors, to people uneasy about money banks. Hamilton wanted to spike Livingston's bank, fearing it would take business away from the Bank of New York and also harm New York state's commercial interests. Hamilton got merchants to work against the bank, action which started a long-standing Hamilton–Livingston rivalry. The two men were relatives, but money is thicker than blood.

In 1792 Alexander Macomb of Hamilton's SUM Corporation (about which we shall hear more) and Hamilton's relative William Duer (Washington Asst Treasury) attempted to corner stocks of the Bank of the United States and Bank of New York. Livingston (Jackson State) became involved in various banking schemes with Duer and Macomb. Livingston was particularly interested in depressing the price of Bank of New York stock. The Bank of New York, however, held a $50,000 mortgage on Livingston's property. The bank foreclosed in 1806 while Livingston was in New Orleans. That sale yielded an excess of $16.96 after satisfying the mortgage debt. Livingston also owed $100,000 to the federal government, a debt which had caused Livingston to flee from New York to New Orleans.

Competition between the Bank of New York and Bank of North America harmed the national credit. That circumstance helped bring about an informal merger of the two banks. By the 1860s the Bank of New York was the central gold depository for Wall Street gold brokers. At one time only the federal government had more gold than did the Bank of New York. Hamilton's bank remained a power in the twentieth century. For instance John Foster Dulles (Eisenhower State, relative of B. Harrison State and of Wilson State) was a Bank of New York director.

After examining experiences of the Bank of England, Bank of North America, and Bank of New York, Alexander Hamilton decided to establish the Bank of the United States (BUS). BUS was capitalized at $10,000,000—$2,000,000 from the federal government and $8,000,000 from private investors. Oliver Wolcott's (Washington Treasury) association with BUS was highly visible. He enabled Bank of New York president Jeremiah Wadsworth to buy forty-eight shares in a brisk market where some potential buyers were shut out. All the stock was bought within a few hours of going on sale.

The year 1791 saw much speculation in BUS scrip. That year Thomas Jefferson asked a correspondent,

> What do you think of this scrippomony? Ships are lying idle at the warfs, buildings are stopped, capitals withdrawn from commerce, manufactures, arts and agriculture to be employed in gambling, and the tide of public prosperity almost unparalleled in any country is arrested in its course, and suppressed by the rage of getting rich in a day. No mortal can tell where this will stop; for the spirit of gambling, when once it has seized a subject, is incurable. The tailor who had made thousands in one day, though he lost them the next, can never again be content with the slow and moderate earnings of his needle.[5]

In 1792 Washington's relative Elbridge Gerry (Madison VP) had thirty BUS shares at $400 each ($10,300 each in 2019 buying power). Hamilton's patron Nicholas Cruger owned stock. So did several delegates to the Constitutional Convention. President Washington declined to invest, feeling it unethical to profit from an institution authorized by his signature. Early directors included several Constitutional Convention delegates, Jeremiah Wadsworth, William Bingham (father-in-law of a Baring brother British banker), John M. Nesbitt (associate of Washington's relative Robert Morris), and Philip Livingston (relative of Jackson State). In 1792 three Bank of Massachusetts directors, an institution where Elbridge Gerry (Madison VP) had modest holdings, resigned and became directors of the Boston BUS branch. Joseph Habersham (Washington PG) was president of the Savannah branch. Bank of North America president Thomas Willing (father-in-law of William Bingham) became president of the central BUS.

Washington's relative Chief Justice John Marshall (Adams State) has been called a "devoted friend" of BUS. He owned four shares in 1796. Robert Morris handled Marshall's purchase of stock, offering to loan him up to $7,000. This was a fuzzy transaction, apparently involving Marshall buying four shares and returning four shares he had borrowed from a Richmond resident.

Alexander Dallas (Madison Treasury and father of Polk VP) was connected with many big money men in Philadelphia. He was a friend of Albert Gallatin (Jefferson and Madison Treasury) and of BUS president David Lenox. In 1808 Gallatin passed word to Dallas on how BUS should word its application to extend its charter, which was due to expire in 1811. Dallas passed the word to Lenox, and the request was drawn up as Gallatin recommended. The question of rechartering BUS, however, was controversial in Congress. Timothy Pickering (Washington State) voted to renew the charter, but the outcome was a tie. George Clinton (Jefferson and Madison VP) distrusted banks and cast the tie-breaking vote that ended the first BUS in 1811. This action cratered the money supply just before the War of 1812. Not until then did Washington's relative President Madison, who had always been a BUS opponent, learn the role of money in warfare. It was a hard experience for him and the country.

Whiskey Rebellion

Alexander Hamilton's determination to create money by having the government go slightly into debt and then pay it off had a drawback. Payment would not be possible without income. One source of government revenue came from sale of public lands. Another big source was tariffs. Even combining them left the federal treasury unable to cover Hamilton's plan. So he (and Congress) resorted to imposing a tax on whiskey, a widespread form of property. Transforming grain into liquor was a convenient technique for long term crop storage before modern preservation methods were invented. Farmers thus wouldn't have to sell grains when prices were low. Also they could transport liquor more economically than grain. Ostensibly at least, federal authorities thought that because such a tax would be spread across the country equally (rather than be focused on any particular region) Americans would be willing to share the burden.

Enforcing Hamilton's whiskey tax was a problem on the frontier. Part of the trouble was that no one welcomes a visit from a tax collector, poking around in a citizen's business. In addition, however, frontiersmen asked why poor people should pay the bills of a rich man's government.

Even if someone was willing to pay the tax, little or no specie was available to pay. Indeed whiskey itself was used as currency on the frontier. For example John Breckinridge used 255 gallons of whiskey to pay a debt owed to the firm Hart & Bartlett in 1805, the year he became Jefferson's Attorney General. When the Attorney General of the United States can't find enough specie to pay an obligation, frontiersmen face a hopeless task. Government agents closed their distilleries and forced frontiersmen to travel to Philadelphia for legal proceedings where they might experience one delay after another from federal courts.

Hamilton's efforts to create money weren't understood in the wilds of western Pennsylvania, near Washington's and Gallatin's land holdings. The Pennsylvanians understood very well, however, that Hamilton and Washington were putting them out of business. In 1794 a revolt known as the Whiskey Rebellion broke out.

President Washington regarded this as a serious military threat and called out the troops. He ordered Secretary of War Knox to take charge, but Knox had other things on his mind. He and Hamilton's relative William Duer (Washington Asst Treasury) had bought 3,000,000 acres in Maine. As usual in his business matters, Duer turned out to be unreliable, and two years before the Whiskey Rebellion Knox found himself suddenly owing $500,000 ($13,000,000 in 2019 buying power). Knox was so distracted by his finances during the Whiskey Rebellion that Washington let Hamilton become *de facto* Secretary of War and granted Knox a leave of absence to deal with his debts. One of Knox's first acts then was to buy several thousand acres more. Upon receiving word of difficulty in putting down the Whiskey Rebellion, Knox refused to return to Philadelphia (the U.S. capital city at the time). Knox finally returned from Maine after being gone eight weeks, overstaying his leave of absence by two weeks. Knox's conduct irked Washington, and coolness set in between them until Knox resigned.

The Whiskey Rebellion was put down, and most participants went unpunished. Several leaders were brought to trial and sentenced to prison. All were pardoned.

The next year, 1795, whiskey distilling was more profitable under the tax law. President Washington then started a comfortable whiskey business of his own. To help finance the operation, Washington sought a loan rating from the Bank of Alexandria in October 1798. His attorney general and relative Charles Lee was an incorporator of the bank, and Washington himself was a stockholder—buying twenty-five shares in 1796 for $5,000 ($94,000 in 2019 buying power). The bank said he could borrow $6,000 to $10,000 ($120,000 to $200,000 in 2019 buying power). Bank president William Herbert offered to be one of Washington's sureties for the loan. Executors of Washington's estate sold five shares of the bank's stock to Herbert for $1,200. Bank of Alexandria organizers John Fitzgerald and William Hartshorne were officers of George Washington's Potomac Company.

Society for Establishing Useful Manufactures

In the 1790s manufacturing was just beginning to be an important source of national wealth here and there in the world. Instead, the produce yielded from the land by the grace of God, was considered the main basis of national prosperity. In America this mental outlook was enhanced by the drain of raw materials from the colonies and by a British prohibition of colonial manufacturing (measures designed to help manufacturers in England). Alexander Hamilton (Washington Treasury) took a conceptual leap over his contemporaries in arguing that manufacturing, by using mechanical power largely unsusceptible to the Deity's whims, could be made the key to American wealth.

Hamilton's *Report on Manufactures* was hailed as demonstrating that industry was as vital to America as agriculture was. Hamilton urged

Congress to encourage industry to blossom. In particular the report described The Society for Useful Manufactures as worthy of support.

Hamilton and his relative William Duer planned that Society, or SUM Corporation (as Hamilton abbreviated it), in 1791. The friendly New Jersey legislature approved the corporate charter Hamilton had drafted. All of the corporation's goods and chattel were made tax exempt forever, with land and buildings exempt for ten years. Employees were exempt from all military duty and from personal taxes (tax breaks for the poor). SUM Corp. was empowered to build canals and roads, charge tolls, exercise eminent domain, and operate lotteries. A board of directors and a governor would control absolutely the thirty-six square mile "Corporation of the Town of Paterson." Duer was made governor.

SUM Corp. was intended to make paper, sail cloth, stockings, blankets, carpets, shoes, cotton, and linen. Even a brewery was planned. At least one observer feared the business enterprise was going too many directions at once, writing to Hamilton, "I repeat it, Sir, unless God should send us saints for Workmen and Angels to conduct them, there is the greatest reason to fear for the success of the plan."[6] Hamilton's correspondent suggested that SUM Corp. reduce its scope to textiles, and raid Europe for a staff, saying there should be eager emigrants due to European events. SUM agents were indeed sent to England, Ireland, and Scotland to scoop up mechanics and artisans. According to a Philadelphia newspaper the British government was so peeved that it passed laws making such recruiting a crime with heavy fine and imprisonment. (Perhaps some British officials still rankled over Washington's pre-revolutionary recruitment of settlers for his Western lands.) Hamilton himself chose workmen and superintendents. Thomas Jefferson and James Madison opposed SUM Corp. because it lured workers from agriculture, increasing the price of agricultural labor. The corporation also exploited the economic situation of the poor, hiring children for low wages. Possibly convict labor was also used. SUM Corp. conducted industrial espionage in Great Britain to get machine designs. Hamilton plugged SUM Corp. (though not by name) in his *Report on Manufactures*, with particular reference to cotton textile production, and went on to advocate measures to help the cotton textile industry.

SUM Corp. was capitalized at $1,000,000 ($26,250,000 in 2019 buying power). This exceeded the assets of all U.S. joint stock companies combined. A quarter of the amount was on hand or promised even before the charter was granted. Hamilton's prospectus said the U.S. government might help, a powerful statement from a man who regularly spoke for the President of the United States. While Secretary of the Treasury, Hamilton contacted the Bank of New York, where federal funds had been liberally deposited. Hamilton got the bank to give SUM low interest loans, on the promise that the bank would suffer no risk. Hamilton's written promise didn't explicitly guarantee government favoritism to the Bank of New York, but such an understanding would be reasonable—especially since the Treasury Secretary was the corporation's founder and the President of the United States had been living in the home of a SUM director, Alexander Macomb. Macomb and Hamilton were real estate associates. Macomb also directed the New York branch of the Bank of the United States. Henry Knox (Washington War) was a SUM stockholder. He, too, was a real estate associate of Hamilton and a close real estate partner of SUM governor William Duer (Washington Asst Treasury). Hamilton's Livingston relatives were SUM stockholders, and Benjamin Walker of Washington's Revolutionary staff was deeply involved in SUM.

Duer was an abysmal choice for SUM governor. He quickly tied the corporation into his Maine real estate speculations with Knox, promising Maine land to European artisans who would come to America for employment by SUM. Duer also speculated with SUM stock and, worse yet, used corporation money for his own speculations. Bookkeeping was soon in a shambles. Duer ruined himself and SUM with unsuccessful speculations. Afterward, in April 1792, Hamilton arranged a five percent (prime rate) loan of $10,000 ($260,000 in 2019 buying power) to SUM and designed a salvage operation. But investors eventually lost everything. After the initial flop SUM revived in a modest way as a textile enterprise with a new board of directors. SUM often squabbled with Morris Canal & Banking Company over water power. In 1885 future Vice President Garret Hobart was president of Passaic Water Company which had acquired SUM's water rights. Hamilton's SUM Corp. itself continued into the twentieth century. In 1937 the New Jersey Supreme Court reaffirmed the corporation's tax exemption. Soon after that the city of Paterson acquired SUM's stock and dissolved Hamilton's corporation.

Jay Treaty

Britain and the United States still had some unfinished business after the Revolution, regarding frontier forts, American property confiscated from British loyalists, West Indies trade, and seizure of American ships on the high seas (along with impressment of American crews into the British navy). In 1794 President Washington sent U.S. Supreme Court Chief Justice John Jay to tidy up these matters in London. Jay had distinguished himself as a diplomat when he served as Secretary of Foreign Affairs for the prior national government operating under the Articles of Confederation. So he was a natural choice for Washington to make. Despite the separation of powers in the three branches of government created by the Constitution, Supreme Court members have accepted special assignments from Presidents, such as Robert Jackson's investigation of Nazi war crimes and Earl Warren's investigation of President John Kennedy's murder. While such work didn't ruin the careers of the Justices, none of these tasks brought them acclaim.

Upon Jay's return to America he presented a treaty allowing the British to continue dealing as they pleased with Indians in U.S. territory. The treaty also let the British continue to seize American ships and crews on the high seas. Critics said Jay was not much of a negotiator. He did, however, get permission for U.S. merchants to trade in the West Indies. Jay was the son of a West Indies merchant, which may help explain his competence with that issue.

Part of his trouble in London may have been his work on an international mercantile plan at the same time. Jay invited three men to join him in the deal: Nicholas Cruger (Hamilton's old employer), Herman LeRoy, and William Bayard (who, like Jay, was both a relative and a law client of Hamilton). Since Jay expected to make £1,000,000 sterling on the deal (having a 2019 buying power of $142,000,000), one could understand if he were to be distracted during the treaty negotiations. He was attentive enough, however, to make sure that the treaty returned estates confiscated from the British Loyalist Bayards during the Revolution.

As might be expected, Jay's treaty met some skepticism. Washington's relative Edmund Randolph (Washington AG and State) was the main cabinet opponent to the treaty, which the President was hesitating to sign. To understand what happened next, one must know that Randolph was a big spender with chronic financial problems, and his money hunger was continuous. While not a crook, he had demonstrated an ability to profit from positions of trust. For example, he was on the William and Mary College board of visitors, and in 1790 he mortgaged his farm to the school for $4,000 (having $110,000 of buying power in 2019). Randolph's relative Thomas Jefferson (Washington State) refused to endorse a note for Randolph in 1793, perhaps aware that Randolph already owed money to Hamilton. Jefferson warned President Washington that Randolph's financial situation could embarrass the government if Washington appointed Randolph to succeed Jefferson in the cabinet. Jefferson was right.

England regarded the Jay Treaty as a high stakes item. In addition to commercial advantages Britain would gain, the treaty would hurt France, which was at war with England. The British knew that Randolph was widely regarded as Jefferson's creature, and Jefferson's friendly sentiments toward France were all too obvious. Indeed, Citizen Edmond Genêt, the French firebrand who was so effective at drumming up American support for

France in its war against England, was the son-in-law of Jefferson's Vice President George Clinton. The British wanted the treaty signed, and they wanted Randolph out of the cabinet. They turned to Timothy Pickering (Washington War) and Oliver Wolcott (Washington and Adams Treasury) who, along with the New England commercial interests they represented, despised Randolph and were incensed at Randolph's ability to give President Washington doubts about Jay's treaty.

The British minister to the United States handed Pickering and Wolcott a dispatch intercepted on its way to France. Pickering and Wolcott raced to President Washington. Apparently none of them paused to ask why the British would supply the American government with such an intelligence coup. Neither Washington nor Wolcott knew French, and they gratefully accepted Pickering's offer to translate. Pickering, however, didn't understand French either. His awkward labors with a dictionary combined with his hatred of Randolph to produce a botched translation suggesting that Randolph had sought funds from the French government to supplement his income. His thirst for money was well known. When Pickering presented his mistranslation to Washington, the President instantly believed it.

Washington had an awesome temper when provoked. He summoned Randolph and handed over the original French document as Pickering and Wolcott looked on. Randolph had known Washington for years and could see that his old friend was furious despite an outward façade of coolness. The façade soon dropped as Washington, Pickering, and Wolcott peppered Randolph with accusatory questions. Randolph was fluent in French and bewildered by his colleagues' reaction to the document, which actually proposed that France fund an espionage mission in the North American wilderness. Angry over the unjust accusation, and recognizing he had lost Washington's confidence, Randolph resigned. The two men were bitter, each feeling betrayed. Washington immediately signed the Jay Treaty.

XYZ Affair

George Washington's successor in the Presidency was his relative John Adams (Washington VP). President Adams appointed Washington's relative John Marshall to the cabinet and the Supreme Court. Marshall was a big real estate operator. His greatest venture was the Fairfax estate, which Marshall's father and Washington had surveyed. Marshall was a lawyer representing the Fairfax family, and Washington paid part of the legal fee when Marshall argued against Randolph (Washington State and AG) in a court case involving the Fairfax estate. As a Fairfax lobbyist, Marshall got the Virginia legislature to annul Revolutionary War confiscation of British-owned estates. Settlers who had bought Fairfax land in good faith from Virginia had to buy it all over again from the Fairfax family. Worse yet, Lord Thomas Fairfax was notorious for taking settlers' money for land titles and then refusing to turn over the titles.[7]

Ca. 1795 Marshall, his brother James, and two other men bought 160,000 acres of the Fairfax estate. After British banker Alexander Baring refused to finance the sale, Marshall's relative Robert Morris (remembered as "financier of the Revolution") backed the loan. To everyone's surprise, Morris went bankrupt, leaving John and James Marshall responsible for paying off the loan. This debt was a terrible burden to John Marshall. It was the reason he accepted in 1797 a diplomatic appointment to France from President Adams—for the money. Marshall got about $20,000 (having a 2019 buying power of $390,000).

In France, Marshall, C. C. Pinckney, and Washington's relative Elbridge Gerry (Madison VP), attempted to negotiate an end to French attacks on the U.S. merchant marine. French officials wanted a bribe of $250,000 ($4,900,000 in 2019 buying power) to settle the dispute. Caron de Beaumarchais, who created *The Barber of Seville* and *The Marriage of Figaro*, apparently agreed to supply the cash. Marshall rejected such a deal and returned to America, where he was greeted as a hero. The slogan "millions for defense, but not one cent for tribute" originated from a toast at a banquet honoring him. The bribery matter is known to history as the "XYZ Affair."

Bribery is a venerable arm of diplomacy. In the XYZ Affair it would have been a cheap way of easing tensions that had almost reached war, particularly since the money would have come from Beaumarchais and cost U.S. taxpayers nothing. Why would Beaumarchais make such an offer, and why would Marshall so firmly reject it? Perhaps because Marshall had been Beaumarchais's lawyer for years, and their finances were intertwined. Ca. 1790 Marshall bought a large Virginia tract mortgaged to Beaumarchais. The Frenchman's XYZ funding offer involved a case Marshall was handling. The lawsuit involved money the United States owed to Beaumarchais for Revolutionary War supplies. During the XYZ Affair Beaumarchais had won in a lower American court, but the case was on appeal. The bribe money was to come from the settlement of that case. This put Marshall in a dilemma. Given the political climate during the Adams Presidency, if Marshall agreed to the bribe, questions would arise about his loyalty if the money's source were ever revealed, and Marshall would be subject to blackmail by the French when Adams made him Secretary of State. If Marshall refused, his honor would be safe at the risk of war.

In 1805 the United States paid $300,000 (with a 2019 buying power of

$6,370,000) on Beaumarchais's claims. Two decades later his heirs sought another $200,000 from the United States ($4,980,000 in 2019 buying power) even though the French government had already paid the sum to the heirs. In Congress John Forsyth (Jackson State) successfully suggested that Congress sidestep the claims and pass the matter on to President John Quincy Adams, son of the man who appointed Beaumarchais's attorney Marshall to the cabinet and Supreme Court.

Marshall's involvement in the XYZ affair resulted from the diplomatic appointment President Adams gave to him in order to provide Marshall with $20,000 to devote to his deal for part of the Fairfax estate. That sum proved insufficient. The Jay Treaty a few years earlier had strengthened Marshall's claim to the Fairfax estate and helped turn the litigation surrounding it into a federal case headed for the Supreme Court. In the final days of the John Adams administration Marshall became Chief Justice. After some years, the case so dear to John Marshall finally arrived before the court. George Washington's relative Charles Lee (Washington and Adams AG) argued for Marshall's side. Samuel Dexter (Adams and Jefferson Treasury) argued against Marshall's side. Both these men were former cabinet colleagues of Marshall. Ostensibly the Chief Justice took no part in the decision, which ruled the Jay Treaty guaranteed Marshall's ownership of land that had comprised part of the Fairfax estate (land which Marshall had finally paid for in full). That was the crucial aspect for the Chief Justice, although the case *Martin* v. *Hunter's Lessee* is famed in jurisprudence for giving federal courts authority over state courts in interpreting the Constitution. Everyone knew of Marshall's stake in the case. The other justices were so deferential toward Marshall that they were known to go along when he would disregard their votes and announce his minority dissent as the court's decision.[8] Justice Joseph Story supposedly wrote the *Martin* decision, but commentators have argued that the Fairfax estate decision showed a knowledge of Virginia law that only Marshall could have. Little surprise but much outrage greeted Story's Fairfax ruling. Marshall's friendliness toward real estate promoters was no secret. He had favorably decided the fraudulent Yazoo land case three years earlier when Story was a lawyer for the Yazoo promoters.

The Yazoo Land Company gained notoriety during the presidency of Thomas Jefferson. The operation began when Georgia sold 35 million superb acres for one-and-a-half cents per acre. The Creek and Choctaw Indians didn't necessarily recognize the Georgia government's title to that region. Supposedly the state sold the land to avoid trouble with the Indians; in theory an Indian war would be the fault of land companies, not the Georgia state government—a delicate distinction to scalped settlers. President Washington was deeply concerned over the way land companies in general aggravated tensions with Indians. U.S. Supreme Court Justice James Wilson and Washington's relative Robert Morris were involved in the Yazoo operation. Corruption was revealed, and the Georgia legislature tried to rescind the sale. Complications arose. Tempers flared. William H. Crawford (Madison and Monroe Treasury, relative of Z. Taylor War) was so angered by the scandal that he murdered one of the backers. Washington's relative Charles Lee (Washington AG) made a report to Congress, referred to a committee headed by Sen. Aaron Burr (Jefferson VP).

Charles Lee's relative Henry had trouble repaying a $20,000 debt to George Washington (having a buying power of $395,000 in 2019) because payment depended on a bond to Lee from U.S. Supreme Court Justice James Wilson. Partly due to Wilson's investments in the Yazoo speculation, he was unable to meet his obligations to Lee and others. Wilson ran away to North Carolina and died. Complications grew as the U.S. government took possession of the disputed land. While in the cabinet Gideon Granger (Jefferson PG, father of J. Tyler PG) was a lobbyist for one Yazoo company, using Post Office patronage to get congressional votes for his company, and even going on to the House floor to clinch deals. Granger was in the middle of similar shady deals stretching from the Western Reserve to Lake Erie.

Other litigation stemming from the Yazoo real estate scheme resulted in the U.S. Supreme Court case of *Fletcher* v. *Peck*, which tested whether the Georgia legislature could invalidate a corrupt contract. The Yazoo speculators were represented by future Supreme Court Justice Joseph Story and future President John Quincy Adams. Chief Justice Marshall (whose relative Robert Morris had been a Yazoo promoter) ruled that a corrupt contract cannot be repealed by a state. This victory for the Yazoo speculators had crucial importance for the American people. It meant that a corporation could use any trick or chicanery to get a contract with a state government, and that the contract was then eternal; the misinformed or corrupt decision of persons long dead bind the living forever. Public treasuries were drained many years before this legal principle finally changed.

Chapter 3

Louisiana Purchase

President Thomas Jefferson's most famous real estate operation was on behalf of the U.S. government. He had his friend Pierre Samuel du Pont de Nemours (father of the founder of the company today known as DuPont) assist in negotiations. Although British banker Alexander Baring had declined to become involved in financing the XYZ Affair bribe he was willing to loan money to the U.S. government for the Louisiana Purchase. Baring brought Dutch bankers Hope & Co. into this real estate project, and together the two banks made a $2,500,000 profit (an amount having a 2019 buying power of $54,700,000) in financing American acquisition of Louisiana. For some persons this transaction yielded still more income, as $3,750,000 of the purchase price was reserved for payment of various claims that assorted U.S. citizens held against the French government. That reserve had a 2019 buying power of $82,050,000. Hamilton's relative Robert Livingston (brother of Jackson State) was in charge of paying these claims in Paris. Livingston pushed hard to get them paid. In effect the U.S. government was paying these debts owed to American claimants by the French regime, as payments were diverted from money being paid for Louisiana.

Burr Murders Hamilton

Soon after the Louisiana Purchase was arranged, Washington's relative Thomas Jefferson was relieved of two political enemies when his Vice President Aaron Burr murdered Alexander Hamilton (Washington Treasury). Various business rivalries complemented political disputes between Burr and Hamilton. They were New York City's top lawyers, competing for the profession's wealthiest clients. For instance, Hamilton represented Holland Land Company when it was trying to get passage of a helpful law through the New York state legislature. The Dutch company had acquired a huge tract of New York state from Washington's relative Robert Morris but was having trouble exploiting it because of restrictions imposed on alien ownership of land. Hamilton enlisted aid from his father-in-law Philip Schuyler, who agreed to help Holland Land if it would loan $250,000 ($5,000,000 in 2019 buying power) to Schuyler's Western Inland Lock Navigation Company, an outfit having trouble in attracting investors. Constructing this canal would increase the value of Holland Land's holdings. Schuyler delivered on passage of the law desired by Holland Land, but the company refused to make the promised loan, fired Hamilton, and replaced him with Burr. Hamilton's relative John Church was so peeved at the turn of affairs that he put a bullet through Burr's sleeve. Burr started Chase Manhattan Bank to compete with Hamilton's Bank of New York, further antagonizing Hamilton. And of course there was the Reynolds affair. Ca. 1791 Hamilton sold his $800 in government bonds, having a buying power of $21,000 in 2019. He also used loans from four friends to pay $1,100 to James Reynolds (a sum having a buying power of $28,800 in 2019). Circumstances were complicated, but a consensus today holds that Reynolds was running a badger game to blackmail Hamilton, threatening to publicize the sexual relationship between Hamilton and Reynolds's wife Maria.

Reynolds was an old political enemy of Hamilton. During the Constitutional convention Reynolds had spread false rumors that Hamilton wanted the new government to be a monarchy. Moreover, Burr (who in hard times would go without food in order to spend his money on sex) was also involved with Maria and may have been James Reynolds's lawyer. President Thomas Jefferson secretly financed, with future President James Monroe as bagman, the man who publicized the Reynolds affair. Hamilton almost fought a duel with Monroe over the matter. Given all these details, the Reynolds affair begins to look like more than a simple badger game. Hamilton's murder not only involved politics, but also derived from years of business and personal rivalries.

War of 1812

As Washington's relative Thomas Jefferson retired from the presidency, and Washington's relative James Madison moved into the White House, relations with England were deteriorating. The basic dispute was money. England's perennial squabbles with France had led to an English blockade of the European coast, cutting off American trade with Europe. Any British slight against American honor, such as kidnapping U.S. citizens and forcing them to serve in the British navy, received wide publicity and was accompanied by much indignation. By 1811 America and England seemed headed toward war.

In such a conflict frontier security would be vital for the United States. Good relations with Indians would seem to be common sense. The governor of Indiana Territory was Washington's relative William Henry Harrison. Governor Harrison effectively carried out Jefferson's and Madison's policy of seizing Indian land. Typically a government agent would get some Indians drunk and have them sign over title to land wanted by the government. Typically the government agent didn't care whether signers had authority to act for Indians residing on the desired land. It was sort of like a city slicker selling an army captain "title" to the Brooklyn Bridge, and the captain shows up with the Fifth Armored Division to take possession. The slicker has his money, the captain his bridge, and 8,000,000 New Yorkers are seething, waiting for revenge.

In 1809 Harrison used this technique to obtain an Indian village (actually a veritable town) on Tippecanoe Creek. This happened to be the hometown of a powerful chief, Tecumseh, who immediately allied a mass of Indians with the British. With the War of 1812 approaching, Tecumseh's action was a heavy blow to frontier safety. In November 1811 Harrison led an inept campaign to chastise Tecumseh and another Indian leader known as The Prophet. Harrison's army camped near the hostile Indian town, lit campfires allowing the enemy to pinpoint all strategic locations, and proceeded to go to sleep. Not pausing to awaken the soldiers, the Indians fell upon the camp and drove Harrison's force all the way back to their home settlements. Newspapers and the public called the incident an example of British villainy and demanded war with England. "Tippecanoe Harrison" was proclaimed a hero, and later became President of the United States.

As noted earlier, Congress closed the Bank of the United States shortly before the War of 1812 began. Thus the U.S. government had difficulty buying weapons. Arms merchants don't give away their wares. Chaotic finances promoted U.S. military defeats. Take the case of New York governor Daniel Tompkins (Monroe War). Since no government money was available to finance New York's defense, Tompkins advanced his own funds, and on his own account raised $1,400,000 in loans from banks and corporations (an amount of money having a buying power of $21,000,000 in 2019). President Madison and Secretary of War Monroe both promised that the U.S. government would pay the loans. The promises, while not worthless, were exaggerated. The government paid only part of the loans, and thereby ruined Tompkins. Creditors seized all his assets. He was sued for years, and eventually he could no longer afford a lawyer. His salary as Vice President was garnisheed, and he may even have spent time in debtor prison while Vice

President. Tompkins died a broken man. Such experiences made patriotic appeals less effective than might have been hoped in raising money to fight the War of 1812. The federal government eventually realized that the war would have to be promoted as a money-making investment.

Washington's relative John Jacob Astor (the fur king) and Madison's Secretary of the Treasury Albert Gallatin planned to finance the war via British bank loans to American banks, who would then lend to the federal government. Yes, the British were going to pay for the American war effort. *American* banks were uninterested, however. Madison's Secretary of the Treasury Alexander Dallas (father of Polk VP) approached various Philadelphia bankers to help Gallatin finance the war. This led to discussions with David Parish in 1813. Parish owned much land on the New York–Canada border, and his family was influential among European bankers in general and British bankers in particular. At first Parish refused to help, but Dallas got him wavering. Then Parish read that Gallatin was offering a commission to anyone bringing in a subscription of $100,000 or more to the government loan, $100,000 having a 2019 buying power of $1,500,000. Seeing a possible profit from financing the war, Parish contacted Alexander Dallas's friend Stephen Girard and Gallatin's friend John Jacob Astor. Then other Philadelphia, New York, and Baltimore capitalists joined the talks. Astor and Girard also had connections with England's giant Baring Brothers bank. Baring joined in financing the American war effort, making big advances to cover American obligations. Of the $16,000,000 loan that the U.S. government was floating, Parish, Girard, and Astor took more than $9,000,000 (which had $135,000,000 in 2019 buying power).

As the war progressed, Madison's morose Secretary of War William Crawford had informal talks with Thomas Baring regarding possible terms of peace. American peace commissioners included future President John Quincy Adams, Henry Clay (JQA State), and Gallatin (Jefferson and Madison Treasury). Adams and Gallatin were both friends of Alexander Baring. En route to Ghent (where all three American diplomats lived in the same house) Gallatin wrote to Alexander Baring, discreetly asking for any information on the situation that Baring might wish to communicate. Baring wrote to Gallatin that Russian mediation was unacceptable to Britain, that peace negotiations would have to be just between the two parties at war. Baring probably told Gallatin other things orally as well—while in London Gallatin resided at Alexander Baring's house. Future President James Monroe, who was Madison's Secretary of State during these negotiations, eventually (perhaps already) owed Baring Brothers a lot of money. Monroe died without paying, and the Barings simply wrote off the debt without attempting to sue Monroe's estate.

Internal Improvements

The "internal improvements" controversy was underway when the War of 1812 ended. This was a fight among advocates of differing transportation systems and also involved debate on the best way to pay for construction of them. Proponents of water transportation favored developing rivers and canals. Proponents of land transit advocated turnpikes and railroads. Debate on paying for these improvements asked whether the public should pay by using tax money to fund projects, or whether capitalists should pay by selling stock. A related issue was philosophical, whether rivers were more democratic than railways: Any farmer could load a raft with produce and proceed downriver to sell farm products, but railroad operators had a monopoly on access to the railway and could force shippers to pay whatever price the operators wanted.

In answer to the question of who was going to pay for internal improvements, in 1816 John C. Calhoun (Monroe War, JQA and Jackson VP) worked hard to get a bill through Congress earmarking revenue from a new Bank of the United States for the purpose of constructing internal improvements. Both houses of Congress approved the legislation, but President Monroe vetoed it the day before he left office. Although Monroe was a member of the so-called Virginia Dynasty of Southern aristocrats who held the presidency for many years, he had married into the Kortright New York mercantile family, a connection that may have influenced his veto decision.

The bottom line in all the rhetoric on this topic was that rivermen didn't want any competing roads. Rivermen traditionally had the edge in government. The edge was partly due to political strength of rivermen. After all, it was George Washington's Potomac River Company which led to the Constitution itself. In large part, however, the rivermen could demonstrate that water transportation was superior to land transportation. This was true in the 1780s and true forty years later. The internal improvements controversy arose mainly because certain rivermen were getting greedy.

In 1787 New York's legislature gave John Fitch a steamboat monopoly although steamboats didn't yet exist. Ten years later Alexander Hamilton's relative Robert R. Livingston (brother of Jackson's Secretary of State) said he knew how to build one. The state legislature then yanked Fitch's monopoly and transferred it to Livingston for twenty years. This switch had to be approved by the state's five-member Council of Revision. Livingston's relative John Jay was one council member. Another was Robert R. Livingston. Approval was granted (so much for John Fitch and for sanctity of contracts with public bodies). Livingston failed to produce a satisfactory steamboat and lost his monopoly. In 1803 Robert Fulton married Livingston's niece and was brought into a new monopoly granted that year, which

Livingston lost for nonperformance again. This was no problem to Livingston, who got still another monopoly granted in 1807. Some years earlier he had hired Washington's relative Nicholas Roosevelt (TR's granduncle) to build a steamboat. Livingston then fired him and proceeded to build the *Clermont* using Roosevelt's design. With the *Clermont* success the monopoly was confirmed and was extended by thirty years.

New York City being one of the nation's two greatest ports, the monopoly on steam navigation was lucrative since Livingston could lay tribute on all steam vessels. Knowing a good thing Livingston decided to expand his monopoly to the Ohio and Mississippi Rivers, and thus control traffic in the other great American port, New Orleans. Robert R. Livingston's brother Edward (Jackson State) was on the scene in Louisiana then, and the Territorial legislature granted the monopoly. As a condition of granting statehood to Louisiana Congress required the Mississippi River to be free to all navigation. Louisiana continued to let Livingston enforce the monopoly anyway. Needing a steamboat to "show the colors" in New Orleans, the Livingston family made amends to Nicholas Roosevelt long enough to have him build the *New Orleans* in 1811. Then they cut him off again, leaving Roosevelt with no money from patent rights.

The monopoly gave Livingston the right to seize any craft that refused to pay the charges he set. Livingston got no cooperation from governments along the Ohio and Mississippi Rivers, with the exception of Louisiana. New Jersey and Connecticut passed retaliatory laws for the New York area, and other states gave monopolies to other persons. A situation loomed reminiscent of epic sea battles, complete with prize crews. Livingston was so strict that New York governor Daniel Tompkins (who was later Monroe's Vice President) had to halt troop transport during the War of 1812 until Livingston was satisfied. In this case Livingston patriotically waived his rights and permitted the nation to defend itself. Tompkins clashed with Livingston in another instance, when Tompkins was providing steam towing for sailing vessels in the New York City vicinity.

The "internal improvements" movement to construct good roads was due in part to the turmoil Livingston caused on the Ohio and Mississippi Rivers, just as the Interstate Highway System was a product of railroad excesses.

Chaos spread by Livingston resulted in a lawsuit fought by prominent New York businessmen and which made its way to the U.S. Supreme Court. Livingston may have thought to gain an edge by hiring as his lawyers William Pinkney (Madison AG) and New York attorney general Thomas J. Oakley. Tompkins, however, hired the *U.S.* Attorney General William Wirt and Daniel Webster (W. H. Harrison, Tyler, and Fillmore State, and son-in-law of important New York merchant Herman LeRoy). Typically,

Webster waited until the last minute to prepare, spending one night and one morning on the case. For this Webster collected a $1,500 fee (having a buying power of $38,000 in 2019). The case of *Gibbons v. Ogden* is famed in jurisprudence for the Court's ruling that broadly interpreted the power of Congress to regulate commerce. Webster could be casual in preparation because in this case (as in so many others) he used his secret weapon—contacting Justice Joseph Story, who was an intimate of Chief Justice John Marshall, by which Webster would learn what arguments the court wanted to hear. Marshall's ruling crushed the Livingston steamboat monopoly. (Was President Jackson's enmity toward Marshall reinforced by Secretary of State Livingston?)

End of the Livingston steamboat monopoly saw government money flow into canals, manmade extensions of rivers and streams. Railroad development started also, but water transportation remained superior to land transit.

Alexander Hamilton's relative George Clinton (Jefferson and Madison VP) helped canal surveys and urged New York legislators to support two canal companies created by a bill drawn up by Hamilton's father-in-law. The Clinton family's big canal project was the Erie Canal. Gideon Granger (Jefferson PG and father of W. H. Harrison's PG) entered the New York state senate in order to promote the Erie Canal, and Peter Porter (JQA War) was a state commissioner to survey a canal route from Lake Erie to the Hudson River. In Congress he urged grants of public land to encourage canal companies, which could then raise capital by selling that real estate. In that era gifts of public land helped finance assorted projects. The national government had acquired the land for a pittance, so donations cost the government little.

William L. Marcy (Polk War, Pierce State) took enough interest in the Erie Canal to become a member of the New York Canal Board. He was also Canal Fund Commissioner. At the Erie Canal hub city of Lockport Marcy's father-in-law and three other persons got water power rights, perhaps 80,000 acres, and set up a bank. Marcy was on the outskirts of this operation. He bought stock in the bank and ca. 1838 got half interest in the water rights.

A suggestion by the grandfather of Henry Gilpin (Van Buren AG) started Chesapeake & Delaware Canal Company. Benjamin Latrobe got construction going in 1804. Gilpin himself was secretary of the company, and Louis McLane (Jackson State and Treasury) was a company attorney. Baltimore merchants opposed the canal because it would open Philadelphia markets to Chesapeake Bay. Farmers *supported* it for the same reason. The canal was intensely important to McLane. It was the biggest reason for his decision to enter Congress. There he pushed Congress to have the national government buy Chesapeake & Delaware stock. John Forsyth (Van Buren State) supported McLane's desire to have the government buy stock, and in the Maryland legislature Roger Taney was a strong supporter of Chesapeake & Delaware canal construction. Ca. 1829 Congress finally approved purchasing $150,000 of stock (2019 buying power of $3,900,000). Richard Johnson (Van Buren VP) supported federal financial help for the Louisville & Portland Canal. Over Forsyth's opposition Congress voted to purchase Louisville & Portland Canal Company stock. Government ownership of business wasn't viewed as a threat to liberty, but these two canals are the only privately owned ones in which the U.S. government invested.

As with railroads, some canal companies dealt more with banking than with transportation. One such operation had the straightforward name of Morris Canal and Banking Company. Directors included author Washington Irving and (in 1836) three members of Congress. The company had a canal (to carry coal from northeastern Pennsylvania to New York City), water power rights (and sold the power to run a Newark factory), a Jersey City bank, and a Wall Street branch bank. Even among the fast operators of Wall Street the company had a bad reputation in the 1820s. "Curses on Morris" was a frequent cry. A conspiracy to corner the market on Morris stock proved so unsavory that all Morrris stock sales were annulled. Foreign money was involved. In 1830 a $750,000 loan from Dutch banker Willem Willink, Jr. (having a 2019 buying power of $20,000,000) was secured by a mortgage on the canal. Five years later the London House of Morrison, Cryder & Company had $200,000 (having a 2019 buying power of $5,600,000) in Morris.

McLane (Jackson Treasury) accepted the Morris Canal & Banking presidency mainly for the $6,000 salary (worth about $150,000 in 2019). McLane did provide service for the money. Under his leadership the company began to pay dividends for the first time. Yet slick financial manipulations continued. Bank of the United States president Nicholas Biddle had an interest in Morris, and the company unsuccessfully attempted to buy the New York branch of the Bank of the United States (BUS). President Martin Van Buren (Jackson VP) ascribed McLane's appointment as Morris president to Biddle's influence. In January 1836 BUS owned over 3,500 Morris shares. Biddle himself secretly bought 400 Morris shares in April 1836. A week later Thomas Biddle & Company bought 3,000 shares. In 1836 Nicholas Biddle bought 650 more shares, and his cousin became a director. James Gordon Bennett of the *New York Herald* said Thomas Biddle & Co. owned over fifty percent of Morris stock in 1837.

Other financial maneuvers occurred. Ca. 1836 Morris and Thomas Biddle & Co. helped finance Indiana's Wabash & Erie Canal. In 1836 Morris started buying Indiana state bonds. One of the Indiana bond commissioners became a Morris stockholder. In three years he made an estimated $100,000 while Indiana lost $3,500,000 on bond transactions, mostly via Morris. Another matter was the conduct of the Morris cashier who defaulted by over $120,000. His assets were seized, reducing the loss to $28,000. The company was able to pay a four percent dividend in February 1837. McLane left the bank presidency that year, receiving a bonus of $9,300 (with a 2019 buying power of $233,000) in addition to his salary. His successor as Morris president was Samuel Southard (Monroe and JQA Navy).

Banks Again

For a time, Morris president Louis McLane (Jackson Treasury) was a central figure in President Andrew Jackson's so-called bank war. This was Jackson's successful fight to cripple the Bank of the United States (BUS). His opposition to BUS is generally interpreted as a clash between frontier and Eastern interests. This is strictly true but somewhat misleading. The clash wasn't between rich Easterners and poor frontiersmen, but between rich Easterners and *rich* frontiersmen. Jackson himself was part of the capitalist establishment, with great prestige in Eastern financial circles. His signature could shake money from Philadelphia sources indifferent to anyone else. Reportedly Boston bankers were willing to loan up to $100,000 merely on his signature, with no collateral. For a time in the War of 1812 Jackson furnished his entire army from his own pocket. In an era when men of immense wealth took care of debts with IOUs and land trades, Jackson paid a $6,000 debt entirely with gold and silver—an incredible feat. Jackson was a member of the U.S. Senate in the 1790s, a job that went only to wealthy aristocrats. He was a sophisticated, knowledgeable capitalist owning diversified general stores in Tennessee. His complaint against BUS was over money supply, which is regulated not by specie reserves but by indebtedness and bank loans. Jackson believed in "sound money," but viewed BUS as overcautious. Jackson moreover suspected that BUS tight-fistedness had less to do with sound money than with stifling Western commerce and preserving Eastern industrial dominance. There were other factors, too. People around Jackson were close to state banks, eager to take over business and deposits from BUS. Such advisers strengthened Jackson's own inclinations. Then, too, with Jackson there was always the possibility of personal grudge. While serving as governor of Florida he had unsuccessfully tried to put a BUS branch there. Jackson remembered who helped or hindered his projects.

From the White House Jackson saw BUS as having more economic power than a private corporation should wield, and he sought to reduce that influence, an effort which had the side benefit of helping Jackson's political friends throughout the country who were running state banks. His war against BUS had two stages. First was Jackson's veto of a bill to extend the life of the BUS charter, which otherwise would expire in 1836 and thereby close the bank. Second was his removal of federal deposits from BUS, crippling the bank's ability to make loans.

To appreciate the fight, remembering the War of 1812 is useful. The first BUS had been closed down just before the war, devastating the money supply. President James Madison then learned the role of money in warfare. It was a hard experience for him and the country. Madison had always opposed the first BUS but now realized how useful it had been. William Crawford (Madison War and relative of Z. Taylor War) had much to do with incorporation of the second BUS in 1816, so much that Madison appointed him as Treasury Secretary. During Jackson's bank war Crawford's son met with Roger Taney (Jackson Treasury) and urged Taney to reconsider his cooperation with Jackson. Another key figure in the 1816 re-creation of BUS was Jackson's future Vice President John C. Calhoun, who said, "I might say with truth that the bank owes as much to me as to any other individual in the country; and I might even add that, had it not been for my efforts, it would not have been chartered."[9] Obviously Jackson and his Vice President were headed for trouble.

The new BUS had a central headquarters in Philadelphia and also operated from various branches around the country. Those institutions touched personal fortunes of several Presidents and cabinet members.

In 1817 former President Thomas Jefferson sought a $3,000 loan (equivalent to $55,500 in 2019 buying power) from the Richmond BUS branch. He needed the money because an audit showed Jefferson owed money to the government for expenses as Minister to France decades earlier. Jefferson's old friend and George Washington relative Wilson Cary Nicholas was a Richmond BUS branch director, and Jefferson got the money. The next year he asked for a renewal on the loan. For this he needed an endorser. Nicholas agreed to sign after everyone else turned Jefferson down. A month later Nicholas asked Jefferson to cosign a $20,000 note for Nicholas (about $400,000 in 2019 buying power). He assured Jefferson that the signature was a mere technicality, that Jefferson would suffer no financial trouble as a result. The bank directors knew otherwise, but did not warn Jefferson. The next year Nicholas defaulted, and Jefferson became responsible for repaying the $20,000 to BUS.

Madison's Navy Secretary William Jones was president of the central BUS, from its re-creation in 1816 until Nicholas Biddle became a director in 1819. That year Jones was forced to resign in disgrace due to his appalling maladministration. At first he was thought a knave, but investigation showed he was a fool. The saga of James McCulloch illustrated one of many problems under Jones. McCulloch was cashier for the BUS Baltimore branch, and his name was immortalized in jurisprudence due to the *McCulloch* v. *Maryland* lawsuit in the U.S. Supreme Court, which staked boundaries of the federal government's powers. Maryland was trying to tax BUS, and on behalf of BUS McCulloch was resisting payment. While the case was being argued, the House of Representatives was considering repeal of the bank's charter. So the case arose in a tense political climate. BUS attorneys for this case included William Pinkney (Madison AG), Daniel Webster (W. H. Harrison State), and William Wirt (Monroe AG). Wirt was U.S. Attorney General while the case was being adjudicated. Chief Justice John Marshall has been called a "devoted friend" of BUS. As soon as he heard of the *McCulloch* v. *Maryland* case Marshall realized it could go to the Supreme Court. He was so interested in this case involving BUS that he immediately got rid of his BUS stock so no one could suggest he should disqualify himself from the proceedings. Marshall was familiar with the original Congressional debates about BUS through research for his George Washington biography. Marshall was also familiar with the points of *McCulloch* v. *Maryland* before it reached the Supreme Court, so familiar that he may have written much of the court's opinion before the case was argued. BUS won.

Up to this point McCulloch was a hero to supporters of BUS. Soon afterward, however, he was exposed as a thief who had been using his inside position to rob the bank. Wirt prosecuted several Baltimore BUS branch officers. William Pinkney was a defense attorney. BUS demanded that McCulloch cover losses that he caused. The businessmen all acted civilly. No public outcry occurred (which could alarm depositors). McCulloch found sixteen Baltimore merchants willing to give notes backing him for $12,500 (2019 buying power of $244,000) each. He didn't tell them the reason he sought their aid, and the scandal remained secret for a while. McCulloch was unable to replace the funds he had stolen, so BUS demanded that one of the merchants, Solomon Etting, pay. Etting refused, saying McCulloch's criminal conduct voided the deal. An unstated reluctance about handing money to BUS might have been because either Etting or his father directed Union Bank—an arch rival of BUS. BUS sued Etting and won in lower court. Etting's Supreme Court lawyers included Webster, Wirt, and Taney. A tie vote among the Supreme Court justices left Etting the loser.

BUS touched other Presidents and cabinet members as well. George Graham (Madison War) was president of a BUS branch. Benjamin Stoddert's (Adams and Jefferson Navy) son-in-law George Campbell (Madison Treasury) directed the Nashville branch. In 1822 Albert Gallatin turned down a feeler about becoming BUS president. He said neither the job nor the salary appealed to him. Instead Nicholas Biddle, who had been a director since 1819, became BUS president and served until 1836. Biddle had been private secretary to John Armstrong (Madison War) and to President Monroe.

By 1825 former President Madison had suffered nine crop failures in ten years and had bad overseas markets for his crops. He needed cash. Biddle turned down Madison's request for a $6,000 BUS loan (2019 buying power of $150,000). Biddle said BUS had to keep its assets liquid and couldn't loan on real estate collateral, as would be necessary in Madison's case. Biddle's position was theoretically strong, but he was known to bend rules for friends. Unfortunately for Madison, Biddle had a long memory about who were friends and who were opponents. Madison had opposed the first BUS.

Contrast Madison's experience with Monroe's. When Monroe retired from the presidency his $43,000 debt (2019 buying power of $1,000,000) to the Bank of Columbia was transferred to BUS. Needing immediate cash to satisfy this debt, Monroe sold 900 acres for $18,000. He turned over to BUS all but 707 acres of his Highland property to cover the remaining $25,000. Those 707 acres were already mortgaged to the Bank of Richmond. BUS was displeased about getting real estate as a loan payment, but Biddle considered Monroe (unlike Madison) to be a friend.

Involvement of Presidents and cabinet members with BUS continued as years passed. When future President John Quincy Adams was serving as Monroe's Secretary of State he owned $9,000 of six percent BUS stock (2019 buying power of $210,000). U.S. Senator Thomas Hart Benton said Biddle used John Quincy Adams as a front for delivering messages to the public about BUS.

President William Henry Harrison was deeply involved in setting up the Cincinnati BUS branch. He and his business associate Jacob Burnet were both directors. Ca. 1817 Harrison pushed to make Burnet the Cincinnati branch president. In August 1828 Harrison got a $10,000 BUS loan (about $260,000 in 2019 buying power) plus renewal of an $8,000 note. In 1830 he owed BUS $19,000 (having a 2019 buying power of $260,000). He sold Indiana and Miami country land to pay off that loan, but those sales didn't yield enough. He still owed $6,000, which grew to $9,000 by 1832. When Harrison took office as President in March 1841 textile king Abbott Lawrence gave him $4,000 ($118,000 in 2019 buying power) to purchase BUS notes.

Henry Clay (JQA State) was a Bank of Kentucky director and involved with Lexington Bank (also called Kentucky Insurance Company). In 1811 both banks wanted BUS killed. Clay strongly argued against BUS then, saying state banks were as good and were even safer. Clay was willing to change his tune for a price. BUS hired him, and he became a key figure in the 1816 recharter action in the House of Representatives. He also became a successful BUS attorney before the U.S Supreme Court. In 1820 Clay owed BUS thousands of dollars, which surely deepened his loyalty. He owned five BUS shares and was appointed as a BUS director but declined the job. He declined because he feared people might question his votes on bank affairs in Congress. This was strictly a public relations concern. In 1820 he was chief counsel in Ohio, heading Ohio and Kentucky legal affairs of the BUS for four years. On behalf of BUS the Whig leader Henry Clay sued Democrat leader Richard Johnson (Van Buren VP) and two other men for about $130,000 ($3,250,000 in 2019 buying power). BUS thereby acquired all their real estate that it could, departing from its traditional abhorrence of real estate as a bank asset. Losing his land to BUS did not stop Johnson from owning $2,000 of BUS stock in 1840 ($58,000 in 2019 buying power). Via lawsuits the bank got 50,000 farmland acres in Ohio and Kentucky, plus much of Cincinnati. These acquisitions generated resentment among the populace.

Ca. 1823 BUS was Clay's main law client, and he pushed through legislation wanted by BUS. He once wrote to BUS president Langdon Cheeves, "The liberality of the allowance which has been made to me is such as to admit of my time, almost exclusively, being applied to its [the bank's] service."[10] Clay told President John Quincy Adams that business from BUS repaired his finances in just four years. In 1825 Clay wrote that he was no longer concerned about debts, and that he expected all to be paid off in two more years. The precise amount that Clay got from BUS is uncertain. One student of Clay's affairs said the retainer was $6,000. Clay tried to pick up still more income from BUS, such as trying to rent to the bank a building he owned. While not immensely wealthy, Clay could live in style. Ca. 1828 he had property worth $100,000 ($2,625,000 in 2019 buying power).

When BUS was chartered in 1816 a twenty-year limit was put on the charter, meaning BUS would have to close in 1836 unless Congress passed a law to extend its life. Clay told Biddle to ask Congress for charter extension four years early, in the midst of Clay's 1832 campaign against Jackson's reelection. Clay said Jackson lacked the courage to veto the extension because a veto would cost him valuable election support from friends of BUS. Clay was lying to Biddle and actually believed Jackson would veto the extension. Clay planned to win the Presidency on the issue. Biddle donated $42,000 to Clay's 1832 presidential campaign against Jackson ($1,213,000 in 2019 buying power).

By vetoing extension of the BUS charter Jackson could not only count on Western support in the 1832 election but also count on support from

Wall Street financiers. New York City businessmen hated BUS because it demanded immediate payment in specie for checks that the New York businessmen drew on the city's banks. This drained New York bank reserves and therefore reduced the credit available to New York businessmen. Destruction of BUS would be a great victory for Wall Street, and Wall Street had a powerful ally in the Jackson administration—Vice President Martin Van Buren.

Henry Clay wanted John Crittenden (William Henry Harrison's Attorney General) to succeed him as chief BUS counsel for Kentucky, but the bank decided to hire no one, due to slack business there. The brother of Harrison's Secretary of War John Bell was director of the Nashville branch and a big borrower. Ca. 1833 Bell himself owed $53,000 ($1,500,000 in 2019 buying power) to BUS, and $7,000 more the next year. To get an extension he wrote to Biddle and promised to support BUS in Jackson's bank war. The House Ways and Means Committee learned that Bell had correspondence with Biddle and demanded that Biddle turn over all correspondence between him and members of Congress. Bell was *terrified* that his solicitation of a bribe would be revealed. At the time he was running against future President James Polk for Speaker of the House. Biddle refused to turn over the correspondence to Congress. Instead he returned Bell's letters to Bell, who presumably destroyed them. Bell won the election for Speaker, and Biddle then had a very grateful and powerful friend in Congress. He was probably not the only member of Congress who was uneasy about revelation of correspondence with Biddle. In 1829 BUS had $192,000 (with a 2019 buying power of $5,134,000) in loans to thirty-four members of Congress. In 1830 the total was $322,000 (2019 buying power of $8,610,000) to fifty-two members, in 1831 $478,000 (2019 buying power of $13,766,000) to fifty-nine members.

A noticeable chunk of that BUS largess went to just one member of Congress, Alexander Hamilton's relative Daniel Webster (Secretary of State for Presidents William Henry Harrison, John Tyler, and Millard Fillmore). Webster was a BUS stockholder, lawyer, and director, and served the bank many years. Less than three weeks after the 1816 charter renewal Webster got a congressional resolution passed requiring that debts to the federal government be paid in specie, treasury notes, BUS notes, or bank notes that were bona fide redeemable in specie. This was a tremendous help to BUS and a great harm to competing banks that issued non-specie currency that was perfectly sound (as was the non-specie paper money residing in American wallets in the 1960s). Moreover, Webster's resolution reduced the money supply in the West, to the advantage of Eastern commercial interests. BUS also appreciated that Webster was chairman of the Senate Committee on Finances, which would handle any proposals to investigate BUS affairs.

Webster received a regular retainer from BUS and took care that its regularity was uninterrupted. In December 1833 he wrote Biddle, "I believe my retainer has not been renewed or *refreshed* as usual. If it be wished that my relation to the Bank should be continued it may be well to send me the usual retainers."[11] In another note Webster urged secrecy in the matter. Biddle replied that he could do nothing about the retainer for a while, otherwise word would get out. Biddle urged Webster, if he wanted his money, to work on expelling three BUS directors who would report Webster's refreshment to President Jackson. The Senate forced all three off the board. Immediately afterward Webster received his refreshment. He also got bonuses in addition to his regular pay for services. These gifts could be substantial; one bonus was $1,500. In addition to all his various fees Webster also received "loans" for which no security was demanded and which were never repaid. Technically Webster might offer "security" such as a Chicago property he pledged for a $10,000 mortgage. He let the mortgage be foreclosed, and the property yielded only $1,067, of which $650 went for taxes. Thus the $10,000 "loan" was actually a gift from BUS.

Here's how one such loan worked, according to a report President Van Buren said he believed. Webster made a resounding speech against the Jackson bank veto in 1832. A few hours after the vote he made a special trip to Philadelphia, arriving on a Saturday evening. Webster went out to Biddle's country home the next day. Monday morning Webster got $10,000 to $15,000 ($290,000 to $433,000 in 2019 buying power) from BUS and left for New York by steamboat the next day. Apparently the money was paid out on Biddle's order and wasn't authorized by the board of directors. This was *in addition* to loans of $32,000 which Webster already had. Webster was nervous lest word leak out about some of his BUS deals. He particularly warned Biddle that Webster's request for a $50,000 mortgage on New England property must remain secret. Considering the way in which Webster flaunted his BUS relationship, that particular mortgage may have been grubby. Possibly Webster's BUS deals made him a blackmail target of James Watson Webb of the New York *Courier & Inquirer.* Yet any such attempt must have had limited success, as the general nature of Webster's BUS relationship was highly publicized at the time. Webster may have had much to be ashamed of, but almost nothing left to hide.

President Van Buren's Secretary of State John Forsyth was described as an intimate friend of BUS president Nicolas Biddle, a friendship perhaps demonstrated by a $20,000 loan Forsyth received from BUS. Lincoln's Treasury Secretary Salmon Chase handled legal affairs in Cincinnati for BUS. The father of Lincoln's Postmaster General Montgomery Blair owed over $20,000 (roughly $500,000 in 2019 buying power) to BUS in the late 1820s. When the father (Francis Blair) and Amos Kendall began the Washington

Globe newspaper BUS allowed him to settle the $20,000 obligation for one-tenth the actual amount. Francis Blair was a close adviser to President Jackson, so Biddle may have been using money in hopes of influencing administration policy. Kendall had $5,375 in BUS loans. Jackson's Secretary of War John Eaton also received BUS loans. According to George Dallas (Polk VP) Eaton's wife accepted gifts from BUS. Dallas was in a position to know; he was a BUS attorney for years and, at Biddle's direction, handled in the U.S. Senate the 1832 effort to continue the BUS charter beyond 1836.

BUS gave Jackson's Postmaster General William Barry an extension on an overdue loan about the time that the BUS recharter struggle began. Jackson's Secretary of State Edward Livingston sought a $2,500 loan to help cover a $3,000 note ($86,000 in 2019 buying power) due in June 1832. Kendall reported that Biddle personally intervened to get an $18,000 loan ($530,000 in 2019 buying power) for Livingston ca. August 1833. Calhoun (Jackson VP) owned BUS stock and borrowed from the bank. Biddle also paid sums to Calhoun.

Jackson felt his reelection in 1832 proved that he had a lot of popular support for his hatred of BUS. Jackson knew enough about banking to realize that he could cripple BUS by simply ordering the Treasury Secretary to withdraw all U.S. government deposits from BUS. The elegance of this was that the federal money could then be deposited in state banks, institutions that Jackson wanted to strengthen. One act could have two beneficial results. (A third benefit was that banks receiving the federal deposits could be expected to support Jackson's political policies, just as Biddle's money had influenced individual politicians.) Jackson' favored banks were called "pet banks."

Jackson ordered Treasury Secretary McLane to remove the federal deposits. Offhand McLane might seem to be no friend of BUS. In 1818 he was on a Congressional committee to investigate BUS. That same year McLane worked hard to wreck any chance of a BUS branch opening in Wilmington, Delaware, where it would compete with Farmers Bank, of which he was president. Yet McLane balked at carrying out Jackson's order.

In 1837 McLane had $5,150 (2019 buying power of $132,000) in outstanding BUS loans, but perhaps BUS stock had something to do with McLane's delay. He had gotten rid of all his BUS stock in 1817, but associates such as Victor DuPont of the great chemical corporation and Sen. Nicholas Van Dyke (brother of the woman McLane jilted) were stockholders. The aunt of McLane's wife had 29 shares in 1818. That same year McLane's relative George Read had the largest private holding of BUS stock in Delaware, 147 shares. At the time Stephen Girard was the largest stockholder of all. He hired Van Dyke as his lawyer to rescue a valuable marine shipment from McLane's clutches. Ownership of BUS stock had larger implications.

President Jefferson worried about how much was owed by foreigners, possibly giving them leverage over the United States in foreign affairs. Jefferson was certainly in a position to know. In 1802 he had the federal government sell 2,220 of its BUS shares to Baring Brothers, the giant British bank. When Stephen Girard wanted to buy $500,000 of BUS stock in 1810 he had Baring Brothers handle the deal ($10,000,000 in 2019 buying power). Ca. 1819 two-thirds of the BUS stock was owned by Englishmen. Frontiersmen often disliked BUS activities, and they knew of the English influence. This knowledge probably helped fuel Western anglophobia. Most American stockholders resided in Eastern and Middle states. In 1809 BUS directors, officers, and American stockholders were all members of the anti–Jackson Federalist political party. This, too, was noted with interest in Andy Jackson country.

President Jackson got tired of McLane's stalling and shifted him to the State Department. The new Treasury Secretary William Duane also refused to remove federal deposits from BUS. Jackson was less patient his time, and soon replaced Duane with Roger Taney, who yanked federal deposits from BUS with gusto, perhaps influenced by his connection with Union Bank of Maryland—which became one of the most favored "pet banks."

Union Bank of Maryland was chartered by Solomon Etting and others. This was the same Etting who lost $12,500 to BUS in the McCulloch scandal. Taney was a director, attorney, and big stockholder of Union Bank. In 1831 Taney and President Monroe's Attorney General William Wirt represented Union Bank officials in a U.S. Supreme Court case over a dispute that began in 1806. That year owners of the ship *Warren*, who were mostly Union Bank directors, sent it on a voyage from Baltimore to Canton, supposedly. But in mid ocean their agent on board opened sealed instructions giving him power over the captain and ordering the ship to Chile for smuggling operations. The captain committed suicide rather than submit to this treachery. The vessel then went to Chile. The crew unsuccessfully tried to leave the agent ashore, but the Union Bank man was colluding with corrupt Spanish colonial officials and had the crew imprisoned four years for disloyalty. The cargo and vessel were sold in Chile, and proceeds were held in a fund for Union Bank's agent. In 1810 ship officers and crew who had returned to the United States sued for their wages. Nine years later the owners went bankrupt, and their interest in the ship was transferred to Robert Oliver, the BUS Baltimore branch, and Union Bank—who acted as trustees, holding the original owners' interest in the ship. In 1824 the trustees got $185,000 from Spain (2019 buying power of $3,870,000) but still refused to pay the crew's wages. Seven years after that award the U.S. Supreme Court ruled unanimously in favor of the sailors, saying, "The seamen were the victims of an illicit voyage, for which they never intended to contract, and in which they had no voluntary participation." Taney tried to evade that finding, asking the court to reconsider and permit the ship's owners to reimburse themselves for expenses by dipping into the fund generated by the *Warren*'s sale, before using it to pay the crew. Such a procedure would minimize the owners' losses by draining the fund on their behalf and leaving no money to pay the crew. The court rejected Taney's plea.

Taney owned $6,000 to $7,000 (having a 2019 buying power of $170,000 to $200,000) of Union Bank stock when he selected the bank for federal deposits during the Bank War. At that time Union Bank had a vast amount of Tennessee bonds, had overextended itself on loans to Baltimore & Ohio Railroad counsel J.H.B. Latrobe (who was a Union Bank director), and was tied to the teetering Bank of Maryland. Union Bank was nonetheless a key instrument in Jackson's plans to wreck BUS, and the Jackson administration wanted Union Bank to be kept healthy. Kendall (Jackson and Van Buren PG) wrote to the Union Bank vice president telling him the Treasury Secretary could help if needed. "We can stand the stopping of other Banks, but if the 'Pets' begin to go, it is impossible to appreciate the consequences.... If there be the least danger to you, for Heaven's sake, fortify yourself so that *you can stand amidst ruin*."[12] To help in the fortification, Taney confidentially made $300,000 of federal funds (2019 buying power of $8,700,000) available to Union Bank for specified emergency conditions. These conditions did not include using $200,000 for stock speculation and support for the Bank of Maryland. This unauthorized use was especially awkward because Ellicott was a financial adviser of Treasury Secretary Taney. The matter was hushed up, and Taney had Ellicott fired as bank president. The firing required skill, as Ellicott and Bank of Maryland president Evan Poultney had 6,000 shares of Union Bank stock. Via court action Taney prevented the voting of this stock, allowing Ellicott to be fired.

Taney was probably unaware of other skullduggery afoot, involving future President Zachary Taylor's Attorney General Reverdy Johnson. Johnson was a Union Bank attorney who Taney asked to look into the Union Bank situation and report. Yet Johnson couldn't be trusted for objective advice. He was a Bank of Maryland director and was involved with several Evan Poultney enterprises. Moreover, Johnson was involved with Ellicott's stock speculation—which Johnson was investigating for Taney. Johnson approached Nicholas Biddle with an offer to scuttle President Jackson's "pet bank" operation. Such sabotage would add great strength to BUS, and since Union Bank was a key part of the pet bank scheme, Johnson was in a position to act. In return, Johnson asked Biddle to bail out Union Bank. Biddle declined Johnson's offer.

Reverdy Johnson was a Bank of Maryland director. This bank specialized in small deposits from the working class. In cooperation with Poultney,

Ellicott & Company, Bank of Maryland also dealt in small loans, for a price of up to one percent interest *per day*. The Bank of Maryland failed, and with it went the savings of its many small depositors. After a year of public recriminations by bank officers, mob action broke out. The brother of Jefferson's Navy Secretary Robert Smith took command of military forces and dispersed the mob attacking Reverdy Johnson's mansion, but too late to save the house and furniture. Taney tried to get the Maryland legislature to compensate Johnson for the loss. Taney took the case partly out of gratitude for Johnson's "help" with the Ellicott Union Bank scandal, not knowing Johnson's treachery. Taney had his brother-in-law Francis Scott Key approach President Jackson, getting Jackson's support for the compensation. The legislature appointed commissioners who ordered the Baltimore municipal government to pay Johnson $40,000 ($1,160,000 in 2019 buying power) from city funds. While acting as Johnson's lawyer in this effort, Taney was being confirmed as Chief Justice of the U.S. Supreme Court.

Regarding bank failures, one should remember that many were no accidents. They were terrible for depositors, but bank officers and their friends could be enriched by loan policies leading to the "disasters." Indeed, that was one reason why so many banks failed before modern regulations were enforced. There were other ways for insiders to profit from bank failures. For instance, someone could run up big debts and pay with notes on the bank. Then when the bank busted, the person could buy up the notes from holders at pennies on the dollar. Thus the debts were legally discharged for a fraction of their total sum. Ire that descended upon officers of a broken bank was sometimes justified.

Involvement of cabinet members with banking was not limited to persons mentioned, but our examples are enough to give a flavor of those involvements.

Chapter 4

American Indians in the Jackson Era

Before leaving the Jackson era we should touch upon the sophisticated use of courts by the "ignorant, savage" Cherokees. A federal contract with the Cherokees guaranteed their residency on their native Georgia land. These "savages" lived in houses, farmed fields, tended orchards and cattle herds, manufactured textiles, ran taverns, built roads, and operated ferries. The Georgia state government decided to run the Cherokees off their land. The Cherokees, however, wanted to work "within the system." On the advice of Daniel Webster (W.H. Harrison State) they went to court. Their lawyer for the U.S. Supreme Court was William Wirt (Monroe and JQA AG), who brought much public outrage upon himself for taking the case.

Georgia didn't bother to send a lawyer to the Supreme Court hearing, reportedly because Georgia didn't intend to obey an adverse ruling anyway. At about this time Georgia executed a Cherokee in defiance of a U.S. Supreme Court order forbidding the execution. In Wirt's case Chief Justice Marshall (Adams State) ruled that the court lacked jurisdiction. Thus the Indians lost.

In 1832 Wirt defended two missionaries that Georgia had convicted of residing among the Cherokees without a license from the governor and an oath to support and defend Georgia law. Considerable feeling existed that the missionaries were successfully encouraging the Cherokees to resist forced emigration. The two were sentenced to four years' hard labor. The U.S. Supreme Court ruled the Georgia law unconstitutional and ordered them released. Georgia kept them imprisoned. This case of Wirt's elicited President Jackson's alleged comment, "John Marshall has made his decision, now let him enforce it." John Berrien's (Jackson AG) work in forcing the Creeks and Cherokees out of Georgia had much to do with his appointment to Jackson's cabinet. Georgia governor John Forsyth (Jackson and VB State) was also active against the Cherokees. Benjamin Brewster (Arthur AG) held a federal position in 1846 dealing with the Cherokees, and Charles Nagel (Taft Commerce and Labor) was attorney for the Cherokee nation.

Gold was one reason that Georgia was so adamant about ridding the state of Cherokees. There was gold on Indian land, discovered in 1828. John C. Calhoun's family (Monroe War, JQA and Jackson VP, Tyler State) sold their interest in Georgia's O'Bar gold mine in November 1832 for $6,000 ($180,000 buying power in 2019). From 1835 to 1836 Calhoun bought gold land, sometimes at sheriff's sales. He was so serious about the investment that he had a British geologist survey the area. Through the 1830s whatever ore the mining operation produced was devoted to paying off the purchase price of the property. Then a fantastic strike was made in 1842. Eight men with no machinery got out over $8000 of ore ($240,000 in 2019 buying power) in two weeks. (This was slave labor of course.) Calhoun abandoned the Senate session in Washington and traveled to Georgia to see the bonanza. The strike soon faded, and Calhoun leased the operation to someone else.

Tippecanoe

The depression under President Martin Van Buren wasn't entirely Biddle's fault. Actions of Jackson contributed also. The Whig political party easily stuck the Democrats with the blame, however, and in 1840 Van Buren lost the Presidency to his relative William Henry Harrison.

We've already encountered Harrison as an Indian fighter. He is sometimes portrayed as nonentity, a minor military figure elevated to office as a Whig tool. He was, however, a noted (if unsuccessful) Western capitalist. Ca. 1818 Harrison and two other men were partners in the Cincinnati Bell, Brass, and Iron Foundry. The firm employed 120 men making boilers, stoves, anchors, screws, bolts, and steamboat parts. This of course made Harrison interested in frontier transportation and internal improvements. He was chairman of the Ohio senate committees examining canal proposals ca. 1819 –1820. White Water Canal Company built a canal through Harrison's North Bend property, boosting the property's value. Harrison also had a contract with the company to supply wood at $2.25 to $2.50 a cord. In addition Harrison started up a quarry and furnished stone for the canal. His metalwork's business soon became unprofitable. After only three years or so in business the concern had lost $60,000. Harrison was held personally responsible for part. Ca. 1824 he was $20,000 ($520,000 in 2019 buying power) in debt from this. Harrison mortgaged his Miami country land and took $8,000 in promissory notes.

Harrison made a fair amount of money from government service in salaries alone. Robert Morris (Washington relative and real estate associate of John Marshall) was Harrison's childhood guardian. Family connections with President Washington got Harrison started in a government career. His salaries in the Northwest Territory government were excellent for the era—$1,200 a year as secretary. Through Henry Clay's (JQA State) influence Harrison later got a brevet commission as major general of the Kentucky militia, with pay and allowances of $6,000 a year. Harrison served twelve years as governor of Indiana Territory at $2,000 a year. Like Lewis Cass (Jackson War, Buchanan State) Harrison was simultaneously Superintendent of Indian Affairs and drew that salary also, $800 a year. Harrison also picked up money as Commissioner of Indian Affairs, a job difficult to separate from Superintendent, perhaps $2,000 or $3,000 in the dozen years. Ca. 1824 Harrison unsuccessfully sought appointment as minister to Mexico, to relieve his finances. Ca. 1825 President John Quincy Adams turned down Harrison's claim for War of 1812 compensation. Finally President John Quincy Adams appointed Harrison as minister to Columbia in 1828 with a $9,000 salary ($234,000 in 2019 buying power) and a $9,000 outfit. (An "outfit" is a bonus paid to a diplomat over and above a salary. Each outfit is a one-time payment, although a diplomat may be granted several outfits over the years.) President Jackson immediately fired Harrison, which left him miffed at Jackson from then on. While a county court clerk Harrison made about $10,000 after 1834.

Despite his comfortable income Harrison had chronic money trouble. He began accumulating debts by 1795, when he borrowed $300 from army surgeon Charles Brown ($6,000 in 2019 buying power). While governor of Indiana Harrison built an expensive brick mansion, surpassing all other Ohio Valley residences in quality. Harrison bartered 400 acres for just the brick. A later mansion was humorously called the "Log Cabin" and was the basis of the 1840 campaign stories that candidate Harrison lived in a log cabin. Harrison's finances began to decline in the War of 1812, but he retained his lavish lifestyle. Ca. 1821 financial burdens, including the foundry noted earlier, forced Harrison to mortgage land for $8,400 ($218,000 in 2019 buying power). Harrison owed thousands of dollars in 1828. In 1829, after receiving perhaps $15,000 from brief service as minister to Columbia, Harrison still owed at least $20,000 ($402,000 in 2019 buying power). He paid the interest but postponed payment of the principal in order to deal with his sons' debts. In 1830 one son had run up debts and another had died, charged with embezzling $12,000 from the government ($321,000 in 2019 buying power). Flooding, summer heat, and theft of livestock reduced farm income. By the mid–1830s farm income no longer met Harrison's expenses. There were taxes, more debts, and $19,000 owed to the Bank of the United States ($530,000 buying power in 2019). He traveled to

Philadelphia in 1832 to meet with bank officials, borrowing $220 at three percent *a month* to finance the trip. Land sales cleared only $13,000 of the BUS debt. In 1833 Harrison still owed $12,000 to various creditors. About this time Harrison was in addition ordered to pay the $12,000 his late son was accused of embezzling. In 1834 Harrison sought money from an "interested backer" in New Orleans. In December 1839 Harrison wrote a letter complaining of his financial strain. "I have a friend in New York who has formed a correct idea upon this subject. He has written to me and authorized me to draw upon him for any sum I might want."[13] One of the last debts Harrison dealt with was the $300 he borrowed in 1795. The note had passed hands over the years, and in 1840 the owner sought to collect with interest. Harrison told him to first prove ownership to Edward Curtis (intimate friend of W.H. Harrison State and brother of a New York banker). Gossip said Harrison was overdrawing his account as President, quite a feat given his time in office.

Why was Harrison's New York friend so generous? There is no question that wealthy businessmen were buying Harrison's friendship and anticipating some return on the investment. For instance, Harrison and textile king Abbott Lawrence became close. Lawrence wanted Harrison to appoint Thomas Ewing, John Bell, and Francis Granger to the cabinet. This was done. Harrison apparently accepted sums of money regularly from Lawrence and other big capitalists. For example in March 1841 Harrison got $5,000 ($142,000 in 2019 buying power),[14] probably one of the final payments since he died the next month. In 1845 negotiations collapsed on a $30,000 loan (buying power $986,000 in 2019) from Lawrence to John C. Calhoun (Tyler State) and Calhoun's son. Calhoun wrote to Lawrence on May 13: "The impression your letter made on my mind is, that your offer is made from a disposition to oblige me on the part of yourself and your friends.... If I am right, as greatly as I am indebted to you and them for their kind feelings, I could not accept, for reasons which I feel sure you will duly appreciate on reflection."[15] By 1847 the Lawrence family was worth $4,500,000 ($135,000,000 in 2019 buying power) and was one of the ten richest families in the U.S. There was a powerful movement to make Abbott Lawrence the Whig Vice-Presidential nominee on the Zachary Taylor ticket, perhaps strengthened by Whig expectation of $100,000 ($3,145,000 in 2019 buying power) from Lawrence if nominated.[16] This would have made cotton king indeed, with both the President and Vice President financially involved in the industry. It also would have made Lawrence President of the United States when Taylor died. Upon Fillmore's succession to the Presidency instead, he appointed high tariff advocate Daniel Webster as Secretary of State. Webster accepted large amounts of money from Abbott Lawrence and other textile manufacturers.[17]

And Tyler, Too

Whigs put John Tyler on the 1840 electoral ticket as a sop to Southern agrarians stupid enough to believe that the Vice President would have any power. When Harrison died after only a month in office the joke was on the Whigs.

President Tyler's family connections to the Whig Party were solid. He was, after all, a relative of Alexander Hamilton. Moreover, Tyler's wealth came from New York City slum property owned by his second wife's family. The family's tenements were notorious for their horrifying conditions. Yet Tyler was a Whig in name only, more comfortable in the Virginia countryside than in the streets of Manhattan. Real Whigs were soon running circles around him. This outcome was foreshadowed by Tyler's lumber and coal business.

In 1837 President Tyler bought about 1,400 acres near Caseyville, KY, at depression prices. Unsuccessful at seeking buyers at $3 an acre, he rented the land to two farmers for $100 a year. He and his brother-in-law Alexander Gardiner helped organize an operation there to sell wood to steamboats. Tyler hoped to get 150 cords an acre and sell the wood for $2.00 to $2.50 a cord. He wanted to use slave labor, but had to resort to whites—who came down with malaria. Eventually Tyler was spending $6.18 to cut each cord and selling it for $1.75 to $2.00 a cord. He was also losing wood—a flood took 100 of 600 cords stored on the riverbank.

Coal was discovered nearby. Expecting his land also had coal, Tyler increased the price to $5.00 an acre. Washington, D.C., bankers Corcoran & Riggs were so optimistic that they accepted one-fourth interest as payment of a $2,000 loan ca. 1845. This was about the time Tyler was President. He then raised the price to $8.00 an acre. At last a good deposit of coal was found on the property, causing Tyler to refuse an offer of $10.00 an acre. He was urged to invest $5,000 to $6,000 for a mine shaft and for a spur railroad to the Ohio River two miles distant. The idea was to establish a wood yard and coal yard for steamboats, selling coal at 8¢ to 10¢ a bushel. Tyler asked his brother-in-law to help finance the enterprise as a partner. Gardiner declined and recommended that Tyler form a joint stock company. This alternative surely had little appeal to Tyler, who was the last President to oppose finance capitalism.

Then Tyler's land was found to have less coal than previously believed. Still in 1846 he turned down an offer of $2,000 ($64,000 in 2019 buying power) for each coal acre. The next year, however, he had to sell all 1,400 acres for a total of $12,000 ($360,000 in 2019 buying power). Then Tyler discovered the buyer didn't have the money. The buyer offered to cancel the contract if Tyler would pay him $3,000. Tyler paid the $3,000 to the welsher! In pity Alexander Gardiner then paid Tyler $6,000 for half of Tyler's interest and also put up $1,500 of the money sent to the welsher. Gardiner expected no profit; in December 1847 he started a joint stock company for the enterprise, which flopped. The bankers wanted out, and Tyler paid them $2,100. He tried to unload that one-fourth interest on Gardiner who refused but retained his three-eighths interest. Finally Gardiner and Tyler decided to sell out, seeking $20,000. Calhoun's (Tyler State) associate Duff Green helped market the property. A Norfolk syndicate bought it for $20,000. Gardiner died before the sale was made, and his share went to Tyler's wife. She used it to buy "Villa Margaret" for $10,000 in 1858 ($300,000 in 2019 buying power). She used this property near Hampton, VA, for summer vacations.

Clearly Tyler's approach to business involved archaic notions of gentlemanly conduct. One easily sees how the Whigs could run circles around him.

Tyler's conduct in the White House enraged businessmen in the Whig Party. The final break occurred over efforts to resurrect the Bank of the United States. Henry Clay (JQA State), we may recall, had been a knave on this issue once before in hopes of gaining the Presidency. Clay repeated his strategy while President Tyler was in office, designing the recharter bill so that Tyler would feel impelled to veto. This cost Tyler his Whig support. Almost all the cabinet resigned over this, and Clay got the Whig Presidential nomination in 1844.

The only cabinet member who remained after the bank veto was Tyler's relative Daniel Webster (W.H. Harrison, Tyler, Fillmore State). Friends defended Webster's refusal to join his colleagues' departure, portraying this as a patriotic sacrifice of political popularity in order to complete the Webster–Ashburton treaty. Anyone familiar with Webster's character, however, will look for the money. In this case the search is short, as the treaty involved the real estate speculation of Knox (Washington War) and Webster's relative Duer (Washington Asst Treasury).

The land in question was around an area claimed by both the United States and Canada. In 1796 Washington tried to appoint Knox as a commissioner to establish the border. Knox declined, admitting his real estate holdings would cause a conflict of interest. The international dispute summered for over forty year until Webster signed a treaty with Britain, in which the United States gave up 3,200,000 acres. The English negotiator, Lord Ashburton, also went by the name Alexander Baring and was a member of the British banking family. The territory in question included land he had bought from Knox and William Bingham (Baring's father-in-law). Webster had been a paid adviser to Baring Brothers before the treaty negotiations began. Moreover, during the talks Webster accepted "expense" money from

Baring. For some reason Webster used outdated maps, ordered the American minister to England to avoid seeking pro–American evidence from British archives, and deceived Massachusetts and Maine officials. Webster also may have had Baring give Jared Sparks about £3,000 to show the Maine legislature false maps supporting the treaty results. Sparks succeeded Washington's relative Edward Everett (Fillmore State) as Harvard University President. Webster, an attorney for Harvard, had Everett appointed minister to England to help smooth the Maine boundary negotiations.

The United States had perfect title to the area Webster gave up to Baring.

In an early abuse of national security privileges Webster was also unable to account for a substantial part of $17,000 ($493,000 in 2019 buying power) he took from foreign intelligence spy funds to illegally influence Maine newspapers.

Mexican War

President James Polk is generally credited with provoking the Mexican War. Unquestionably he and many other Americans were looking for an excuse to make off with some Mexican territory. We must not, however, underestimate the influence of one American in particular, Polk's Treasury Secretary Robert Walker.

Walker became Treasury Secretary partly because the West wanted him to control land agent appointments. His brother Duncan made big Texas land purchases ca. 1834. Robert's father-in-law later moved there and sent back real estate speculation tips. Duncan was jailed by the Mexicans for his Texas activity and died from the effects. Walker hated Mexico after that. All this was directly related to Walker's enthusiastic support of Texas independence first, annexation to the United States later, and finally the Mexican War.

Chapter 5

California Gold

"Of all lives on earth a banker's is the worst, and no wonder they are specially debarred all chances of heaven." So said banker William T. Sherman (Grant War), who also reflected that "I ought to have had sense enough to keep out of such disreputable business."[18]

When Sherman's father died, Corwin (Fillmore Treasury) was at his side. Sherman was adopted by Ewing (W.H. Harrison and Tyler Treasury, Z. Taylor Interior,) and later married Ewing's daughter. President Zachary Taylor, Henry Clay (JQA State), and Daniel Webster (W.H. Harrison, Tyler, and Fillmore State) attended the wedding.

Sherman was on the scene at Sutter's Mill in California soon after the gold discovery, helping to write the official U.S. Army report to the federal government. He began making high interest loans in California. Sherman also saw what big profits merchants could make off gold seekers. He urged his brother John (Hayes Treasury, McKinley State) to rush goods to San Francisco so they could make a killing. John didn't act fast enough so W.T. Sherman, Dr. Murray Warner, and California governor Richard Barnes Mason each chipped in $500 to purchase goods and open a store. W.T. Sherman was in the Army at the time, but this partnership was legal. Each partner made a $2,000 profit. Ten years later Sherman and his father-in-law Ewing decided to make a killing by selling provisions to Pike's Peak gold rush wagon trains going by Leavenworth, KS, where Sherman was a law partner of Ewing's son. All roads from Kansas City, St. Joseph, and Leavenworth passed within four miles of the Ewing family property near Leavenworth. Sherman got his wife to sell her St. Louis property to provide capital. Ewing tossed in $5,000 ($90,000 in 2019 buying power). After Sherman had spent $2,000 of his own money and $3,340 of Ewing's they concluded the project wouldn't succeed. It folded.

Mrs. Sherman's tastes were costly. "My household expenses are beyond my means," Sherman told his brother John. "I thought that gradually I might compromise but it's impossible."[19] His in-laws pressed Sherman to resign from the Army and go into business for more money. He even took another family into his St. Louis house to split expenses. Still Sherman went into debt. In 1852 he borrowed from his brother John and father-in-law. Sherman's letters were about possibilities for speculation. Mention of his military career was completely absent. In 1852 Sherman held an important Army position in charge of military supplies at New Orleans. This work involved big money, and Sherman became acquainted with the financial elite of one of the nation's greatest ports. Sherman found the pay insufficient.

Sherman was a friend of Maj. Henry S. Turner, partner in the Lucas & Turner bank of San Francisco, which was a branch of the St. Louis bank Lucas & Symonds. Ca. 1853 Sherman sought a partnership in the New Orleans branch. This was unavailable, but he was offered a partnership in the San Francisco branch. His resignation from the Army hadn't taken effect, and Turner said Sherman should get transferred from the New Orleans to the San Francisco Commissary. "I know that you possess an extraordinary business capacity," Turner wrote. "Your situation as Commissary at San Francisco would throw you continually in contact with business men; you would, sooner than any man of my acquaintance find out and become familiar with avenues of trade and speculation. You would thus be on hand to avail yourself of the thousand and one opportunities which, as we learn from every quarter, are there presented for making a fortune."[20] Sherman's brother John was enthusiastic. "From your business habits and experience, you ought in a few years to acquire a fortune."[21]

Turner (a West Point graduate) got W.T. Sherman a six-month leave to go to California and give it a try. If successful, Sherman would resign from the Army since he couldn't do both jobs full time. His status as the son-in-law of a former Treasury secretary was of some value in the San Francisco banking community, as was his decision to employ Schuyler Hamilton (grandson of Washington Treasury). Another top aide to Sherman was Benjamin Nesbit, whose father was prominent at the Bank of Kentucky (as were Henry Clay and the father-in-law of Abraham Lincoln). Sherman's banker salary was $5,000 (buying power of $160,000 in 2019) plus one-eighth of the profits. This was better than Sherman's $1,560 Army salary. He promised to stay with Lucas & Turner until at least 1860. He started with $100,000 of capital, but the financial jungle of San Francisco was so hungry that Sherman called for and got another $200,000. He made a hat full of money and spent it in a first-class lifestyle.

Sherman became San Francisco's leading citizen and was irked that his wife wanted to return to their old Ohio home to be near old friends. Sherman hoped to save $5,000 to $10,000 a year in San Francisco and decided he would rather have his wife leave him than lose out on all that money. He bought one side of a brick duplex for $3,500. Ca. 1855 he borrowed $7,000 (2019 buying power of $202,000) to buy a $9,000 house. This became a financial strain. Sherman said, "I cannot confide to Mrs. Sherman the fact that I am not saving money,"[22] especially since money was Sherman's excuse for staying in San Francisco! The St. Louis headquarters of Sherman's bank offered to buy the house and let the family stay without rent, as thanks for his great work. Sherman declined, but felt tied to San Francisco by the money invested in the house. He felt uncomfortable about that. He felt obligated to display a scale of living appropriate to the city's leading citizen, spending all his income. "I don't think I am one dollar's richer this day than when I left New Orleans."[23]

During an 1855 San Francisco bank run Wells Fargo stayed closed, letting Lucas & Turner take the blows. The father of John Hays Hammond (mining engineer who worked with future President Herbert Hoover) helped save Lucas & Turner in the run. Lucas & Turner withstood the run, but Sherman never forgot that Wells Fargo had left him hanging, to twist slowly, slowly in the wind. "War is fool's play compared to this," Sherman remarked once.[24] After the run Louis McLane (son of Jackson Treasury) became Wells Fargo president, and Charles McLane was San Francisco agent. Louis had served in the Army under John Frémont (1856 Republican Presidential nominee). Sherman had a nephew of Pacific Mail agent William F. Babcock working at Lucas & Turner. William Seward's (Lincoln State) multimillionaire law partner was president of Wells Fargo Express Company, and Leland Stanford (Central Pacific RR) was a Wells Fargo Express Co. director. Wells Fargo was a top client of the law firm in which President Grover Cleveland clerked in 1855. Other directors over the years included W. Averell Harriman (Truman Commerce) and his father, and banking associates of Strauss (Hoover Pvt. secretary, Eisenhower Commerce). President Jimmy Carter's associate Ernest Arbuckle was Wells Fargo Bank Chairman.

Sherman's Lucas & Turner bank became a powerful and respected West Coast financial institution. Sherman suffered from asthma and expected to die from the San Francisco climate. He was determined to kill himself, if necessary to make money. When Sherman declined to run for City Treasurer, fearing conflict of interest, the Lucas & Turner firm raised his salary by the same amount the City Treasurer was paid, $4,000.

Sherman was in heavy debt when the San Francisco bank was closed by the St. Louis headquarters. He was then sent to the New York City branch, taking a total loss on all his California real estate. Ca. 1859, however, a member of the firm paid Sherman $6,150 ($185,000 in 2019 buying power) for the San Francisco house. Sherman left his wife and family in Ohio, saying they bothered him too much. Columbus Delano (Grant Interior) was a member of New York City's Delano, Dunlevy, & Co. at about this time and may have known Sherman as a fellow New York banker. Sherman's wealthy New York acquaintance William Scott helped provide contacts with New York and Boston circles. Henry Hitchcock (brother of McKinley Interior) was a wealthy friend and associate of Sherman. Sherman eventually became friends with top capitalists Moses Taylor, Peter Cooper, A. Stewart (Grant Treasury nominee), and William H. Aspinwall (grand uncle of FDR).

Sherman knew Aspinwall from San Francisco, where he offered to help with Mrs. Sherman's trip back to the East. Aspinwall was in a good position to help, since he had founded Pacific Mail Steamship Co. in 1847. That year Pacific Mail started bribing Congress for mail subsidies. In 1872 alone the company spent nearly $1,000,000 ($20,000,000 in 2019 buying power) to get a ten-year subsidy of $500,000 a year. Pacific Mail had a western coast monopoly from 1859 to 1869. Evarts (A. Johnson AG, Hayes State) was a Pacific mail lawyer, and Samuel Tilden (1872 Democratic Presidential nominee) was interested in the company.

In October 1857, the Lucas & Symonds banking firm (of which Lucas & Turner was part) collapsed. Sherman had invested Army friends' money in Lucas & Turner, among other places. Happily, all depositors were paid in full after the firm flopped. Ethan Allen Hitchcock (uncle of McKinley Interior) was one of the Army friends who entrusted his money to Sherman in San Francisco. In Sherman's banking career he did well for his firm but not for himself. In 1859 Sherman declined a $7,500 salary job ($217,000 in 2019 buying power) establishing a bank in London, England. He eventually returned to his Army career, and won fame for his march to the sea.

Quicksilver

While a San Francisco banker, Sherman was familiar with the New Almaden Quicksilver Mine, having visited it as early as 1849. A British–American syndicate Barrow, Forbes & Company comprised New Almaden. They bought out the Andres Castillero claim and the Jose Reyos claim to the property. And Charles Fossat had bought part of still another claim to the mine, that of Justo Larios. Enter the Quicksilver Mining Company, organized by Robert Walker (Polk Treasury), banker W.W Corcoran (whose firm had been involved with President Tyler's coal and lumber operation), and other Eastern capitalists. Stockholders included Jeremiah Black (Buchanan AG and State), Frederick P. Stanton (law associate of Polk Treasury), and Reverdy Johnson (Z. Taylor AG). Walker's friend and Mississippi Indian land syndicate associate William Gwin (now a U.S. Senator from California) was also involved. The group's lawyer was former U.S.

Supreme Court Justice Curtis, who had been succeeded on the court by Walker's cabinet colleague Nathan Clifford (Polk AG). Quicksilver Mining Co. wanted the New Almaden mine.

Walker challenged Fossat's claim in court. At the same time, however, the U.S. government also challenged Fossat's claim. Walker thus needed to support Fossat's claim in the federal suit or all factions of capitalists would lose the mine to the government. This made things tricky. Fortunately, Walker's old cabinet colleague President James Buchanan (Polk State) ordered Attorney General Black to help Walker. In 1857 Black sent Edwin Stanton (Buchanan AG, Lincoln and A. Johnson War) to California as a special federal attorney to deal with this and other matters. The United States paid Stanton $25,000 ($700,000 in 2019 buying power) plus expenses, more salary than anyone but the President received from the government. Stanton had already been lawyer for one of the groups the government was challenging in various California matters. Stanton soon returned to Washington, where he joined Buchanan's cabinet as Attorney General, with Black becoming Secretary of State. Stanton now abandoned some U.S. claims to the mine.

With the coming of the Lincoln Administration, Fossat hired Black as attorney. Stanton had joined Lincoln's cabinet by the time the Supreme Court decided the government's case in 1863. Reverdy Johnson (Z. Taylor War) was now an opposing attorney. Justice Clifford (Polk AG) delivered the opinion against the Castillero claim and thus against the British-American New Almaden company. Such a declaration favored Fossat. Somewhere along the line Walker's Quicksilver Mining Co. bought Fossat's claim. Walker reportedly sold his share of the claim for $500,000 in 1863 ($10,000,000 in 2019 buying power). The matter was yet to be settled, however, for Edward Bates (Lincoln AG) had renewed U.S. claims that his cabinet colleague Stanton had dropped as Buchanan's Attorney General. Bates urged Lincoln and John Usher to have the government seize the mine. Lincoln gave the go-ahead pending a Supreme Court decision on the final elements of the controversy. Lincoln sent his associate Leonard Swett to do the job. This was against the advice of David Davis (Lincoln associate and U.S. Sup Ct J), who described Swett as "crazy to make money."[25] Before Swett left for California Usher learned that Walker's Quicksilver Mining Co. was seeking to hire Swett. Swett's behavior in California was so outrageous that Usher suspected Swett had been bribed by Quicksilver Mining Co., possibly in connivance with company attorneys Black and Stanton. Relations between Usher and Salmon Chase (Lincoln Treasury) soured over New Almaden. The outcry in California forced Lincoln to retreat, and he ordered Gen. Henry Halleck to restore the mine to the British–American New Almaden Co. Halleck was a partner in New Almaden Co. and was the company's engineer. Halleck also headed a California law firm which represented the company. Moreover, one of the law firm's members was Frederick Billings, Frémont's (1856 Republican Presidential nominee) attorney. This immediately suggested a tie-in with Black, who was hired as Frémont's attorney while a member of Buchanan's cabinet. Bates was suspicious that the capitalist factions were outwitting the government.

Bates personally argued the government's case before the Supreme Court. Caleb Cushing (Pierce AG) had now joined Black in representing Quicksilver Mining Co. Black's associate J.B. Williams, however, apparently joined with the British–American New Almaden Co. and opposed Black. This may have been genuine opposition or evidence of a private accommodation among the parties. Williams had been Black's associate handling California litigation for Frémont. Bates was irked by the conduct of Black and Cushing. In his Supreme Court argument Bates took pains to suggest the possibility of corruption permeating the whole affair. Seward's (Lincoln State) intimate Wall Street associate Thurlow Weed (relative of Garfield PG) and Lincoln's associate Leonard Swett then moved in for a stock market operation as the Supreme Court decision neared. Justice David Davis (Lincoln associate) and Weed were in contact at this point. Although whether Davis leaked is unknown, such conduct by court members had occurred before. At any rate on March 20, 1864, Weed and Swett began buying Quicksilver Mining Co. stock like crazy. On April 4, the court announced its decision regarding Fossat, which sent the mine to Quicksilver Mining Co. Weed and Swett had bought stock at 65⅝ to 67¼. The price was 91 on March 31. The exact point at which the two speculators unloaded is unknown, but they must have made big money. "Stunned, Bates darkly speculated on the motives of the Court."[26] Black's fee in the case was $180,000 in gold. In 1881 New Almaden produced over twenty percent of the world's total yield of quicksilver.

In November 1860 Black became permanent agent for Frémont's (1856 Republican Presidential nominee) California land claims. The hiring of Black was marked by feverish communications, such as, "Fix the amount of your *retainer* and advise me of it by *return Pony* [*Express*]."[27] Part of the excitement, surely, was because Black was still a member of Buchanan's cabinet. And Buchanan had defeated Frémont for the Presidency in 1856. Crittenden (W. Harrison, Tyler and Fill AG) had been a lawyer for Frémont's land claims ca. 1855, as had George M. Bibb who had worked in the Attorney General's office under Caleb Cushing (Pierce AG). As Attorney General, Black had been arguing for the U.S. government side in California land claims. As Frémont's agent Black was opposed in court by Edwin Stanton (Buchanan AG, Lincoln and A. Johnson War) and Reverdy Johnson (Z. Taylor AG).

Slavery

Once there was much debate on whether slavery or free labor was better for the laborer. After all, so much money was invested in a slave that the owner had a strong incentive to keep the slave healthy and adequately fed, clothed, and sheltered. Northern capitalists didn't care if a worker was maimed on the job—there were plenty of shivering, unemployed "free men" to take his place. Slaveowners knew that fleeing bondsmen were all making a terrible mistake that they would always regret, but few if any ever felt enough regret to return to slavery.

"Slaves are capital; the slaveholder is a capitalist. Free labor will be the first to demand the abolition of slavery; capital will be the last to concede it."[28] Those were the words of George Bancroft (Polk Navy) in 1834. Although racism and slavery became intertwined in the United States, traditionally slavery was looked upon as merely an ownership of labor. Slaves could be of the white race, and slave owners could be black. Apprentices and indentured servants were slaves with time limits on their bondage. The issue of labor, not racism, concerned antebellum Americans. The law treated slaves as property, but owners thought of them as laborers. The terms "black" and "worker" were interchangeable. The debate about slavery continued after the Emancipation Proclamation, transformed as the issue of labor unions. Both controversies involved the question of workers' rights, which continues today.

One other aspect of slavery merits notice. Large planters were robber baron capitalists, ruining land and moving on. Slave plantations were a cancer on the South, crowding out needed small farmers and industry. The general planter attitude was to just plant more cotton. Antebellum plantations were reminiscent of latter twentieth century "growth" corporations, continually reinvesting capital in nonproductive ways. Slaves are normally thought of agricultural workers, but they worked in mining and smelting operations, canal construction, factories, and wherever else Southern capitalists needed labor. Slaves were owned by corporations and churches. The capital of the South was tied up in ownership of labor. Prime field hands sold for $1,800 to $2,000 ($53,200 in 2019 buying power). Little money was available for highways, canals, railroads, and industry. The economic advance of the North over the South was due to the more efficient use of Northern capital. Slavery sucks up so much money that a slave economy cannot compete with a free labor economy.

To appreciate the difficulty of ending slavery in America, we must appreciate how deeply government leaders were involved with slavery. This involvement not only showed how alien the idea of abolition was, but what a tremendous financial commitment Presidents and cabinet members had in the slave system. Clearly slavery couldn't end without a tremendous battle.

George Washington owned about 300 slaves while President. He brought along some slaves when he went to the nation's capital of Philadelphia. In 1791 Edmund Randolph (Washington AG) noted a Pennsylvania law that freed slaves who remained in Pennsylvania six months. This was a standard provision in free state laws. Randolph advised Washington's wife to take slave servants out of state for a while. He knew Washington could ill afford the financial loss from losing slaves who stayed too long in Philadelphia. The story is told of a slave who was so badly injured in a survey job that he couldn't walk or even ride a horse. Rather than leave the slave to his fate and lose all the money invested in him, Washington had him transported on a sled. Such acts are supposed to show Washington as a kind taskmaster. Nonetheless several of his slaves fled to the British lines and freedom during the Revolution. He was still losing runaways as President. Washington's "kindness" with men who were a financial investment should be contrasted with floggings of 100 to 300 lashes he dished out to Revolutionary War enlisted men, sometimes ordering the person's flayed back to be washed with salt and water. Floggings were even meted out for card playing, a pastime Washington enjoyed but which he felt unsuitable for the enlisted men. Such double standards and rough treatment were widely known and accounted for some recruitment difficulty.

Randolph (Washington AG and State) owned about 200 slaves while a cabinet member. He took an oath of Pennsylvania citizenship in order to pick up some extra money in private law practice in Pennsylvania courts while U.S. Attorney General. He took some slaves to Philadelphia and became troubled by the same law he had warned Mrs. Washington about. President Washington felt Randolph had nothing to worry about, but Randolph decided to take no chances. He sent his slaves back to Virginia, keeping the reason secret lest they learn that they had almost become free. The mother of Hamilton (Washington Treasury) owned ten to fifteen slaves. Hamilton himself directed West Indies slave transactions for prominent New York City merchant Nicholas Kruger ca. 1772. As a prize agent for cargo captured by privateers, Pickering (Washington and Adams State) sold off slave cargoes. Pickering hated slavery and was distressed by the inconsistency of his business actions with his moral ideals.

After losing forty-six slaves to the British lines and freedom during the Revolution, President Thomas Jefferson (Washington State and Adams VP) owned 200 in 1789. As Secretary of State he wanted the British to pay for part of his loss. Hamilton told the English not to worry about it. Jefferson sold some slaves and mortgaged others to pay debts. His father-in-law had been a slave trader and ran up large debts via loans to purchase slaves.

Jefferson wrote in the summer of 1787 during the Constitutional Convention, "Nor would I willingly sell slaves as long as there remains any prospect of paying my debts with their labor." Aaron Burr (Jefferson VP) was an owner, slavery being legal in New York up to 1827. John Breckinridge (Jefferson AG) sent most of his slaves from Virginia to his Kentucky lands, splitting families. He hired them out in Kentucky for the income it would bring him. His slaves worked in a Kentucky sawmill, rope factory, paper factory, and also manufactured tombstones. Breckinridge ridiculed the idea of abolition. John Marshall (Adams State) owned slaves.

President James Madison (Jefferson State) was an owner; William Crawford (Madison War) had about forty, and George Campbell about twenty. The mother of Alexander Dallas (Madison Treasury) mistreated her slaves. The wife of Paul Hamilton (Madison Navy) inherited twenty-three slaves. President James Monroe (Madison War and State) sold some of his to provide his brother with urgently needed funds in 1787. Monroe also sold several for $5,000 to help pay a $9,000 debt he owed John Jacob Astor. John McLean (Monroe, JQA and Jackson PG) once refused to sell a slave even though the money would have wiped McLean's debts clean. In May 1811 slaveowner Henry Clay (JQA State) announced a slave auction to be held in front of the hotel he owned, to satisfy a debt owed to a law client. Clay himself owned up to sixty slaves. The family tutor Amos Kendall (Jackson PG) noted that Clay's thirteen-year-old son pulled a knife and threatened to stab one slave, and that a twelve-year-old son attempted to kill several. These were examples of slave owners who were indifferent to the well-being of their bondsmen.

John C. Calhoun (Monroe War, JQA and Jackson VP, John Tyler State) owned up to eighty. Calhoun's wife felt offended by a house slave and threatened to have him whipped. He thereupon ran away but was caught. Calhoun ordered, "Have him lodged in jail for one week, to be fed on bread and water, and to employ some one for me to give him 30 lashes well laid at the end of the time.... I deem it necessary to our proper security to prevent the formation of the habit of running away, and I think it better to punish him before his return home than afterwards."[29] In 1845 Calhoun offered to buy a group of slaves for $14,000 ($460,000 in 2019 buying power).

President Jackson was a large slaveholder. A visitor to one of his plantations in 1818 reported a field "white with cotton and alive with negroes."[30] Jackson found a slave to be acceptable collateral for a loan he gave out, though he was irked when a debtor offered slaves after an opportunity had passed to sell them "down the river" at New Orleans. In 1839 he urged his son to get slaves in legal action against a Jackson debtor and use them to pay for a piano. Like Calhoun, Jackson was alert to safety of slaveowner families; once Jackson ordered fifty lashes for his wife's maid. Jackson wasn't always insensitive, however. Despite being pressed for funds, ca. 1817 he spent $1,800 to unite a slave family. In the 1840s he spent $34,000 to unite a slave husband and wife. After Jackson died his son sold them apart to two different buyers. One purchaser then found and bought the other spouse to unite them again. After that they stayed together until death. In 1816 Edward Livingston (Jackson State) offered $24,000 for forty of Jackson's slaves ($425,000 in 2019 buying power). William Barry (Jackson PG) owned slaves, as did the wife of Louis McLane (Jackson Treasury and State). McLane sought to sell one so he and his wife could get together while he was in Congress.

Jackson cabinet members were involved with a notable dispute on the slavery question. The slave cargo of the Spanish-registry ship *Amistad*, led by the charismatic Cinqué, managed to take over the vessel and sail it to the United States. John Forsyth (Jackson State) favored turning the "mutineers" over to Spanish authorities for Spanish style justice. Levi Woodbury (Jackson and Van Buren Treasury), Felix Grundy (Van Buren AG), Amos Kendall (Jackson PG), and Henry Gilpin (Van Buren AG) concurred with Forsyth's stance. Former President John Quincy Adams (Monroe State), however, led a monumental fight to save the blacks, winning a federal court order to free them and send them back to Africa. Forsyth then spearheaded an unsuccessful appeal. Reports that Cinqué later became a wealthy and influential slavetrader himself have been challenged by historians. John Quincy Adams was feisty in slavery controversies, putting up with outrage from Congressional colleagues and hatred (including death threats) from the public. Such threats had to be taken seriously. Vice President Van Buren presided over the Senate with pistols, and one anti-slavery Senator was beaten nearly to death on the Senate floor some years later.

A controversy involving several cabinet members was the Dred Scott case decided by slaveowner Roger Taney (Jackson AG & Treasury). James Campbell (Pierce PG) was a lawyer in the case. Scott's attorney was Montgomery Blair (Lincoln PG). The lawyer who got Scott returned to slavery was Reverdy Johnson (Z. Taylor AG). In 1821 Johnson successfully defended the manumission of ten slaves that Taney was trying to return to bondage. Three years later Taney was a lawyer for an indicted slavetrader. This was a hanging offense. Taney argued that the indictment should be dismissed due to defects. For instance it failed to say the slave ship prepared to sail or departed from U.S. territory. Also the indictment read, "with the intent that the vessel *should be employed* in the slave trade" while the statute read "with intent *to employ*."[31] Justice Story ruled that the slavetrader committed the illegal acts, but agreed with Taney that the case should be dismissed due to the indictment's defects, such as those noted above. This case helped generate slave state support to make Taney Attorney

General and later Chief Justice. John Eaton's (Jackson War) family-owned slaves.

An 1841 lawsuit asked whether a slave buyer had to pay for slaves illegally brought into Mississippi. Henry Gilpin (Van Buren AG) along with Polk's Treasury Secretary Robert Walker, whose slave empire was based on other persons' money, argued that the contract was invalid, that their client could keep the slaves without paying. Clay (JQA State) and Webster (W.H. Harrison, J. Tyler, and Fillmore State) argued that the contract was valid, that a deal is a deal. The U.S. Supreme Court got around the arguments by ruling that the slaves were brought in legally.

President Van Buren's father was a slave owner. Joel Poinsett (Van Buren War) and Felix Grundy (Van Buren AG) owned slaves. Grundy liked one of his slaves so much that Grundy had him buried at Grundy's feet. President William Henry Harrison had slaves, as did his Secretary of State Daniel Webster, who bought one of President Madison's. John Crittenden (W.H. Harrison, J. Tyler, and Fillmore AG) was an owner. President Tyler (W.H. Harrison VP) owned about seventy, borrowing from Richmond banks to buy some. Bell (W.H. Harrison and J. Tyler War) was a wealthy slave owner. John Bell lost $10,000 in lynched slaves when an "insurrection plot" was discovered at the Tennessee iron mines and mills where they worked. Abel Upshur (J. Tyler Navy and State) was a slaveholder, and Wickliffe's (J. Tyler PG) father was the greatest slave owner in Kentucky. President Polk and Robert Walker (Polk Treasury) were owners. President Zachary Taylor owned over 100, valued at about $50,000 ca. 1848 ($1,600,000 in 2019 buying power). His son-in-law Jefferson Davis (Pierce War and CSA President) was a slave owner, as were all members of the CSA cabinet, and Davis's brother Joseph owned 1,000. President James Buchanan (Polk State), John Breckinridge (Buchanan VP), and Lewis Cass (Jackson War, Buchanan State) were owners. John Floyd (Buchanan War) owned forty in 1837. Howell Cobb (Buchanan Treasury) had over 1,000.

The father of Montgomery Blair (Lincoln PG) was a slave owner, as were the father and brother of Edward Bates (Lincoln AG). James Speed (Lincoln AG) was a slave owner. President Andrew Johnson (Lincoln VP) had slaves, as did the father of Orville Browning (Johnson Interior). Future President Grant was a slave holder in 1859, and his wife owned several. While president of Louisiana State University in 1860 W.T. Sherman (Grant War) urged his brother John (Hayes Treasury, McKinley State) to be more discrete in anti-slavery utterances lest they cause trouble for W.T. Sherman. His function at LSU was made clear by Louisiana planter Braxton Bragg: "Give us well-disciplined masters, managers, and assistants, and we shall never hear of slave insurrections."[32] W.T. Sherman felt slavery was necessary, stating, "Rice, sugar, and certain kinds of cotton cannot be produced except by forced negro labor."[33] Sherman wanted to buy a few slaves himself, noting, "Niggers won't work unless they are owned."[34] Although Henry Wilson (Grant VP) was a prominent anti-slavery spokesman his personal fortune came from manufacturing cheap shoes probably intended for slaves. In 1847 he had 109 employees, who put out well over 120,000 pair. The father of Hamilton Fish (Grant State) was a slave owner, as was Benjamin Bristow's (Grant Treasury) father. David Key's (Hayes PG) in-laws owned slaves, and Richard Thompson's (Hayes Navy) aunt owned 100.

The family of President Arthur (Garfield VP) owned slaves, and his wife owned one. The father-in-law of Walter Gresham (Arthur PG, Cleveland State) was an owner, as were the fathers of Hilary Herbert (Cleveland Navy) and William Wilson (Cleveland PG). William Wilson himself was an owner, as was Lucius Lamar (Cleveland Interior). One of Lamar's relatives was hoping for a $480,000 profit on one (just one!) slaver expedition he was planning to send to Africa from New York City ca. 1859 ($14,400,000 in 2019 buying power). This was a capital crime. Lamar's relative was the son of the president of New York City's Bank of the Republic. The *Wanderer* was ostensibly sold to a member of a yacht club, but actually went to the relative of Lamar for use in African slave trade. Captives were landed in Georgia on Jekyll Island. U.S. Senator Thomas Hendricks (Cleveland VP) opposed the Thirteenth Amendment to the Constitution. Augustus Garland (Cleveland AG) overturned that part of the 1868 Arkansas constitution which had prevented collection of money from old slave sale contracts. President Theodore Roosevelt's (McKinley VP) mother had slaves, as did the father of William McAdoo (Wilson Treasury) and the father of Col. Edward House (Wilson adviser).

Quite possibly more cabinet members owned slaves, but information becomes sketchy for cabinets after the Buchanan Administration—slaveholding was no longer something to brag about.

Our leaders have a meager anti-slavery record up to the Lincoln Administration. Prominent cabinet members belonged to the American Colonization Society, but this wasn't an anti-slavery organization. Its goal rather was to ship free blacks out of the country. President Lincoln endorsed a plan of Ambrose W. Thompson to colonize free blacks in Panama, having them work coal mines. The U.S. Navy was to get the coal for half price. Richard Thompson (Hayes Navy) was a lawyer for the colonization planners. The plan was soon revealed as merely a scheme to milk the U.S. Treasury, and Lincoln terminated federal support in 1862. Again, however, this was no abolitionist activity.

A few cabinet members were involved in anti-slavery court cases. Ca. 1847 Illinois law freed slaves who were brought into the state by their owners. Abraham Lincoln represented a slaveholder who thereby lost his title to his slaves and who sought to send a slave family to Kentucky for sale as Deep South plantation labor. This was a well settled point of law, but Lincoln took on the case, albeit reluctantly, perhaps knowing that his client couldn't possibly win. Montgomery Blair (Lincoln PG), Salmon Chase (Lincoln Treasury), and William Seward (Lincoln State) all had widely publicized roles attacking slavery in court—but again none of these men served in cabinets before Lincoln. President Rutherford Hayes was a prominent anti-slavery lawyer. William Evarts (Johnson AG, Hayes State) and future President Arthur (Garfield VP) took anti-slavery positions in court as lawyers for New York state. As New Mexico Territory Attorney General, Stephen Elkins (B. Harrison War) prosecuted violations of anti-slavery laws in the 1860s and 1870s, but he was partly motivated by the $25 fee from the federal government for each indictment (conviction was unnecessary to get the fee)—which added up to a tidy amount. Cabinet members who took a stand against slavery outside of court cases can almost be counted on the fingers of one hand. President John Quincy Adams, as noted earlier, was a courageous public opponent of slavery. John Frémont (1856 Republican Presidential nominee) refused to use slave labor in his California mines, and his wife refused gifts of slaves offered by her family. Zachariah Chandler (Grant Interior) raised $1,900 for abolitionists in 1848 ($61,000 in 2019 buying power).

This is roughly the extent of the anti-slavery record accumulated by Presidents and cabinet members. The meagerness is understandable as a matter of economics. Almost every President and cabinet member was a well-to-do capitalist, most of them sharing the antipathy or downright prejudice of employers against laborers. As long as the work got done, few of our leaders cared about the workers. Abolitionists were regarded as Communists, subversives who agitated the workers—subversives who sometimes supported acts of violence against slave owners and their plantations and factories, subversives who defied constitutional government.

Worker Rights

Anti-slavery agitation publicized exploitation of workers, raising the consciousness of many Americans. Abolitionists started the movement for workers' rights, in which the end of slavery was a great victory. This invigorated the movement instead of quieting it, and an era of vicious labor–management strife began. As might be expected, our national leaders generally continued to support employers over workers.

Future President Pierce (who was a relative of textile king Abbott Lawrence) was an attorney for New Hampshire textile mills fighting the ten-hour work day in 1848 and 1849. Textile workers in Pittsburgh, PA, struck for a ten-hour day. Mill owners responded with a lock out and with scabs. Some fights occurred, and strikers organized a boycott. On behalf of mill owners Edwin Stanton (Buchanan AG, Lincoln War) sued the strikers for damages. Stanton won and even got some women strikers jailed. This success attracted more wealthy clients to him.

President Buchanan (Polk State) was nicknamed "Ten Cent Jimmy" for his advocacy of reduced wages to improve sales of American exports. In the Civil War Congress passed a law allowing capitalists to import foreign workers and use their labor until the transportation cost had been paid from their wages. Anyone familiar with "company store" operations will see how this could be a lifetime proposition. Salmon Chase (Lincoln Treasury) and Gideon Welles (Lincoln Navy) endorsed the American Emigrant Co., which was formed to expedite this.

Orville Browning (Grant Interior) was a CB&Q Railroad attorney against the grangers. William Evarts (Johnson AG, Hayes State) duplicated this service for the Chicago and Northwestern Railway Co.

When Congress reduced the federal workday to eight hours in 1868, the War Department made a corresponding cut in wages. This was contrary to the law's intent, but Evarts (Johnson AG) and Ebenezer Hoar (Grant AG) both ruled in favor of the reduction. President Grant, with the strong support of Vice President Henry Wilson, ordered the wages restored to the law's intended level. In 1877 President Benjamin Harrison and six other men formed an armed vigilante committee to suppress railroad strikers in Indianapolis, IN. U.S. District Judge Walter Gresham (Arthur PG, Cleveland State) promised to take no administrative action without vigilante approval. In 1887 the Cravath law firm represented Old Dominion Steamship Company in crushing a strike, beginning a long string of labor cases for the law firm. Cravath was an ex-law partner of Charles Evans Hughes (Harding and Coolidge State). Cravath law firm affiliates over the years included the son-in-law of Benjamin Butler (Jackson and Van Buren AG), Richard Blatchford (tutor in Robert R. Livingston family, executor of Daniel Webster's will, adviser to Zachary Taylor), Abraham Lincoln (local counsel for Springfield, IL, litigation, father of Garfield War), William Seward (Lincoln and A. Johnson State), Samuel Blatchford (U.S. Supreme Court Justice and private secretary to Seward), the son of William Evarts (Johnson AG, Hayes State), James McReynolds (Wilson AG, U.S. Supreme Court Justice), Russell Leffingwell (Wilson Asst. Treasury), Joseph Cotton (Hoover Undersecretary of State, law partner of Wilson Treasury), Roswell Magill (FDR Undersecretary of Treasury), John J. McCloy (FDR Asst. War), William O. Douglas (U.S. Supreme Court Justice), Roswell Gilpatric (JFK Deputy Defense), John Conner (LBJ Commerce), Eugene V. Rostow (LBJ Vietnam adviser) and William Miller (Carter Treasury).

John Hay (Lincoln private secretary, McKinley State) hated railroad strikers and felt they brought shame to America. President Taft (TR War) called coal and railroad strikers' tactics Bolshevistic, a minority choking off a vital service to compel the majority to submit. Taft admitted issuing anti-labor injunctions "almost by the bushel" as a judge. His judicial opinions destroyed Congressional efforts to limit child labor. In the mid–1920s Taft called the U.S. Senate a "Bolshevik body" and grimly decided in 1929 to remain Chief Justice as long as possible, to keep the "Bolsheviki" from controlling the Supreme Court. As an employer Henry Payne (TR PG) was anti-union. Josephus Daniels (Wilson Navy) felt the union demand for an eight-hour day was excessive and would hurt labor's cause. Ca. the 1920s Henry Stimson (Taft War, Hoover State, FDR and Truman War, law partner of McKinley War and of TR State) on behalf of the New York attorney general prosecuted a union group as violators of anti-monopoly laws! The father of Andrew Mellon (Harding, Coolidge, Hoover Treasury) said labor unions were okay, but it was impermissible for them to shut down an employer's operation. The father visited an antebellum Mississippi plantation and noted how similar the slave quarters were to the miners' quarters provided by his coal company. Secretary Andrew Mellon's companies had a twelve-hour day: Union Steel, Alcoa, Gulf Oil. While cutting wages and discharging workers in the Great Depression, Gulf Oil had reserves of $280,000,000, Alcoa $85,000,000, and Koppers $50,000,000. Frank Murphy (FDR AG) was a vigorous anti-labor lawyer in his younger days. Michael Blumenthal (Carter Treasury) said reviving child labor and reducing the minimum wage were ideas that should be examined.

As in slave times, few cabinet members supported workers in labor disputes. William B. Wilson (Wilson Labor), Martin Durkin (Eisenhower Labor), Arthur Goldberg (JFK Labor), and perhaps a handful of others appear to have solid records in support of workers.

Today slavery is generally viewed only in a moral context. Biographies of slaveholders usually deal only with the capital investment represented by the victims. In terms of worker exploitation, however, Presidents and cabinet members share a consensus right up to modern times.

Incidentally, this record shows why Republicans, "the party of Lincoln," turned against blacks. The Republicans were an uneasy alliance of Whig capitalists and abolitionist social revolutionaries. Both factions were committed to ending slavery. Once this happened the alliance disintegrated, splitting the party. Abolitionists wanted to continue and expand social reforms. Whigs merely wanted to liberate the capital invested in slaves, and were positively opposed to improving the lot of workers. The showdown between these two elements of the party was President Andrew Johnson's impeachment, with Johnson as the Whig champion. With the

Whig impeachment victory the abolitionists were expelled from the Republican Party. "The party of Lincoln" ceased to exist in 1868, and that is why blacks had no political influence for the next century despite Republican dominance in national politics. The brevity of abolitionist power in national politics (1856 to 1868) is no surprise, given our leaders' basic hostility toward workers dating from the 1700s. Abolitionists were useful to the immediate purpose of Whig capitalists, and were discarded when that usefulness ended.

Chapter 6

Transportation

As the Civil War approached, division between North and South was reflected in business interests of men who eventually led the Union and Confederacy.

For years rivers were the main inland transportation system. This commerce brought together many interested persons at the 1847 Rivers and Harbors convention in Chicago.

Schuyler Colfax (Grant VP) was principal secretary at the meeting. Edward Bates (Lincoln AG), who had been president of the 1844 convention, also attended—as did Lincoln and Elihu Washburne (Grant State) who chatted together there. Lincoln also attracted attention from conventioneer Norman Judd (Lincoln minister to Russia) who, ten years later, convinced his associates to hire Lincoln as their lawyer in the Rock Island Bridge case.

In the middle of the Mississippi River was a speck called Rock Island, owned by the U.S. government. Railroads wanted to use it in building a bridge. Rivermen feared this would obstruct navigation. A test of strength began between the two factions. In defiance of a law permitting bridge construction, Jefferson Davis (Pierce War) yielded to river interests and to interests including himself, who favored a southern route for the proposed transcontinental railroad. The bridge would strengthen proponents of the central route. Davis forbade using Rock Island for a bridge support and sought a court injunction to settle this matter permanently. In 1855 the U.S. Supreme Court ruled in favor of the bridge. It was built to carry the Chicago, Rock Island & Pacific Railroad from Illinois to Iowa, where it became the Mississippi & Missouri railroad run by John Dix (Buchanan Treasury). The steamboat *Effie Afton* hit a bridge pier and was a total wreck. The railroads were sued, and brought in attorney Abraham Lincoln. Since considerable evidence indicated that the boat had rammed the bridge deliberately, trying to knock it down, Lincoln was able to keep a jury from reaching a decision. The case was dismissed, and Lincoln's railroad clients were in the clear. Already Lincoln and Jefferson Davis were on opposite sides.

Cotton

For many years cotton was crucial to the U.S. economy, bringing in a lot of money from Europe, with European investors funding much of American's economic expansion. Part of this money disappeared into slave purchases. Yet part also went into banks, thereby providing capital for other business enterprise. Much cotton money stayed in the North, with bankers, brokers, and merchants. Although North and South worked together in cotton, the South viewed the partnership as lopsided: The South grew the cotton, and the North kept the profits. Indeed, there is reason to view the North, particularly New York City, as ruler of the cotton economy. The North and South division of business interests can be seen among government leaders who dealt with cotton and textiles.

The father of Joseph Habersham (Washington PG) was Georgia's first great cotton grower, sending exports to England. William Crawford (Madison War, Madison and Monroe Treasury, relative of Z. Taylor War) was a grower, as was John C. Calhoun (Madison War, JQA and Jackson VP, J.Tyler State, relative of Van Buren AG and of Taft War). A fire ca. 1825 cost Calhoun his ginhouse and a season's crop. This left him pressed for money and may account for a large debt he owed to Joel Poinsett (Van Buren War) about this time. Calhoun paid that off in two years. Clay (JQA State) was proprietor of Madison Hemp Company, with 1,200 water powered spindles for flax and hemp.

President Jackson had several cotton plantations in Mississippi, Alabama, and Tennessee—including one on land he bought from reputed river pirate John Melton. Ca. 1804 one shipment alone was over 56,000 pounds. Jackson even exported cotton to England, thus having a financial stake in British trade policies. Ca. 1804 he was one of the few planters in his area who owned a cotton gin, paying a special tax on it and allowing his neighbors' cotton to be worked in it. In 1823 Jackson devoted almost all his energies to the cotton crop, and two years later he attributed excellent prices to the tariff had had voted for. As President a decade later, Jackson left plantation management to his son—whose incompetence harshly damaged Jackson's finances. In vain Jackson hoped his presidential salary would allow him to recover from the blow. After leaving office Jackson saw his 1841 crop fail, his 1842 profits wiped out by shipping charges, and his 1843 crop at the Halcyon Plantation in Mississippi destroyed by flood. These were on top of simultaneous financial disasters caused by his son.

John Forsyth (Jackson and Van Buren State) raised nankeen cotton. President Polk had a Tennessee cotton plantation, supervised by his brother-in-law. Hugh Legaré (Tyler AG) was a cotton grower.

President Zachary Taylor helped incorporate Taylor Cotton Mills of Cannelton, IN, an operation which failed before producing anything. Nonetheless Taylor made big money from cotton production. In 1824 his first crop yielded a $1500 profit ($39,000 in 2019 buying power). His boyhood friend Mannsel White was a prominent banker and cotton broker who sold Taylor's cotton. By the 1840s Taylor generally had at least $20,000 deposited in White's New Orleans bank all the time, over $50,000 in June 1849 ($1,600,000 in 2019 buying power). Taylor's son-in-law Jefferson Davis (Pierce War) was a planter, as were his father and very rich brother. Cotton men supported future President James Buchanan (Polk State) for the 1852 Democratic presidential nomination won by Pierce. The uncle of Pierce's wife was Amos Lawrence, brother of textile king Abbott Lawrence—whose influence on American government was noted earlier. John Floyd (Buchanan War) was a big Arkansas planter, and the wife of Howell Cobb (Buchanan Treasury) had several excellent cotton plantations. Robert Toombs (CSA State) was the son of a wealthy planter, and George Trenholm (CSA Treasury) had great cotton interests. Lucius Lamar (Cleveland Interior) was a grower, and the father of Oscar Straus (TR Commerce & Labor) had most of his money in cotton while living in Georgia during the Civil War.

Presidents and cabinet members were active in the manufacture of cloth. Washington made and sold cloth, doing especially well in the Revolution when British imports were cut off. To promote the U.S. textile industry President Washington wore a homespun suit at his first inauguration. Oliver Wolcott (Washington and Adams Treasury) was a woolens manufacturer in Litchfield, CT. He invested in Jeremiah Wadsworth's wool cloth factory. Wadsworth was an associate of William Duer (Washington Asst Treasury) and John Church—men close to Alexander Hamilton (Washington Treasury). The father of Gideon Welles (Lincoln and A. Johnson Navy) was a real estate associate of Wolcott and a partner in a woolen mill. Welles's father also turned his store into a yarn manufacturing enterprise called Eagle Company. While a diplomat in France, future President John Adams sent various gauzes, linens, threads, and ribbons to his wife back in the United States. She had friends sell the items on commission.

Louis McLane (Jackson Treasury and State) and his brother-in-law rented out a cotton factory. McLane, the DuPont family, and others sent Isaac Briggs to Washington, D.C., to lobby for a higher textile tariff in 1815. McLane's operation had sixty employees in 1832. He and his brother-in-law sold out three years later for $16,500 ($470,000 in 2019 buying power).

William March (Polk War, Pierce State) and a partner owned a cotton mill. Ca. 1840 it burned, and neither partner had enough money to rebuild. Cornelius Bliss (McKinley Interior), James Gary (McKinley PG), and the son-in-law of Benjamin Bristow (Grant Treasury) were rich textile manufacturers.

In 1851 Levi Morton (B. Harrison VP) was a junior partner in J.M. Beebe & Company. Beebe was a Boston importing and jobbing house that had a big cotton trade, along with railroads, banking, and insurance connections. In 1854 Morton became head of Morton, Grinnell & Company, a wholesale drygoods commission house, which went bankrupt in May 1861 due to Southern customers refusing to pay their tabs. This refusal had much to do with rallying Northern capitalists behind Lincoln's war measures. Buchanan didn't have such encouragement since neither the extent nor the effect of Southern debt repudiation had been felt during the final weeks of Buchanan's presidency. Morton's creditors got fifty cents on the dollar. He restarted his business by the end of 1861 and remained the firm's head until 1863, when he began devoting more energy to banking. Around 1868 Morton paid off the old creditors in full, even though all had been settled legally via bankruptcy proceedings. This generated much good feeling toward the banking firm of L.P. Morton & Company. Morton became a partner in Morton, Rose & Co. of London. That British firm was run by Sir John Rose (Canadian Minister of Finance). Presidents Grant, Hayes, and Benjamin Harrison made Morton, Rose & Co. fiscal agent for the United States. All U.S. government finances in Europe passed through the bank, from consular fees to diplomatic salaries to bond sales. This lucrative Republican arrangement ended with President Cleveland's resumption of power in 1893.

Cornelius Bliss (McKinley Interior) joined Morton's J.M. Beebe & Co. in 1848 and stayed until 1866. About that time Bliss became a partner in John S. & Eben Wright and company, a Boston textile mill operation with a New York branch. The New York operation eventually became greater than Boston's. Wright, Bliss, & Fabyan became one of the nation's top textile firms. After the Wrights died the company name became Bliss, Fabyan & Co. Bliss ran the company until he died. The firm became known throughout the world. Bliss was also director of American Cotton Company. Wealthy capitalists would come to Bliss for help. He left McKinley's cabinet to spend more time with his business, and even McKinley's offer of the vice presidency in 1900 failed to lure Bliss away.

Improved agricultural technology boosted grain yields in the Midwest, so much that by the mid–1850s the North no longer needed money from Southern cotton. Although Southern leaders were emboldened by the belief that cotton could still coerce the North, agricultural economics had drastically changed. The North was superior to the South in industry, and now at least an even match in agriculture. Probably most persons didn't realize this. Gradual developments are often unnoticed as they happen. Three Northern leaders in particular, however, had become acutely aware of the changed circumstances. Through patent litigation involving the McCormick reaper, Abraham Lincoln, Edwin Stanton (Lincoln War), and William Seward (Lincoln State) knew that the North need no longer tremble at threats from King Cotton. They also knew that the reaper could free much agricultural manpower for military service. All this knowledge may have stiffened the resistance and resolution of these three key leaders, and emboldened them to stand up to the Southern aristocracy. (The South, incidentally, also miscalculated in thinking England would have to come to terms over cotton). The war-induced boom in iron, armaments, and marine affairs balanced the injury to the British textile industry. The British gross national product was thus largely unaffected by any loss of American cotton, which eliminated leverage that Confederate leaders had anticipated.

Another way to make money in wartime is trading with the enemy. Lincoln authorized select individuals to engage in cotton trade with Confederate sources. His associate Leonard Swett and William Seward's (Lincoln State) associate Thurlow Weed operated together in this trade. Orville Browning (A. Johnson Interior) got Lincoln's help in Confederate cotton deals involving Lincoln's sister-in-law Emily Todd Helm. Before the war Lincoln's father-in-law, described as a smooth operator, was a member of the cotton manufacturing firm Oldham, Todd & Co. Lincoln handled several law cases for his father-in-law. General Grant protested Browning's project to Edwin Stanton (Lincoln War), who went to Lincoln about it. In the end Browning's project flopped. Grant wasn't in the best of positions to protest. His father was shipping cheap cotton north from occupied territory to make speculative profit on high Northern prices. And Grant's real estate partner James Russell Jones was also involved with cotton trading in occupied territory.

A dramatic Confederate cotton deal was engineered by the son-in-law of Salmon Chase (Lincoln Treasury) with a permit issued by Chase. The son-in-law's inherited fortune was based on the largest textile plant in New England, the Sprague Manufacturing Company. The Confederate deal included use of counterfeit Confederate money and sending large quantities of guns to the rebels. The brother of Montgomery Blair (Lincoln PG) said Chase's son-in-law stood to make $2,000,000. The cotton–munitions deal was smashed by Gen. John Dix (Buchanan Treasury), the same Dix whose railroad was connected with the Rock Island bridge case which Lincoln argued. Evidence of the cotton–munitions deal was covered up by Stanton (Lincoln War).

After the Civil War, the U.S. Supreme Court ruled that every Confederate cotton trade permit issued by Lincoln was illegal.

Railroads

The more agricultural products the Midwest had to ship, the more money Chicago and railroads would make. Railroads' self-interest dictated support for Cyrus H. McCormick and his reaper. Indeed McCormick reaper sales, railroad construction, and wheat production seemed interlocked from 1849 to 1859.

In 1854 John Manny challenged McCormick's patents. McCormick's lawyers included Reverdy Johnson (Z. Taylor AG) and Thad Stevens (later leader of radical Republican Congressmen in the Civil War). Manny's lawyers included Lincoln, Edwin Stanton (Lincoln War), Peter Watson (Lincoln Assistant War), and George Harding (to whom President Lincoln offered the Commissioner of Patents job). Lincoln had been hired in anticipation of a Chicago trial, but the case was moved to Cincinnati. Although Lincoln traveled there, the other lawyers seemed to resent his presence on their turf, and his assistance was rejected. So he just sat and watched, collecting a fee of $400 to $1,000 ($11,600 to $29,000 in 2019 buying power).

In the 1860 Presidential election the main choice was between Abraham Lincoln and Stephen Douglas, both of Illinois, both of railroads in general, and both of Illinois Central in particular. Again in 1864 the choice was between two Illinois Central men, Abraham Lincoln and George McClellan. The background of Lincoln and his associates made them immediately aware of strategic use of railroads in warfare, a new concept in military strategy, giving the North yet another edge over Southern leadership. In the Confederate cabinet only George Trenholm, John Breckinridge, and Judah Benjamin had railroad experience, and not all of that was pre-war.

Abraham Lincoln was a railroad man. He is often portrayed as a backwoodsman who emerged from the frontier at the hour our nation needed his leadership. Actually his adult career was spent amid Western capitalists and politicians. His reputation was such that he was offered high public office by President Zachary Taylor in the 1840s. Lincoln's service in Congress during that decade brought him into contact with the Eastern establishment, as did his law case work. His in-laws were part of Kentucky's elite.

Lincoln's business activities were intertwined with many railroads. Even his involvement in challenging the McCormick reaper patent can be viewed as railroad-related, to open the plains to more farmers and to thereby increase agricultural freight shipments. As an example of railroad interest in agricultural technology, Illinois Central Railroad offered a

$1,500 prize ($43,500 in 2019 buying power) for the best steam plow at the 1859 state fair, in addition to the fair's prize of $3,000 ($87,000 in 2019 buying power).

Robert Walker (Polk Treasury) was heavily involved with starting the Illinois Central Railroad and in 1850 considered accepting the company's presidency. In 1851 he went to London to negotiate with the Peabody banking house and with Baring Brothers. President John Tyler's banker W.W. Corcoran helped Walker get a friendly reception in London. Walker was IC RR's key money raiser in England. His salary was the interest on all deposits made in the IC RR account. Rothschild U.S. agent August Belmont helped Walker's negotiations with the Rothschilds. Baring Brothers recognized that IC RR success would aid other Illinois investments and help the state government's finances. Illinois securities and particularly public infrastructure bonds were badly declining, and IC RR construction was expected to perk them up. Indeed, Daniel Webster's (Fill State) support for IC RR was probably related to the Illinois security holdings of his friends. Heavy presence of British investment in Northern corporations and government bonds, and desire to protect those investments, was another factor that Southern leaders seemingly failed to consider when anticipating that England's need for cotton would force that country to aid the Confederacy.

IC RR was also expected possibly to help Cairo City & Canal Company which was in trouble. British money was in that enterprise, as were funds from three of Webster's close friends. Yet Baring Brothers refused to help IC RR despite all these reasons for financing the road. This refusal was based on the advice of Baring Brothers' U.S. railroad expert William H. Swift who was also trustee of a canal operation that IC RR would injure. In 1852, however, a British syndicate began financing IC RR. British and Dutch investors largely owned the road at one time. In 1864 the English held three-fourths of all IC RR stock. Prime Minister William Gladstone was on a committee of stock and bondholders. Walker (Polk Treasury) found yet another wrinkle to promote English investment. He used the English money to buy thousands of tons of British railroad iron, which he shipped to America. Thus prosperity of the English iron industry became linked to IC RR.

In 1850 U.S. Sen. Stephen Douglas, Representative and future governor William Bissell, and allies got Congress to make a land grant to Alabama, Mississippi, and Illinois. The states would then turn over the land to railroads. Through this deal IC RR got 2,600,000 acres along its right of way. The railway sent recruiters overseas to sell land and bring over immigrants. Its colonization work changed the Illinois political composition enough to allow a Republican victory in 1860.

When Lincoln went to Congress in 1847 his Springfield house was occupied most of the time by a friend who was IC RR's general solicitor. After IC RR retained Lincoln in one lawsuit, a corporation director wrote: "This is the more fortunate, as he proves to be not only the most prominent of his political party, but the acknowledged special advisor of the Bissell administration." Lincoln was not an employee of IC RR (or any other railway) but did handle about forty law cases for IC RR. His fees were modest; in 1853 he charged $25 for one IC RR case ($800 in 2019 buying power). Lincoln seems to have lobbied the Illinois legislature to pass the IC RR charter in 1851. The charter exempted the road from all taxes except five percent of the gross revenue in the first six years and seven percent thereafter. In 1853 a county tried to tax IC RR. Lincoln followed his lucrative custom of offering his powerful services to each side and was hired by IC solicitor Mason Brayman. Lincoln won the tax exemption case for IC RR and billed the corporation the biggest fee he ever charged—$5,000 (about $145,000 in 2019 buying power). The railroad balked on paying, and this fee arrived just in time to fund Lincoln's 1858 U.S. Senate campaign. Lincoln's law partner summarized the Lincoln–Illinois Central connection: "Much as we deprecated the avarice of great corporations, we both thanked the Lord for letting the Illinois Central Railroad fall into our hands."

President Lincoln made Illinois Central president N.P. Banks and IC vice president George McClellan (1864 Democratic presidential nominee) Civil War generals. McClellan made $3,000 a year ($85,500 in 2019 buying power) as IC's chief engineer in 1857 and $5,000 as vice president in 1858 ($150,000 in 2019 buying power). During the panic of 1857 McClellan developed sidelines to create income for the railroad, such as harvesting Lake Michigan ice and later shipping it to Cairo in southern Illinois during the summer. McClellan even set up an IC line of packets to New Orleans. In 1858 a big Louisville lawyer strongly recommended that McClellan hire W.T. Sherman (Grant War), but McClellan had no job to offer. He cleared all of IC's debts in just two years. McClellan proved himself an expert organizer of men and material for vast undertakings. People marveled at how he left nothing to chance, erecting the strongest possible bridges. For some reason, however, McClellan was reluctant to permit the bridges to prove their strength through use. He stalled on having the first train run across the spans. This character quirk seemed unimportant at the time.

The Civil War allowed IC to recover from its failure in the Panic of 1857. Due to military transport the war guaranteed IC's financial health. IC also sold rolling stock to the government. In 1862 IC's *net* earnings were $1,830,000 (about $45,000,000 in 2019 buying power). Troop transport alone accounted for one-fourth of that sum.

Civil War

Only human ingenuity limited our leaders' ability to make money off the Civil War. What follows is merely a sample.

The most obvious way to make money from a war is from armaments sales. James Blaine (Garfield, Arthur, and B. Harrison State) was a Civil War military agent for the state of Maine. In November 1861 he discussed the Spencer rifle with Warren Fisher, who was seeking a federal contract. They agreed that Blaine would use his influence as Maine's military agent to urge the rifle upon the Secretary of War. Fisher got a contract for 20,000 rifles. Blaine was given a free gift of $10,000 ($290,000 in 2019 buying power) in Spencer rifle company stock. J.P. Morgan's purchase of condemned guns from the government and subsequent profitable resale back to the government is well known. Less known is the participation of Simon Cameron's (Lincoln War) associate Alexander Cummings and Simon Stevens (law partner of Thad Stevens) who reportedly anticipated a $50,000 profit ($1,450,000 in 2019 buying power) on Morgan's deal. Incidentally, Cameron stopped vital orders to foreign arms manufacturers so as to encourage American industry. Other cabinet members and senior General Winfield Scott (1852 Whig presidential nominee) approved Cameron's "Buy American" policy. After the Union defeat at Bull Run the government turned to foreign sources for arms. Baring Brothers helped finance those purchases, and the government of Austria was helpful. Austria was especially interested in friendly relations with the United States since Archduke Maximilian was trying to rule Mexico at the time. Montgomery Blair's (Lincoln PG) brother pushed war contracts for friends. When the war began Gideon Welles (Lincoln and Johnson Navy) appointed several men to send military supplies to Washington, D.C. One was Welles's brother-in-law, who got a 2½ percent commission on contracts for materiel, $95,000 ($2,750,000 in 2019 buying power) in just four and a half months. General Grant made an enemy of Leonard Swett (Lincoln associate) by correcting quartermaster department abuses despite the interest Swett had in the contracts. George Bancroft's (Polk Navy) Civil War investments included iron, railroads, and armaments. At the war's end his income was $9,500 ($145,000 in 2019 buying power) in a four-month period (although this may have included other income sources such as book royalties). Samuel Tilden (1876 Democrat presidential nominee) sold 6,000 tons of gun and machinery metal to the government. Tilden's brother ran a chemical factory and got a big War Department order for "coffee extract" paste. The War Department cancelled the order after the brother was caught smuggling quinine into New Orleans. In 1864 President Chester Arthur (Garfield VP) was a lawyer for Thomas Murphy—a rich, fast, and loose New York hat manufacturer charged with providing inferior products to the U.S. Army in the Civil War. Murphy was a key New York conservative Republican in the mid–1860s. John Wanamaker (B. Harrison PG) and his brother-in-law Nathan Brown put up less than $4,000 ($116,000 in 2019 buying power) to start a Philadelphia men's clothes store in 1861. They made uniforms for federal and local governments, did custom tailoring, and bought unclaimed clothes from wholesalers. The latter were sold cheap, a complete suit for three dollars. Wanamaker's slogan was "No shoddy sold here." Patriotically he sold only wool goods in 1861, no cotton. Wanamaker was a pioneer in "one price" merchandising—the same item was the same price to everyone. He was also a pioneer in allowing people to return unused merchandise for exchange or refund. Wanamaker was an innovator in advertising, using aerial balloons, toy balloons, pencils, picture postcards, calendars, and clocks. He was known to use chicanery. For instance he switched labels on hats, marketing American-made hats with fake British labels. He also obtained a big bunch of President Grant's memoirs when first published in 1886 and offered them for retail sale, so people didn't have to use publisher Mark Twain's subscription agents. "That unco-pious butter-mouthed Sunday school-slobbering sneak-thief," Mark Twain called Wanamaker, "now of Philadelphia, presently of hell."[35] Theodore Roosevelt also disliked Wanamaker, referring to him as "That hypocritical haberdasher! ... He is an ill-constitutioned creature, oily, with bristles sticking up through the oil." President Roosevelt declared, "You may tell the Postmaster-General [Wanamaker] from me that I don't like him for two reasons. In the first place he has a very sloppy mind, and in the next place he does not tell the truth."[36]

An important Confederate armaments transaction was construction of the cruiser *Alabama* which destroyed U.S. shipping around the world. The CSA admiral who built *Alabama* was an uncle of President Theodore Roosevelt. The ship's commander was the father-in-law of Luke Wright (TR War). TR's mother was a slave owner, and his relative George Randolph served as Confederate Secretary of War. The brother of Oscar Straus (TR Commerce and Labor) became wealthy by financing the CSA government with European money. Straus was a relative of Paul Morton (TR Navy). TR had plenty of ties to the Old South.

Alabama was built in England, and after the war the United States sought compensation for damage caused by the ship. Persons involved in negotiations included William Meredith (Z. Taylor Treasury), Caleb Cushing (Pierce AG), James Harlan (A. Johnson Interior), William Evarts (A. Johnson AG, Hayes State), Hamilton Fish (Grant State), John Creswell (Grant PG), George Williams (Grant AG) and Redfield Proctor (B. Harrison War). At first there was talk of demanding over $2 billion from England, but the United States settled for $15,500,000. Payment was handled by Jay Cooke & Co., L.P. Morton & Co., and Morton, Rose & Co. (of London).

Another way to make money is by financing a war. Banker Jay Cooke offered a handsome present to President Lincoln's financially pressed Treasury Secretary Salmon Chase. Chase felt that accepting such a gift would be an impropriety, and declined with thanks. Instead Cooke made expensive gifts to Chase's daughter, who lived with Chase in Washington. Cooke's brother soon had open access to the Treasury Department. He would get inside information on military plans and telegraph it to Jay, who could then conduct sharp stock market operations. The brother also used Chase's influence in a crooked scheme with quartermaster supplies in Ohio. Stanton (Lincoln War) suppressed that story. In February 1862 Chase asked Cooke to loan $2,000 ($50,000 in 2019 buying power) to Chase's daughter. A month after the loan was made, Chase appointed Cooke as the loan agent to sell Treasury bonds—a tremendous financial boon to Cooke. At the same time Chase asked Jay to "invest a few dollars for me so as to make the best profit. " Chase also told Jay to be careful in writing, so that Chase's official files would be uncluttered with information on Jay's help with Chase's personal finances. Cooke wrote to Chase:

> I will take great pains to lay aside some choice "tid bits" managing the investments for you and not bothering your head with them, other than once in six months. I hope to make up the deficiency in your account … for it is a shame that you should go "behind hand" working as you do.… My use of the balance your deposited in J[ay] C[ooke] & Co. need not interfere with your drawing on it as you may have occasion.[37]

Correspondence talks of over $1,000 profit on another investment and projected tripling or quadrupling of $5,000 in railroad stock. These loans and investments smack of favoritism as best. Chase was continually nervous lest his correspondence with Cooke attract an investigation. Cooke approached Chief Justice Chase about becoming a partner in Jay Cooke & Co. while Chase remained on the Supreme Court. The idea fizzled.

When Jay Cooke & Co. failed it was heavily in debt to the Navy Department. Edwards Pierrepont (Grant AG) urged that prosecution of a brokerage firm be dropped lest it reveal activities of Jay Cooke & Co. William Chandler (A. Johnson Assistant Treasury, Arthur Navy) became a friend of Jay Cooke in the Civil War. As one person delicately phrased it, this "was to mean much to Chandler in the six years which followed his retirement from office" as Assistant Secretary of the Treasury.[38]

Still another road to Civil War wealth was via rails. Railroads continually cheated the government on freight and troop transport charges. The range of abuses that inspired the postwar Grange movement—pools, short and long haul abuses—were perfected by railroads in their knavery against the men dying to defend the government. Railroads were also reluctant to lend rolling stock to the U.S. Army, so the government had to manufacture cars and locomotives.

A comprehensive recital of Civil War railway activity is beyond this book's scope, but a few samples will give a flavor of what occurred.

Montgomery Blair (Lincoln PG) was a Baltimore & Ohio lawyer. He was an intimate friend of the B&O president in the Civil War and worked to spike Simon Cameron's (Lincoln War) wartime plans to send B&O traffic to Pennsylvania Railroad with which Cameron had ties. Thomas Scott (Lincoln Assistant War) was Pennsylvania Railroad vice president while a member of the subcabinet. Scott overcharged the government in military transport contracts with Pennsylvania Railroad. Ca. April 1861 Chase (Lincoln Treasury) urged Ohio to send more troops and to send them via Pennsylvania Railroad.

President Garfield condemned Camden & Amboy railway for complaining that Civil War troop transport was violating the monopoly granted in Camden & Amboy's charter, reminiscent of Livingston and his steamboat monopoly in the War of 1812. Earlier, the *Albany Journal* newspaper of Thurlow Weed (associate of Lincoln State) criticized Camden & Amboy for safety problems. This criticism may have been politically motivated, as Weed ignored safety problems of the New York Central Railroad.

New York Central president Dean Richmond helped bankroll the successful Stephen Douglas effort to get the 1860 Democratic Presidential nomination, but New York Central men were indifferent after the convention. Richmond supported George McClellan against Lincoln in 1864.

In contrast to some other railroad executives, Louisville & Nashville president James Guthrie (Pierce Treasury) gave total cooperation to General William Sherman (Grant War) who wrote, "I have always felt grateful to Mr. Guthrie who had sense enough and patriotism enough to subordinate the interests of his railway company to the cause of his country."[39]

The most famous railroad operation of the era was the transcontinental railway.

Three routes (northern, central, and southern) were promoted by various railroad companies and cabinet officers, but only one could receive federal subsidies. These subsidies included money, land grants, and guarantees to creditors. These subsidies meant fortunes instead of ruin for railroad promoters, land for farmers, profits for real estate speculators, and large orders (with guaranteed payment) for the lumber and iron industries. Moreover, whatever the choice of route, the choice could affect the economic growth of the South for decades, perhaps forever. With such stakes the rivals sometimes ignored standards of gentlemanly competition.

The Atlantic & Pacific Railroad company was a New York corporation strongly pushing for the southern route. New York capitalists were part of the Southern cotton economy, perhaps the senior partner. In 1853 Cave Johnson (Polk AG) told his former cabinet colleague and future President James Buchanan (Polk State) that the New York railway company had $100,000,000 to work with ($3,200,000,000 in 2019 buying power) and would bribe Congressmen with stock. Robert Walker (Polk Treasury) was a key figure who reportedly subscribed $10,000,000. The specific route desired by Walker's group went through Mexican territory. This surely delighted Walker who always wanted to encroach on Mexico. The state of Texas agreed to give the railroad sixteen sections of land (over 10,000 acres) for every mile constructed. This meant Walker's group could get up to 12,800 square miles. Walker began negotiations with Mexico for part of the route. His loose talk inspired the Mexicans to up the price and reduce the size of the Gadsden Purchase, the name for a land acquisition that became part of Arizona and New Mexico and which involved the same territory that the railroad sought. There was open talk of a connection between the Gadsden Purchase and Walker's railroad plans, and indeed Jefferson Davis (Pierce War) promoted the Purchase partly to enhance appeal of the southern transcontinental route. Davis owed much of his political rise to Walker. And Walker's brother-in-law was an important officer in the Army Corps of Topographical Engineers which was doing the official government surveys of potential transcontinental railway routes. While U.S. Army engineer Joseph Johnston (CSA general) was scouting a Texas route in 1853, his fellow army engineer George McClellan (1864 Democratic presidential nominee) was surveying the northern route, with John Frémont (1856 Republican presidential nominee) running an independent survey of a more central path.

Jefferson Davis also proposed $100,000,000 of U.S. government funding for Judah Benjamin's (CSA AG, War, and State) Pacific railroad route across Mexico's Isthmus of Tehuantepec. As early as 1847 Walker's relative George Dallas (Polk VP) urged that a canal or railroad be put across the isthmus, and that the Mexican War peace treaty should force Mexico to give up the necessary territory. Dallas said, "Mexico in sober truth should not be permitted to be the dog in the manger—to keep selfishly useless that which without injury to her, may be converted into the means of bringing closely together, of improving and of enriching the whole human family." Judah Benjamin and other New Orleans capitalists became involved in a railroad project in that area. When trouble arose between Mexico and Benjamin's company President Fillmore (Z. Taylor VP) rejected Benjamin's demands that the U.S. government show Mexico who was boss. Benjamin then said he would force a war in order to protect the $100,000 he had invested. President Fillmore replied that Benjamin could start a war between his company and Mexico, but that Benjamin lacked the power to involve the U.S. government. In all the excitement Walker's New York syndicate wound up in the commanding position for the isthmus railroad operation. Fillmore was not only the chief representative of the federal government, but a New Yorker, too. Could the circumstances of this financial loss have affected Benjamin's decision to help lead the Confederate government? Benjamin was still nursing an interest in the outmaneuvered company in 1858 when President Buchanan (Polk State) asked Congress to seize the isthmus.

In the end Walker's transcontinental railroad scheme flopped.

Sen. Stephen Douglas (1860 Democratic presidential nominee) promoted the northern route. Douglas, John Breckinridge (Buchanan VP), and others were set up to make a fortune from real estate if the northern route were chosen. Walker was also involved in that real estate operation, perhaps as a personal financial hedge if the southern route lost.

Douglas had an extravagant notion of how to proceed and in 1854 introduced a bill to build three transcontinental railroads simultaneously on all three routes. This meant he was cordial to central route promoters, a cordiality with grave portent. The profitability, and therefore the attractiveness, of the central route would increase if more settlers (i.e. railroad customers) could be put in the Kansas–Nebraska area which comprised a much larger region than the later states having that name. Douglas was in a position to move on this since he was chairman of the Senate committee on territories. In 1854 Douglas began pushing for the organization of a territorial government in Nebraska. He agreed to divide Nebraska in two, creating a Kansas territorial government as well, partly because Iowa residents feared the capital of a new single territory would be so far south as to preclude a transcontinental railroad through Council Bluffs. Formation of two territorial governments would also aid getting land grants in Kansas for Missouri railroads, helping them push toward the Pacific. Douglas needed Southern support to organize the Kansas and Nebraska Territories. This contributed to creation of his Popular Sovereignty doctrine which wrecked the Compromise of 1850 and the Missouri Compromise of 1820. Thus efforts to promote the central route increased tensions that led to the Civil War.

The central route was chosen. Elihu Washburne's (Grant State) brother had been on the House Select Committee for years, and James Harlan (A. Johnson Interior) personally directed passage of the Pacific Railroad Act. Caleb Smith (Lincoln Interior) appointed Tilden (1876 Democratic presidential nominee) as a commissioner to help build the transcontinental railroad. Two railroads, Union Pacific and Central Pacific, would construct the transcontinental railway simultaneously. President Lincoln ordered that Council Bluffs, IA, be made the eastern terminus of the road. He owned a quarter section of land there, acquired from Norman Judd who was involved with Lincoln in the Rock Island bridge lawsuit. John Usher (Lincoln Interior) said Lincoln expected accusation of conflict of interest in that decision. At Usher's urging Lincoln set the transcontinental gauge at five feet. This matched the non-standard gauge of Usher's Leavenworth, Pawnee & Western Railroad, thus giving it an edge in transcontinental traffic. Congress, which contained many friends of standard gauge, went into an uproar. Lincoln retreated and made the transcontinental railroad standard gauge.

Lincoln's concept of railroad financing was used. There were two mortgages on the railway. The railroad companies' bonds were the first. Many of these were sold to foreigners. Foreigners owned over fifty percent of Central Pacific, and one-third of Union Pacific. This may have influenced diplomatic responses to the Civil War. The second mortgage was a six percent U.S. government bond loan of $16,000 for every mile of plains track, $32,000 for hilly land, and $48,000 per mile through mountain regions. This put the federal government in the middle of the "private enterprise" operation and gave the Secretary of the Interior much patronage.

John Dix (Buchanan Treasury) was Union Pacific president while he was a major general commanding the Department of the East. That year he bought $20,000 ($400,000 in 2019 buying power) of UP stock. John Floyd's (Buchanan War) associate Alexander Majors (of Pony Express fame) helped grade UP roadbed and supplied ties and telegraph poles. W.T. Sherman's (Grant War) friend Maj. Gen. Grenville M. Dodge was in charge of UP construction and received continual advice from Sherman regarding the construction. Dodge was also a spokesman for Jay Gould. Other top Union Pacific positions were held by Army officers who served under Sherman. His brother John (Hayes Treasury, McKinley State) may have extended the influence of Dodge and Union Pacific. Salmon Chase (Lincoln Treasury) sought the UP presidency while he was Chief Justice, intended to hold both offices simultaneously. Chase and James Harlan (A. Johnson Interior) helped UP get financing from New York's Bank of Commerce.

Like other great railways, UP wasn't a monolith. A UP subsidiary which involved several cabinet members was Leavenworth, Pawnee & Western Railroad, soon known as Union Pacific–Eastern Division. In 1861 John Usher (Lincoln Interior) was lawyer for Delaware Indians in Kansas, against LP&W RR. Usher's law team argued the LP&W hadn't paid the Indians for their land and that the federal government should cease to aid the railroad. The Indians lost. Since the lawyers' fee was contingent on money obtained in the settlement, Usher got no fee. Subsequently Usher was hired by LP&W to grab more Indian land. He was called a turncoat, but Usher said his behavior was proper since he received no fee from the Indians.

The brother-in-law of W.T. Sherman (Grant War), while a Kansas Supreme Court justice, bought up Indian land along the LP&W route. This was in cooperation with the railroad. The Washington, D.C., agent for the judge and his associates was Usher, whose fee was an option for 250,000 Kansas acres. After becoming Secretary of the Interior Usher appointed J.C. Stone (agent for LP&W) as a commissioner to deal with Indians of Kansas and Nebraska. Since the LP&W was stealing timber from Delaware land in Kansas, this appointment may have reduced the chances of Indians receiving satisfaction. Two of Usher's friends were made agents for the Sac and Fox tribes in that area. When those two tribes gave up a big chunk of land in 1864, Usher's two friends got land certificates as a fee. Scrip for 76,000 acres was offered to Usher, Hugh McCulloch (Lincoln, A. Johnson, and Arthur Treasury), John Nicolay (Lincoln private secretary), and others. Usher may not have accepted any, but he did help persons in Indiana take part in the deal (probably to bring business to his Indiana law practice). In 1864 Usher fired Fielding Johnson as a Delaware agent. Johnson had been associated with Usher and Wright in 1861 but now belonged to the wrong faction in the LP&W. Johnson went public, making a big stink about Usher's connection with LP&W and resultant harm to Indians and other land owners.

Usher got his old law partner William Griswold appointed to the Board of Commissioners supervising Union Pacific matters, and also got R.W. Latham appointed; Latham was financial agent of the New York man who handled some transactions of W.T. Sherman's (Grant War) brother-in-law, the Kansas judge. Griswold and Usher helped organize the Terre Haute, Alton & St. Louis Railroad. Tilden's (1876 Democratic presidential nominee) crooked role in that road was exposed by the *Chicago Tribune* in the 1876 campaign and hurt Tilden politically.

Richard Thompson (Hayes Navy) asked Usher to cut him in on a Union Pacific stock deal. In 1863 Sherman's brother-in-law had controlling interest of LP&W. Over Usher's objection the other two men sold out to John Frémont (1856 Republican presidential nominee) and New York banker Samuel Hallett.

Frémont's LP&W was renamed Union Pacific Railway–Eastern Division. In October 1863 he gave public support to the railroad, support which was regarded as an official position of the Lincoln Administration. Union Pacific–Eastern Division was now the Kansas branch of the UP main line. In 1864 Hallett asked Usher, Edward Bates (Lincoln AG), and Salmon Chase (Lincoln Treasury) to help arrange financing of UP–Eastern Division. Usher and Montgomery Blair (Lincoln PG) publicly declared the government would provide "every lawful facility in its power that will tend to forward the early completion of the enterprise."[40] Company records indicate that by this time Usher had been given 10,000 shares of stock, par value

$500,000. Par value of a stock is printed on the stock certificate. This has no relation to the market value. The market value of UP–Eastern Division stock was below par value but could be expected to increase as the railroad prospered. Thus Usher had a strong motive to help the road.

In 1864 Congress began federal subsidy of UP–Eastern Division. The former acting chief engineer of the road, Orlando Talcott, warned Lincoln that line construction was below federal standards. Usher was told of the charges and informed his railroad associates. Latham had Talcott physically chastised. Sometime later Talcott murdered the banker Hallett.

As a further complication in UP–Eastern Division affairs, there were two competing boards of directors, a Hallett faction and a Frémont faction. Each claimed to be the real corporation. The railroad needed official government inspectors to certify the work was done properly. Only then could the railroad get payment of the federal subsidy. Usher appointed Richard Thompson (Hayes Navy), Leonard Swett (Lincoln associate fresh from the California New Almaden mine) and the governor of Kansas as the inspectors. Usher hoped Swett would show gratitude by relieving Usher's personal financial difficulties. Thompson declined to serve and was replaced by a former Kansas governor. After leaving the cabinet Usher briefly and nebulously (due to the competing boards of directors) functioned as the railroad's president, though his formal title was "general solicitor." His cabinet successor James Harlan (A. Johnson Interior) found that Usher's railroad inspectors had done an inadequate job and the UP–Eastern Division failed to meet the requirements for federal money.

UP–Eastern Division and UP were considered strategically important for crushing Indians who lived between the two railways. Both roads had powerful allies in the Army. The military-industrial complex had begun to evolve. UP–Eastern Division tried to beat UP to the 100th parallel, with UP–Eastern Division hoping to thereby get the federal subsidy to go the rest of the way across the continent. In other words, the subsidiary was trying to replace the parent corporation, a neat caper had it succeeded.

W. Chandler (Arthur Navy) was a UP–Eastern Division lawyer in 1867. He declined a $5,000 job as solicitor and agent, not wanting a full time UP–Eastern Division job, since he was the parent UP's Washington, D.C., agent. Chandler charged big fees and used inside information for no-risk stock speculation. An 1868 memo to UP's president said that W.T. Sherman's (Grant War) relative Jim Blaine (Garfield State), Sherman's brother-in-law, and C.T. Sherman had received UP–Eastern Division bonds. Blaine's share of the bonds may have reached a monetary value of $250,000 ($4,250,000 in 2019 buying power). Court records were mutilated at the time to disguise Blaine's name. The original document, however, proved that the person listed as a bond recipient was James G. Blaine (Garfield State).

In 1868 UP–Eastern Division was renamed Kansas Pacific Railway and Telegraph Co. and eventually was absorbed into UP.

UP was constructed by Crédit Mobilier Co. of America. Crédit Mobilier was incorporated by John C. Calhoun's (Monroe War) associate Duff Green to raise money for a southern route transcontinental railroad. When Green's project folded, UP backers acquired Crédit Mobilier. There are two theories about why the UP backers did this. One theory is that the deal was legitimate. This theory notes that it was very hard to sell UP stock and thereby raise money to build the railroad, because UP wasn't a limited liability corporation. This meant investors could lose more than they invested. Crédit Mobilier did have limited liability, and was interlocked with UP so that Crédit Mobilier could gradually acquire UP's assets. The people who owned Crédit Mobilier stock would eventually own UP, making Crédit Mobilier an attractive stock to buy.

The other theory about Crédit Mobilier says it was a successful ploy by big capitalists and politicians to make a fortune by looting UP. Jeremiah Black (Buch AG) was a lawyer for a UP executive who claimed he was entitled to 250 shares of Crédit Mobilier. Black warned UP management that unless they paid $100,000 to their colleague he would release letters detailing distribution of Crédit Mobilier stock to members of Congress. Black went away empty-handed, and the letters were released. Investigation showed that some members of Congress got free Crédit Mobilier stock, presumably to influence any legislation affecting UP. Crédit Mobilier thus acted as a front for Congressmen, who could truthfully say they were uninfluenced by owning any UP stock. Controversy exits on whether Blaine (Garfield & B. Harrison State) owned stock. Blaine, Vice President Colfax, and Garfield all lied about their involvement.[41] Garfield denied receiving a cash gift. He explained the money was merely a loan that never had to be repaid.

Crédit Mobilier acquired UP's assets by charging outrageous amounts for construction work. UP president John Dix (Buchanan Treasury) opposed this, and soon found himself ousted as president and director of the railroad. He was miffed about losing the $8,000 president's salary. He owned 500 UP shares, partly (if not all) acquired as gifts. He apparently demanded that UP buy the stock from him at $100 a share (market value was $20 a share). Otherwise, Dix allegedly said, UP would have no luck getting financing from Europe. While Dix was UP president he was in Europe serving as U.S. Minister to France, where he was supposed to promote the railroad among Europeans. UP gave in to his blackmail and bought the stock to get rid of him.

While it is true that Crédit Mobilier overcharged UP for railroad construction, it is also true it accepted payment in UP stock at par value. Since the market value was less than the par value, Crédit Mobilier had to overcharge or go broke. The overcharge was only on paper. One investigator reported that in terms of the UP stock's market value, construction contracts were reasonable. Of course if UP developed into a thriving railway, Crédit Mobilier would reap a fortune. Crédit Mobilier insiders didn't expect such a happy outcome, and they were right. They intended to make their money by building the railroad, not by owning and running it.

There were still other ways to make money from UP, as Blaine (Garfield State) showed. Little Rock & Ft. Smith Railway was owned by Atlantic & Pacific Railroad, Robert Walker's (Polk Treasury) land hungry New York corporation that promoted the southern transcontinental route. Benjamin Bristow (Grant Treasury) was general counsel of Atlantic & Pacific. While Blaine was speaker of the House he pushed land grants that saved Little Rock & Ft. Smith. One of the men involved with Little Rock & Ft. Smith was Warren Fisher, the same Warren Fisher who Blaine favored with rifle contracts in the Civil War. Regarding the railway, Blaine wrote to Fisher, "I do not feel that I shall prove a deadhead n the enterprise if I once embark in it. I see various channels in which I know I can be useful." "Deadhead" is railroad slang for someone who gets a free ride. In another letter to Fisher, Blaine said, "Your liberal mode of dealing with me the last eight years has not passed without my full appreciation." In more than one letter of October 1869 to Little Rock & Ft. Smith figures Blaine stated that he had done the railway "a great favor."[42] Blaine unsuccessfully tried to get financier Jay Cooke to participate in maneuvers affecting Little Rock and Ft. Smith, saying, "I may say without egotism that my position will enable me to render you service of vital importance and value."[43]

Real Estate

The relationship of iron, coal, and lumber to railroads was obvious. Other relationships were less apparent but crucial. Above all was the matter of land.

Up to the 1820s real estate seemed the major business enterprise of Presidents and cabinet members. In the 1830s a shift occurred toward banking and railroads. Normally we think of railroading as a business far different from real estate, but many railways (especially the transcontinental Pacific ones) were dependent on land sales to generate revenue—land which the railways acquired free from Congress. Several cabinet members were offered jobs as railroad land agents. These were crucial job positions, a sign of how highly the railroads regarded these men. The scale of railroad real estate operations was tremendous. Railroads owned a piece of Minnesota two times the size of Massachusetts and a piece of California three times the size of New Hampshire. One railroad had a piece of Montana the size of Maryland, New Jersey, and Massachusetts combined. Railroad land grants in Kansas equaled the size of Connecticut and New Jersey. Connecticut and Rhode Island would have fit into railroad property in Iowa with room to spare. There would have been about as much room for Connecticut and Rhode Island on railroad holdings in Michigan, Minnesota, or Washington. That was how much the railways owned outright. They controlled access to even larger areas. A little money could go a long way on the Great Plains for well-connected unscrupulous persons. In fact genuine plains settlers felt at times that they were in a fiefdom controlled by New Yorkers.

Since railroads could make big money from land sales, the railroads were interested in promoting Western expansion. And since Indians intimidated potential settlers, railway capitalists felt that Indian civilizations had to be destroyed. The great bison slaughter wasn't thoughtless, but calculated to deprive Indians of sustenance and drive them out. Buffalo Bill Cody shot bison for the UP–Eastern Division. Railroads also were strategically important for rapid troop movement. Hollywood movies glory in the cavalry, but in the Old West hard pressed fighters were looking for smokestack puffs. Troop transport even created railroad revenue while soldiers fought the railways' battles against Indians.

Railroads also had much to do with the great nineteenth century immigration of Europeans to America. This great human migration is usually thought of in terms of Ellis Island and urban ghettos. The vast open spaces of the Great Plans would be an image just as appropriate. Many Europeans came to nineteenth century America via a package deal which included purchase of and settlement on railroad land. Not all European capital acquired by railroads came from investors in securities. European settlers brought over by Illinois Central helped Lincoln win Illinois electoral votes and the Presidency. Such settlement was especially important because it foretold future railroad revenue from agricultural freight shipments. The long and short haul abuses, whereby railroads extorted higher rates from rural areas, had the ironic effect of encouraging persons to leave the countryside and live in urban areas. Thus did some railroads hurt themselves and contribute to the process of urbanization. Railroads supported President Theodore Roosevelt's "conservation" movement to close the public domain, because settlers would be forced on to railroad land. Railroads had no genuine commitment to conservation. Since railways could make money by transporting ore, washing away mountains via placer mining was good for railroads. Devastating the land with strip mining was also good for railroads. Clear cutting vast forests, destroying wildlife that lived there, and wrecking the forest floor through erosion—all that was good for railroads. Shortcuts on deep mine safety that produced more ore but killed more miners were good for railroads. Reducing passenger service and increasing shipments of oil for private automobiles was good for railroads. Railroads did not decree that such things happen, but were part of the zeitgeist that promoted such effects. What was good for railroads was good for the President and cabinet members.

Chapter 7

Abraham Lincoln's Estate

Lincoln's father was one of the wealthiest men in his county, admittedly a distinction less notable when the poverty level of his neighbors is factored in. Lincoln married into Kentucky's aristocracy, giving him entre into Virginia's elite. Edward Everett (Fillmore State) knew something about aristocracy, and said Lincoln was a highly refined person.

As a country postmaster Lincoln abused his franking privilege. He cleaned up as an Illinois legislator. The pay of $3 a day (later $4) was excellent for the period, especially for a part time job. Lincoln was paid for Sundays and Christmas when the legislature didn't meet. He illegally drew pay for days when he didn't attend the legislature. Mileage allowance was $3 for every twenty miles on trips between a legislator's home and the state capital. After moving to Springfield Lincoln continued to draw mileage as if he still lived in New Salem, miles north of Springfield. As a U.S. Congressman he got $8 per 20 miles. A round trip for him by postal route would have been 624 miles. Lincoln, however, figured mileage by a route through Chicago, IL, and Buffalo, NY. He thereby picked up an extra $675 ($21,900 in 2019 buying power), a tidy sum when $1,500 was a handsome salary.

President Lincoln was not rich, but lived very comfortably. He declined appointment by President Taylor as governor of Oregon Territory, which carried a $3,000 salary ($97,400 in 2019 buying power). Lincoln's income in the 1840s was under $2,000 a year, which may not sound like much. Yet at that same time his brother-in-law spent under $1,200 a year giving superb entertainments, with his house continually open to state legislators and to strangers. Lincoln's own table "was famed for the excellence of many rare Kentucky dishes, and in season, it was loaded with venison, wild turkeys, prairie chickens, quail, and other game."[44] Lincoln had a fine Springfield, IL, house, with two live-in servants. Lincoln took vacation trips to New York City and Canada in the 1850s, an uncommon luxury for Midwesterners. In 1850 he declared his assets as over $17,000 ($540,000 in 2019 buying power). His law income alone reached $5,000 a year in that decade. Lincoln also loaned out money at ten percent interest. In fifteen years he made seventeen loans, totaling over $12,000, yielding about $200 a year in interest payments.

One loan in 1857 was $2,400 to Norman Judd, who convinced associates to hire Lincoln as attorney in the Rock Island bridge case that year. One report says Lincoln got no interest on it, and that the principal was repaid in 1865 after inflation had reduced the debt by about forty percent. Another report says Judd paid back $5,400 including interest.

In his second term President Lincoln planned to save all his salary and live off the income from his investments. Much has been made of Mrs. Lincoln's "foolish extravagances" which "burdened" Lincoln's finances in the White House. Lincoln's estate was $15,000 ($430,000 in 2019 buying power) when he became President, $90,000 ($1,377,000 in 2019 buying power) when he died. The estate was so strong that after all of Mrs. Lincoln's bills were finally paid the estate had *risen* in value to $111,000 when it was finally distributed to heirs in 1867 ($1,885,000 in 2019 buying power). Any anguish Lincoln suffered from his wife's spending could be explained by the following comment from his law partner William Herndon: "He had none of the avarice of the *get* but he had the avarice of the *keep*."[45]

Andrew Johnson Impeachment

The impeachment of Andrew Johnson (Lincoln VP) after the Civil War has already been examined as a power struggle between Whig and abolitionist factions of the Republican Party. Intertwined with the impeachment were side issues such as bird excrement, also known as guano. Guano was a valuable fertilizer, and coastal islands of Latin America had hills of it deposited over the centuries.

Toward the end of the Pierce Administration, Congress passed a law that U.S. citizens could take possession of any guano island they discovered, and the President could use military forces to protect the seizure. In 1860 the Baltimore company Patterson & Murguiondo discovered Alta Vela island, fifteen miles south of Haiti. The Dominican Republic attacked the Baltimore operation. Jeremiah Black (Buchanan State) delayed military assistance until the Dominican Republic claim to the island was settled. Just after Lincoln became President, William Seward (Lincoln State) heard that the Dominican Republic gave up its claim. Black was now attorney for the Baltimore company and wanted U.S. military protection of the guano operation. Seward stalled the matter seven years. It turned that the Dominican Republic had sold the guano rights to Root, Webster, Clark & Co.—a New

York firm in which Seward's intimate associate Thurlow Weed had financial interest. The New York company had been removing guano from the island all those years. Now, two days after President Johnson got the impeachment summons, his defense lawyer Black (Buchanan State) asked Johnson to act under the 1856 law and send federal forces to the island to protect the Baltimore company's rights. Johnson was reluctant to do so, as this would antagonize both Seward and Congress. Apparently independently of Black, several impeachment prosecutors in Congress, and others including future President Garfield, endorsed the Baltimore claim. Black again asked Johnson for military action, and he again refused, fearing to offend ex–Whigs in Congress who were led by Seward. Black then decided to try getting Congressional action for the Baltimore company. This was a direct violation of his impeachment client's wishes and therefore a conflict of interest. Black realized this and quit the impeachment defense team, feeling that bird excrement was more important than the President's fate. Reportedly the Baltimore company pushed for U.S. annexation of the Dominican Republic, a move supported by President Grant and Hamilton Fish (Grant State).

The request for U.S. military protection for guano operations was nothing unheard of. For example, in 1852 New York City capitalists staged a 100-ship raid on Peruvian guano islands. Unknown to President Fillmore (Z. Taylor VP), the businessmen got Webster's (Fillmore State) promise of U.S. Navy protection in the operation, a promise confirmed by William Graham (Fillmore Navy). Fillmore was irritated when he learned of Webster's action, and the President yanked Navy protection after the fleet had sailed. Fillmore insisted the businessmen would have to attack Peru at their own risk. The merchants then quickly reached an accommodation with Peru, being allowed to take guano if they paid for it. The merchants then descended on Fillmore, arguing the federal government (rather than the merchants) should pay Peru since the expedition would never have sailed without Webster's commitment of U.S. government support. Fillmore agreed to have taxpayers foot the bill, mainly because the guano men had enough influence to get the money from Congress anyway.

Presidency of Grant

Railroads and many other corporations began to expand greatly in the 1860s, often with little regard for the public interest. The Civil War is often credited for this because large sums went to defense contractors, which included railroads, iron, lumber, textiles, agriculture, and other businesses besides armaments. Just as important, however, was the absence of Southern states from the U.S. government in the 1860s. Southerners in Congress traditionally obstructed Northern businessmen, but this obstruction was now gone from the government. Yet Congressional representatives of Northern business interests still operated with the same force that had built up over the decades in an attempt to smash through Southern opposition. Big business interests now hurtled through the nation without control.

President Grant and great capitalists were mutual admirers. The capitalists liked Grant because he paid no attention to their activities. He liked them because they gave him presents. W.T. Sherman (Grant War) estimated Grant took $100,000 from rich New Yorkers from 1865 to 1868 ($1,600,000 in 2019 buying power). Sherman declined such generosity when it was offered to him, fearing it would put him under too heavy an obligation to the donors. The Union League Club of Philadelphia gave Grant's wife a completely furnished Philadelphia mansion, including velvet carpeting and a piano. Adolph Borie (Grant Navy) was a highly visible donor in the Philadelphia transaction. Fifty Bostonians donated a $75,000 library. President-Elect Grant's $30,000 Washington home was a gift, and shortly before assuming office Grant sold it to rich friends for $65,000 ($1,144,000 in 2019 buying power). The day before the inauguration A.T. Stewart handed Grant the check, and Grant soon nominated him for Secretary of the Treasury. The house then passed to W.T. Sherman (Grant War). Ebenezer Hoar gave Grant a library and was appointed Attorney General. Judge Edwards Pierrepont gave Grant $20,000 and was appointed Attorney General and ambassador to England. Grant regularly took free rides on railroad and steamship lines. He accepted a resort house in Long Branch, NJ, and built another next to it which he rented out for $3,000 per season. The money continued to come in as ex–President, while Grant was still a third term possibility. New Yorkers including J.P. Morgan, Joseph Drexel, and Hamilton Fish (Grant State) gave $100,000 to buy a New York City house. William H. Vanderbilt, Jay Gould, John Mackay, and George W. Jones gave the ex–President $100,000 to buy a New York City house. William H. Vanderbilt, Jay Gould, John Mackey, and George W. Jones gave the ex–President a $250,000 trust fund intended to provide a permanent income. When the Grant & Ward banking firm failed, leaving Grant with almost no assets, William H. Vanderbilt gave Grant an unsecured loan of $150,000.

The Grant administration's tolerance of and participation in business scandals became legendary. For instance Jay Gould, James Fisk, Jr., and President Grant's brother-in-law decided to corner the gold market in 1869. On Gould's recommendation President Grant appointed Daniel Butterworth head of the New York subtreasury. Butterworth had been a key aide in helping A.T. Stewart (Grant Treasury nominee) collect $105,000 ($1,650,500 in 2019 buying power) which was handed over to Grant as a gift in 1866, before he became President. Butterworth seemed to help the gold conspiracy by sending secret information. George Boutwell (Grant Treasury) knew of the conspiracy but made no attempt to stop it. The operation, however, quickly halted foreign trade and forced Boutwell to act. During the most critical period Grant couldn't be reached by anyone in DC for several days. During the conspiracy, the wife of Grant's brother-in-law got a letter from Grant's wife that the President "is very much annoyed by your speculations. You must close them out as quick as you can."[46] Grant knew what was going on.

Orville Babcock (Grant private secretary) was in the Whiskey Ring, as was John A. McDonald (Grant Supt. Internal Revenue) who headed it. William Belknap (Grant War) floated about on the fringes of the Ring. Basically the ring would blackmail distillers and defraud tax collections. Grant had accepted various gifts from McDonald and continued to do so during the criminal investigation. At that time Grant also purchased from McDonald a horse team, carriage, set of harness with gold heartplates, and buggy whip—all for $1,758.50. After McDonald was indicted Grant met publicly with him and expressed sympathy. McDonald was convicted. As Babcock's trial went on, some witnesses were willing to give evidence against higher-ups if the government would refrain from prosecuting those witnesses. Grant had Pierrepont (Grant AG) refuse the requests for immunity, which kept the evidence under wraps. Grant also made a deposition to the court that he and Babcock were so close that Grant would know if Babcock engaged in criminal acts. This was a powerful statement for a jury in those days. A conviction would mean that the jury believed the President of the United States was, at the very least, a criminal involved in perjury and obstruction of justice. The jury found Babcock innocent, though his guilt was widely believed. All the key figures in the prosecution soon resigned under pressure or were fired. Zachariah Chandler (Grant Interior) donated at least $1,000 for Babcock's trial expenses.

George Williams (Grant AG) used Justice Department money for living expenses, purchase of a carriage and of liveries for two servants, and for cashing checks that banks wouldn't honor. After these illegal acts came out Grant retained Williams as Attorney General.[47] Apparently his wife was involved with Grant's brother-in-law in accepting a $30,000 bribe to halt investigation of the New York commercial firm Pratt & Boyd. Grant's private secretary also seemed involved. Williams's wife apparently tried to blackmail Grant with the John Davenport scandal, in which Grant had provided Davenport with about $44,000 in Justice Department funds. Davenport may have pocketed the money or may have used it to buy New York City votes in the 1872 election. Pierrepont (Grant AG) was nervous about Grant's involvement. Grant nominated Williams to the Supreme Court.

William Belknap (Grant War) took large bribes from persons who wanted to run Indian trading posts, $20,000 according to House impeachment proceedings. Belknap said he wasn't involved in bribery. He said his wife took all that money, not him. President Grant' wife, in tears, begged cabinet members to show their support and regard for Belknap. Reportedly some of the bribe money went to one of her relatives. President Grant's brother got some of the bribe money. Grant knew this because Grant had gotten four trading post positions for the brother.[48] Belknap resigned, and the Senate then refused to convict him in the impeachment. General Custer's testimony against Belknap so outraged Grant that the President exiled him to Indian territory with command of one 600-man regiment. Custer knew he would have to take some daring risks to re-establish his Army career. Future President James Garfield, incidentally, learned of the Belknap scandal four years before the impeachment. He made a less than thorough investigation and reported Belknap had been exonerated.

While serving as a cabinet member George Robeson (Grant Navy) was affiliated with A.G. Cattell & Co., a Philadelphia grain, flour, and feed commission firm. Its business came largely from fees it collected from Navy Department contractors, who paid because of Secretary Robeson's connection with Cattell & Co. Not only the company, but Robeson himself, prospered. He entered the cabinet with a $20,000 estate ($365,000 in 2019 buying power). In four years Robeson deposited $320,000 ($6,400,000 in 2019 buying power) in three banks. A member of the company also bought Robeson some Long Branch, NJ, property—President Grant's vacation town. Robeson also got $3,000 outright from the same company member. The firm's books were haphazard, and some records were destroyed.

W.T. Sherman's (Grant War) friend Maj. Gen. Grenville M. Dodge was in charge of Union Pacific Railroad construction. Dodge and some friends bought a house for John Rawlins (Grant War) to reside in as a cabinet member. Dodge said,

> I am able to do this through the kindness of a few friends, most of only know you by reputation, but who have watched your course through your entire public life. Their respect and high regard for you as a gentleman and a soldier, your strict integrity and ability, your disinterested services to your country and your Chief alone has prompted this gift. I trust you will receive it I the same kindly spirit it is given, and at some future time more appropriate than this I will furnish you the names of the gentlemen.[49]

(Since Rawlins was a poor man, perhaps Dodge and his friends may have expected some return favor.)

In one biographer's words Rawlins was "deeply sympathetic with all misgoverned people" and felt the United States should encourage, perhaps protect, Cuban rebels. Rawlins pushed to have the United States recognize Cuban rebels as "belligerents"—a step with precise meaning in international law, and a step that might have thwarted U.S. proceedings against England in the *Alabama* claims case. Fish (Grant State) and Hoar (Grant AG) stopped President Grant from following Rawlins's advice. Rawlins died. Grant was executer of the estate and ordered the burning of $28,000 of Cuban rebel bonds which Rawlins had owned. Perhaps Grant felt uneasy about Rawlins having bonds that were worthless unless the United States aided the rebels. Somehow the bonds were spared, and the Cuban rebels donated yet another $20,000 of the bonds to Rawlins's family. The rebel "minister to the U.S." was a close friend of Rawlins's physician. The Cuban rebel headquarters was at 71 Broadway, New York City—rather a distant staging point for invasion, although close to J.P. Morgan. Yet in truth the rebels did start their military operations from Gardiner's Island in New York City. This was the property of President John Tyler's in-laws, who were involved with the raids on Cuba.

Another matter, the "Perkins claim," was described as "perhaps the most malodorous of the many claims upon which lobbyists, shysters, and political harpies fed during the Gilded Age."[50] Benjamin W. Perkins claimed to have made a Crimean War contract with Russia for arms, plus a verbal contract with Baron Eduard de Stoeckl, Russian minister to the United States, for gunpowder. Russia repudiated both. Perkins's lawyer was Crédit Mobilier figure Joseph B. Stewart, aided by two of President Grant's brothers-in-law. They got Lewis Cass (Jackson War, Buchanan State) to seek arbitration of the claim. Russia indignantly declined. Part of the indignation may have been because Russian money to American newspapers had helped promote the appointment of Cass to President Buchanan's cabinet. Buchanan himself was a former ambassador to Russia. Caleb Cushing (Pierce AG), William Evarts (A. Johnson AG, Hayes State), and William Seward (Lincoln State) all pressed the claim upon the Russian government. Stoeckl apparently agreed to arbitration if the United States would buy Alaska in return. Stoeckl then had Cass's cabinet successor Black (Buchanan State) act as bagman for bribing Congress. Seward's law firm subsequently took on the Russian government as a client.

James Watson Webb (editor of *New York Courier & Enquirer*) was U.S. minister to Brazil under Seward (Lincoln & A. Johnson State). Webb successfully pressed that nation to pay a shipping loss claim. President Grant and Fish (Grant State) decided the claim should be paid back to Brazil. Webb then admitted bribery and appeared to have used extortion in the settlement, in which he apparently pocketed a few thousand dollars for himself. William Evarts (A. Johnson AG, Hayes State) was Webb's lawyer. A hung jury allowed Webb to go free.

President Grant deposited his Presidential paycheck at Sherman & Grant, a DC bank run by U.S. Grant, Jr. The son's unsavory banking associates cheated the Grants. Theodore Roosevelt said that Grant's son Fred "is one of the most interesting studies that I know of, from the point of view of atavism. I am sure his brain must reproduce that of some long-lost arboreal ancestor." Ex-President Grant himself became a banker, establishing the New York City firm Grant & Ward. James Fish (father-in-law of Ward and president of Marine Bank of Brooklyn) was a silent partner. President Grant invested all his liquid capital in the operation, $100,000. U.S. Grant, Jr., put in $50,000, and other family members put in hundreds of thousands more. Other rich persons put their money into Grant & Ward. The firm had an excellent reputation for a while. New York City put $1,000,000 of city funds on deposit with the firm, and Grant & Ward marketed various railroad bonds. Unfortunately, Ward was a crook running the pyramid game. President Grant's friends who knew of Ward's crookedness were afraid to say anything, knowing Grant's harsh reaction to criticism of people he trusted. Grant thought the $100,000 he invested had risen to $1,500,000 through Ward's talents, and that sort of thing could generate a lot of trust and regard in Grant. On May 5, 1884, Ward persuaded Grant to get a $150,000 personal loan from William H. Vanderbilt. Vanderbilt refused any collateral, and later said, "I gave him my check without question, not because the transaction was business-like, but simply because the request came from General Grant."[51] Grant turned over the money to Ward. The next day the bank failed, and Ward had disappeared. Grant lost $350,000 in the failure. This wiped him out financially. His New York home and trophies were consigned to Vanderbilt, who offered to give them to Grant's wife. The offer was made to save the property from other creditors. Vanderbilt gave the property to the government. Grant's wife sold her DC houses, and Grant's $250,000 trust fund was tied up and untouchable. Grant's family is often described as impoverished by this experience. That characterization is incorrect. Their scale of living became less grand, but remained comfortable. For instance, soon after the bank failure the Grant family summered at their favorite Long Branch, NJ, resort.

Ward later turned up and admitted his financial misdealings. U.S. District Attorney Elihu Root (McKinley and TR War) prosecuted James Fish for embezzling Marine National Bank. Root also got Ward indicted. One of Root's private clients was Theodore Roosevelt. Both Ward and Fish were imprisoned for long terms. Seward's (Lincoln State) nephew was Grant's attorney in the aftermath of the bank failure.

Election of 1876

In the presidential election of 1876 Democrat Samuel Tilden seemed to have an edge over Republican Rutherford Hayes. The popular vote was 4,300,000 for Tilden and 4,036,000 for Hayes. The electoral college vote was 184 for Tilden and 165 for Hayes. But a funny thing happened to Tilden on the way to the White House. He didn't reckon on the Texas & Pacific Railroad.

In the 1870s Union Pacific president Thomas Scott (Lincoln Assistant War) was president of still another line, Texas & Pacific. Texas & Pacific had been started before the Civil War by John Frémont (1856 Republican Presidential nominee) who shared controlling interest in UP–Eastern Division. Most Texas & Pacific officials were Northerners. The chief engineer of Texas & Pacific was Grenville Dodge, previously UP chief engineer. Benjamin Bristow (Grant Treasury), who had been general counsel of Atlantic & Pacific Railroad (in which Frémont had invested heavily after withdrawing from UP–Eastern Division) was Texas & Pacific counsel in 1872. Pierrepont (Grant AG) was director, counsel, and treasurer of Texas & Pacific, going to London and Frankfurt on railroad business in 1872. That same year Bristow was president of California & Texas Railway Construction Co., a Crédit Mobilier style operation associated with Texas & Pacific Railway. Bristow used political influence on Congress and Belknap (Grant War), trying to get military posts established along the railroad route for protection of settlers and generation of freight revenue. Also in 1872 future President Garfield got an offer to head the land bureau of Texas & Pacific. Bristow was middleman in the negotiations. Garfield needed the money and was sorely tempted, but decided to remain in Congress. The land bureau would have been a full-time job, forcing Garfield to leave Congress. Railroads' land operations, as noted earlier, were tremendous. This job offer was therefore a sign of special confidence in Garfield.

In 1873 Texas & Pacific began a big push to lay track in order to save its land grants. The state of Texas rented black convicts to the railroad for pennies per day. Texas had been a slave state, and free blacks didn't have to be guilty of much to wind up in prison. Chief engineer Dodge had wanted to round up Indians for use as slave labor on another railroad. Dead workers were quickly buried in trackside dumps.

In 1876 Texas & Pacific was still in danger of losing its land grants. To help construction Scott sought federal guarantee of Texas & Pacific bonds—$200,000,000 including interest, a stupendous sum for the era. There was much support for this guarantee in the South. So much support that powerful Democrats were willing to help throw the Presidency to Hayes despite the election's outcome, if the GOP would pledge support of the Texas & Pacific subsidy. Hayes maintained a discrete distance but didn't oppose the subsidy. More wheeling and dealing occurred, and when the dust settled W.T. Sherman (Grant War and friend of Texas & Pacific chief engineer Dodge) was found using the Army to enforce a ballot count that left Hayes the winner instead of Tilden. President-Elect Hayes rode to his inauguration in Scott's private railroad car.

The rivalry between Southern Pacific and Texas & Pacific worsened after Hayes became President, with work gangs attacking one another. George McCrary (Hayes War) finally ordered both sides to halt construction. Southern Pacific sought no federal subsidy, and President Hayes told railroad magnate Collis Huntington to continue. Thus the South could get its Pacific railroad, and the federal government wouldn't have to pay a subsidy to satisfy the South's railroad ambitions—an interesting turn of events. Hayes then came out publicly against Scott's subsidy request.

Jay Gould was involved with Texas & Pacific. Gould, as noted earlier, gave money to President Grant, who in turn ordered W.T. Sherman (Grant War) to enforce the ballot count that made Hayes President. Gould took over Scott's interest in Texas & Pacific in 1880. Gould and Huntington then cooperated in finishing the system. Relations between the two railroads became cordial indeed, and Texas & Pacific eventually operated Southern Pacific from Sierra Blanca to El Paso.

Tilden may have felt some satisfaction over the betrayal of Texas & Pacific, since he and Scott had been close business associates. Scott had $100,000 and Tilden $50,000 of stock in Continental Improvement Co., a Crédit Mobilier style operation that we have encountered before. Fort Wayne Railroad (part of the Pennsylvania Railroad system) was used to grease the financing of Continental Improvement Co. Tilden was lawyer for Ft. Wayne Railroad and a giant operator in its stock. English capital was also involved. In the end Continental Improvement wound up with parts, at least, of the 1,600,000-acre land grant given to Grand Rapids & Indiana Railroad. In one set of sales 90,000 acres were sold for a profit of just under $1,300,000. Tilden argued, incidentally that this land was tax free since it was granted for railroad purposes, i.e., not for the purpose of being taxed. No taxes were paid for twenty years, but in the end the courts ruled against this argument. Tilden had railroad activity with Jay Gould, James Fisk, Oakes Ames (Crédit Mobilier), Dean Richmond (New York Central), William Ogden (UP RR and Chicago & Northwestern), and Walter Gresham (Arthur PG, Cleveland State). Tilden made an enemy of Whitney (Cleveland Navy) by looting St. Louis, Alton & Terre Haute Railroad. Whitney decided to fight Tilden by becoming corporation counsel of the railroad. Whitney's father controlled Massachusetts delegates at the upcoming 1876 Democratic convention, and Tilden did nothing to Whitney. Reportedly

Whitney made $1,250,000 by consolidating Chicago & Northwestern with Peninsular Railroad in 1864 ($20,000,000 in 2019 buying power). On Tilden's recommendation, freight rates were raised so the watered stocks could produce earnings. This directly encouraged formation of the Granger movement. In 1866 James Parton gave details of Tilden's Chicago & Northwestern activities in *Manual for the Instruction of "Rings," Railroad and Political*. Tilden suppressed the book by court order and by buying up copies. After Tilden's death his papers were searched four or more times to find and destroy all documents that might harm his reputation. His railroad and business papers were especially singled out for destruction. This elimination of evidence was in accordance with Tilden's will.

Rutherford Hayes

Ca. 1875 future President Hayes administered an estate that gave $5,000 to Oberlin College. Instead of delivering the money, Hayes borrowed it and paid no interest. Oberlin College consented to both the borrowing and the zero interest. Hayes married into a wealthy family. His brother-in-law had a $500,000 estate in the 1840s. Much of Hayes's capital was tied up, and he preferred to postpone bill payment rather than sell property at a loss to generate cash. Hayes did much entertaining in the White House. One month's bill was $6,000. Each year as President he spent $8,000 to $9,000 on food. His stable cost $6,000 the first year in office. He often gave away small sums. Hayes spent all but $1,000 of his $200,000 total salary. He could well afford it, leaving an estate of $1,000,000.

Chapter 8

Pennsylvania Railroad

A nationwide railroad strike during the Hayes administration was suppressed with difficulty and bloodshed. In 1877 Pittsburgh riots damaged the Pennsylvania Railroad and several other firms. The Pennsylvania Railroad had great influence in the state legislature, and the state voted a $3,000,000 bond issue to reimburse the corporations for the damage. This way taxpayers took the loss instead of corporation investors. Wealthy persons bemoaned the tax burden rioters had forced upon law abiding citizens. Apparently the roles of the legislature and corporation stockholders were regarded as insignificant in laying blame.

William H. Vanderbilt, Andrew Carnegie, and the grandfather of Nelson Rockefeller (Ford VP) decided to break Pennsylvania Railroad's monopoly in the Pennsylvania oil fields. Carnegie's motive was to sell steel to a new railroad. Rockefeller's motive was to reduce costs. Vanderbilt's motive was to harm Pennsylvania Railroad. They bought the planned South Pennsylvania Railroad (also called Southern Pennsylvania Railroad) which would also harm Baltimore & Ohio Railroad. The syndicate also included Vanderbilt's son-in-law, Rockefeller's brother, Francis Lynde Stetson (Cleveland law associate), William Whitney (Cleveland Navy), Whitney's law partner, Henry C. Frick (associate of Harding Treasury), and the grandfather of Ogden Mills (Hoover Treasury, relative of 1892 GOP VP nominee). Whitney lobbied the Pennsylvania legislature and got favorable legislation over Jeremiah Black's (Buchanan State) opposition. In 1884 Vanderbilt planned to sell South Pennsylvania Railroad so he could buy West Shore Railroad. Stephen Elkins (B. Harrison War) was involved with the negotiations. Anthony Drexel of Drexel, Morgan & Co. was unable to arrange the sale for Vanderbilt. J.P. Morgan then bought West Shore for New York Central, which he directed. Vanderbilt thereupon made a deal with Pennsylvania Railroad that cut off many syndicate members, including Carnegie and Whitney (Cleveland Navy). The whole episode has been called "a very remarkable piece of profitable manipulation and duplicity."[52]

Marine Industry

The great European emigration to America was occurring during the Hayes administration and grew ever stronger through the rest of the century. This of course was profitable for steamship companies. Carl Schurz's (Hayes Interior) brother-in-law was a Meyer Brothers partner in Hamburg, Germany. In 1888 he got Schurz hired by Hamburg-American Packet Company, also known as Hamburg-American Steamship Company. Schurz had no business experience and was ignorant about the marine industry. He was paid the biggest salary he had ever made simply for the benefit of his name. Schurz astonished everyone by doing a good job. Schurz quit in 1892 because he felt tied down and wanted to spend time on other things.

William Preston (Z. Taylor Navy) and Ambrose Dudley Mann (Pierce Asst. State) were among those who helped make Norfolk a great port, connecting railroad and steamship lines. In 1857 M.J. Kelley sold shares in a steamship operation to President Buchanan (Polk State), Howell Cobb (Buchanan Treasury), John Floyd (Buchanan War), Isaac Toucey (Buchanan Navy and Polk AG), and Robert McClelland (Pierce Interior). Buchanan and Cobb were eager buyers, but the rest less so.

U.S. Sen. Judah Benjamin (CSA AG, War, State) worked for the interests of Edward K. Collins, George Law, and Cornelius Vanderbilt. President Pierce tried to end the Collins steamship line mail subsidy. Instead Congress continued it, freed Collins from some previous conditions, and gave up the right to terminate the contract. Collins could end the arrangement, but Congress couldn't. Pierce's veto of this legislation was sustained. Businessmen said this was an example of Pierce's "unfriendliness" toward business. Sen. William Seward (Lincoln State) supported government subsidies for steamship companies, in particular the Collins line. Stephen Douglas (1860 Democratic presidential nominee) advocated Cuban annexation, which would help steamship companies. They appreciated this and were the bulwark of support for Douglas's 1852 Democratic presidential nomination hopes. George Law himself supported Douglas for the 1852 nomination. Seward's intimate associate Thurlow Weed had a good relationship with George Law and Edward Collins. When Russell Sage ran for Congress in 1852 he asked Weed to keep Collins and Law from financing Sage's opponent. Weed was also on good terms with Commodore Vanderbilt, getting him to provide Seward's transportation to Europe in 1859. Note that U.S. Senators Seward and Benjamin were both involved with the same steamship interests, providing a business link between the U.S. and Confederate cabinets.

George Trenholm (CSA Treasury) headed John Fraser & Co., a shipping and commission firm of Charleston, SC. Trenholm's company had fifty blockade runners in the Civil War. The company exported cotton, tobacco, and turpentine. Salt, coal, iron, arms, ammunition, and other items were imported. Trenholm's business made big money.

James Garfield

President Garfield (father of TR Interior) had saved $1,200 by the time he married. His savings reached $5,000 during the Civil War ($75,000 in 2019 buying power), but then his expenses in Congress destroyed that sum. In 1865 Garfield and four other men set up an "oil company" which was actually a real estate operation. First they had someone pose as a Quaker looking for sheep pasture. With this falsehood the agent was able to buy up much Kentucky land at pennies an acre. This was deeded to Garfield and the partners at $100 an acre, and the "oil company" was to use investors' money to buy the "oil land" from the partners at that price. The goal was to turn the partners' $4,000 investment into $100,000 with suckers' money. Garfield was in charge of rounding up suckers, but only found enough for the partners to break even. Also in 1865 Garfield sold stock in genuine Pennsylvania oil land owned by the Phillips brothers. The next year the Phillips brothers and other Pennsylvania oil men got Garfield to help repeal an oil tax. They offered Garfield $2,750 in thanks, but Garfield declined the money ($41,250 in 2019 buying power). An 1867 trip to Europe was so expensive that Garfield drew several months' Congressional salary in advance and sold forty acres of Wisconsin land. The burden may have influenced his conduct in the Crédit Mobilier scandal. In 1869 he decided to build a house in Washington, as he had been paying $6,000 a year in rent. Garfield put about $13,000 into the house, which he couldn't afford. He borrowed half from his Army associate David Swain and paid it back. Swain sent many gifts to Garfield over the years, and Garfield worked to advance Swain's Army career. Ca. 1873 Garfield wanted to buy a $350 horse but couldn't meet the price ($7,000 in 2019 buying power). In 1875 Garfield took a train trip West, riding in a private car provided by Jay Gould. White House expenses burdened Garfield, as he depended mainly on his salary to meet living costs. President Hayes offered to sell his matched team of horses to the new President, but a veterinarian warned Garfield that the animals had been used so hard that not much was left in them. Hayes loaned his $1,150 landau to Garfield, who didn't own horses or a carriage. When Garfield was assassinated he left an estate of about $61,700 ($1,480,800 in 2019 buying power). "Prominent New York citizens" raised another $300,000 for the family before Garfield was buried. Congressional payments boosted the grand total to $500,000.

Robert Lincoln

The corporation law practice of Robert Lincoln (Garfield and Arthur War, son of Lincoln) was already highly profitable in 1868, three years after his father died. Robert Lincoln early learned to value himself highly, reportedly charging $250 for a half hour title search. Eventually Robert Lincoln's law practice may have been the biggest in Chicago. His firm handled the wills of Walter L. Newberry, Marshall Field, and Joseph Medill (*Chicago Tribune*). Robert Lincoln personally handled Newberry's will and related litigation. Robert Lincoln was close to McCormick, Pullman, Marshall Field, and other great capitalists of the era, being an official in many corporations himself. His close relationship with David Davis (US Sup Court J) surely did Robert Lincoln's law practice no harm. He made a lot of money as a corporation lawyer but noted in 1878, "Like any lawyer I manage to live up to all I make."[53] When J.D. Cameron (Grant War) suggested to Garfield that he appoint Robert Lincoln Secretary of War, Lincoln was very reluctant to give up his lucrative law practice, but was eventually persuaded to accept the cabinet post. In 1887 Lincoln said he would refuse the Vice Presidential nomination. "To take any office at all would be a great sacrifice to [my] business interests."[54] In 1871 he inherited about $18,000 ($360,000 in 2019 buying power). When his mother continued to spend so much that it jeopardized the size of his expected inheritance, Robert Lincoln had her certified as a lunatic. The certifying physician was the uncle of Robert Lincoln's law partner. Although those aspects of the proceedings are literally true, they may be too stark; Robert may have been trying to do the right thing. Robert Lincoln inherited $84,000 from the mother. In 1926 Lincoln transferred over $1,250,000 in stocks and bonds to his wife to reduce the income tax bite. Much of that wealth came from Lincoln's involvement with the Pullman railroad car company.

Pullman Railroad Cars

Pullman's Palace Car Co. was later known as Pullman Co. and as Pullman, Inc. Pullman's cars were leased (not sold) to railroad companies. The company, like any large business, wanted friends in high places. The Pullman Company put walnut paneling with gold leaf trim in Uaher's (Lincoln

Interior) house. Usher, as noted earlier, had an important role in the transcontinental railroad. Robert Lincoln's law firm had various railroad clients, including the Pullman concern. By 1872 Robert Lincoln had enough influence to get Gen. Horace Porter made New York representative of Pullman Co. He was eventually company vice president.

Pullman dividends in 1893 had been $2,500,000 ($70,000,000 in 2019 buying power) on capital of $36,000,000. There was a surplus of $25,000,000 in undivided profits. In May 1894 Pullman stock sold above par. Pullman then decided that it was time to economize and began to fire workers. Union leader and socialist Eugene Debs called a strike, and American Railway Union members refused to handle Pullman cars. This had nationwide impact, and the railroads decided to show the workers who was boss. Richard Olney (Cleveland AG) and George Pullman were fellow directors of Boston & Maine Railroad. Olney was prejudiced against the strike due to years as a railroad attorney and director. Even historian Allen Nevins agreed with that, and Nevins took care to avoid even gentle criticism of great men unless the evidence for utter condemnation was compelling. Olney appointed Edwin Walker (Chicago, Milwaukee & St. Paul railroad attorney) as special counsel to help the federal district attorney in Chicago to deal with the strike. This appointment came within two hours of Walker's recommendation by the General Managers' Association, a railroad group of which Olney was a member. Olney had appointed many U.S. marshals recommended by railroads. In turn, "Federal marshals had appointed some 3,600 deputies who were selected by the General Managers' Association, who were armed and paid for by the railroads, and acted in the double capacity of railroad employees and U.S. officers. The press described them as "'toughs' and Marshal Donnelly as in part 'worthless' and drunken."[55] Daniel Lamont (Cleveland War) directed federal forces in Chicago. Walter Gresham (Cleveland State) was so horrified by conditions that he called for George Pullman to resign from the company. George Pullman wasn't universally admired among capitalists. Gresham's wife noted that Pullman's wealthy enemies would probably use the strike to sell Pullman stock short and worsen the situation. Robert Lincoln accompanied George Pullman here and there during the strike and acted as George Pullman's attorney in defending him for avoiding a subpoena. Robert Lincoln and another man got $425,000 as executors of Pullman's will.

Robert Lincoln was Pullman president from 1897 to 1911 and board chairman later. Ca. 1915 Pullman porters were paid $27.50 a month. One porter testified that his tips were $87.50 a month. Robert Lincoln was asked in 1915, "Would you or any self-respecting member of your Board of Directors be willing to take your pay in the same way, Mr. Lincoln?" The reply: "Oh, no, and I must say that this arrangement of tips is not a nice one at all.

But it is an old one." Robert Lincoln then chuckled, going on, "and one to which the colored race is accustomed. The public seems to be fond of it." In effect railroad ticket holders were paying the salaries of Pullman employees (via tips), relieving Pullman stockholders of that expense. Robert Lincoln was asked if employee complaints about labor conditions would ever be considered by the board of directors. He replied, "It would be rather hard to get the board together for such a purpose." Robert Lincoln also admitted that no porter would ever be promoted.[56] About this time the U.S. Supreme Court ruled that the Pullman corporation could require employees to release from personal injury liability Pullman Co. and all railroad corporations with Pullman cars.

Chapter 9

Chester Arthur

Future President Arthur (Garfield VP) was making $56,000 a year as Collector of the Port of New York when Congress altered the pay system from a percentage of revenue collections to a straight $12,000 salary. He was a big spender but left an estate of $161,000.

Young Theodore Roosevelt

Arthur's job as Collector of the Port of New York would be a historical blip except that it helped bring Theodore Roosevelt (McKinley VP) to the Presidency. President Hayes nominated Roosevelt's father to replace Arthur as Collector. Arthur was a duke (if not king) of the New York spoilsmen, and the Senate confirmation battle was raw and bloody. In the end Roosevelt's father lost and soon died from the strain. Young Roosevelt wasn't the sort of person to forget this. In a few years Roosevelt would descend upon Washington as Civil Service Commissioner, obsessed with destroying the spoils system that killed his father.

During the Arthur Presidency Roosevelt fled to the West where he could be away from Eastern political intrigues.

> Roosevelt could ride a hundred miles a day, stay up all night on watch, and be back at work after a hastily gulped, 3:00 a.m. breakfast. On one occasion he was in the saddle for nearly forty hours, wearing out five horses, and winding up in another stampede. He roped steers till his hands were flayed, wrestled calves in burning clouds of alkali-dust and stuck "like a burr" to bucking ponies, while his nose poured blood and hat, guns, and spectacles flew in all directions. One particularly vicious horse fell over backwards on him cracking the point of his left shoulder. There was no doctor within a hundred miles, so he continued to work "as best I could, until the injury healed itself." It was weeks before could raise his arm freely.
>
> "That four-eyed maverick," remarked one veteran puncher, "has sand in his craw a-plenty." And Sourdoughs everywhere allowed that he was "one of our crowd," "not a purty rider, but a hell of a *good* rider," and (highest praise of all) "a fearless bugger."

TR became a prominent figure among Bad Lands stockmen. In 1885 there was talk off him becoming Dakota's first U.S. Senator when the Territory achieved statehood.

In this period Roosevelt, like many other Westerners, learned some of the limits of Western agriculture. Being wealthy and a free spender, TR plunked $5,000 into Cheyenne Beef Co., ca. 1884 ($125,000 in 2019 buying power). He then decided to start his own Bad Lands cattle operation and put $85,000 into the project in 1885 ($2,210,000 in 2019 buying power). This seems to have been about half his capital. By the next year, his two herds were clearly losing money, a lot of money. In the terrible winter of 1886–1887 TR lost perhaps 65% of his herds. "The losses are crippling," he said. "I am planning to get out of it." He had lost about $52,000 in three years. By 1899, however, twelve years of careful management had cut his loss to just over $20,000. As he left to take charge of the Rough Riders in the Spanish-American War, TR sold the meager remnant of his steers and gave his Elkhorn Ranch to ranch employee Sylvanne Ferris, whom TR later made Land Officer of North Dakota.

Grover Cleveland

Cleveland served two terms as President, but they weren't consecutive. He was first elected in 1884. In 1888 he was defeated by Benjamin Harrison. Four years later ex–President Cleveland returned for a grudge match against President Harrison, and this time Cleveland won. So Cleveland's Presidency spanned twelve years.

In his pre–Presidential days Cleveland wanted to be a sheriff in New York state for the money, expecting (and apparently achieving) $40,000 in fees over three years. In 1881 his savings were $75,000 ($1,875,000 in 2019 buying power). His fortune in 1897 was $300,000 ($9,000,000 in 2019 buying power) to $350,000.

Cleveland was with President Fillmore's (Z. Taylor VP) law firm in the 1850s. President Cleveland and Wilson Bissell (Cleveland PG) were law partners, just as Fillmore and *his* Postmaster General were law partners. Cleveland surrounded himself with great capitalists such as William Whitney (Cleveland Navy). Whitney loved to spend money and was bothered by his wife's attempts to economize. He could well afford it, dying with over $21,000,000 still unspent. Ex-President Cleveland was a legal consultant for big corporations. Ca. 1889 Cleveland was with the law firm of Bangs, Stetson, Tracy & MacVeagh. Tracy was the brother-in-law of J.P. Morgan.

Whitney made his money by participating in New York City's streetcar wars. Other participants included Thomas Fortune Ryan (associate of

TR's brother-in-law) and FDR's father. Elihu Root (TR State and War) and Whitney were irked by Gov. Theodore Roosevelt's actions involving taxes on Whitney streetcar company franchises. This had much to do with Roosevelt's nomination as Vice President. TR himself felt that both Whitney and Ryan were involved with getting him the nomination in order to get him out of New York politics.

George Harvey (key man in getting Woodrow Wilson the 1912 Democratic Presidential nomination) was an executive in Metropolitan Street Railway. With the help of Levi Morton (B. Harrison VP) Metropolitan Securities Co. replaced Metropolitan Street Railway. Directors of the new company included James Hazen Hyde (Equitable Life Assurance). Whitney personally guaranteed $5,000,000 of the stock subscription in forming the new company; if not enough stock was sold, Whitney would have to buy up to $5,000,000.

Tobacco

Whitney was also a big tobacco man. John D. Rockefeller (grandfather of Ford VP) organized American Tobacco Company. Ca. 1896 Whitney and Thomas Fortune Ryan decided to move in on American Tobacco. Whitney and Ryan formed Consolidated Tobacco Co. of New Jersey, a holding company that took control of American Tobacco. Whitney's Consolidated Tobacco security holdings were $7,600,000 in 1901 ($243,200,000 in 2019 buying power) and $9,200,000 in 1904 ($257,600,000 in 2019 buying power). American and British capitalists then divided the international tobacco market between them. At a banquet celebrating formation of British-American Tobacco, with American tobacco king James Duke as guest of honor, ex–Navy Secretary Whitney "laid his hand on Duke's shoulder and said: 'It is such marvelous merchants as these men who make a great navy necessary to carry and protect trade which seems to know no bounds.'"[57] James McReynolds (Wilson AG) quit prosecuting American Tobacco for anti-trust violations in 1911. McReynolds gave up because he felt George Wickersham (Taft AG) was too lenient with American Tobacco. McReynolds complained, "Since when has property illegally and criminally acquired come to have any rights?"[58]

Railroads Again

CB&Q Railroad lawyer Richard Olney (Cleveland AG and State) was making perhaps $50,000 a year when he entered the cabinet ($1,400,000 in 2019 buying power). When he left, his estate was about $1,400,000 ($42,000,000 in 2019 buying power). Olney became a CB&Q director in 1889. The future Attorney General was a CB&Q lobbyist against the Interstate Commerce Act of 1887 and advised the railroad's president to commit crimes if that would help business.[59] While Attorney General, Olney continued to get a $10,000 salary from CB&Q ($290,000 in 2019 buying power). The railroad president wrote to Olney regarding his appointment as Attorney General, "It shall make no difference in our relations except as you may think it expedient to make."[60] The board chairman wrote to the railroad's president about Olney's appointment as Attorney General, "It seems to me rather for our advantage to have him at Washington."[61]

Chapter 10

Sherman Anti-Trust Law

For years the sugar industry was in essence the American Sugar Refining Co., known as the Sugar Trust, which produced about ninety-eight percent of U.S. sugar ca. 1891. Elihu Root (McKinley and TR War) was attorney for the powerful Havemeyer sugar family and helped them form American Sugar Refining Co. In an anti-trust suit against American Sugar, Richard Olney (Cleveland AG) deliberately neglected to have the government prove that interstate commerce was involved This caused the case to collapse. Olney had been a key defense attorney for the Whiskey Trust in anti-trust action prosecuted by the Benjamin Harrison administration. Olney was unopposed to criminal trust activity and actually brought suit against American Sugar in hopes that the Supreme Court would strike down the Sherman Anti-Trust Act. After leaving the cabinet Olney became an American Sugar official.

American Sugar forced railroads to pay rebates. Since according to some estimates sugar was forty percent of all western freight from New York, the railroads were in a position to be influenced. American Sugar used low freight charges (via rebates) to compete against Western sugar-beet growers. Ca. 1907 Root's law partner Henry Stimson (Taft War, Hoover State, FDR War, and Truman War) got American Sugar and New York Central Railroad convicted for their rebate arrangement. The law partner of William Evarts (A. Johnson AG) was a defense lawyer in that case. Stimson was U.S. District Attorney for Southern New York at the time. He also successfully sued American Sugar et al. for defrauding customs duties by $3,500,000 from 1901 to 1907. The defendants had tampered with the customs scales. Rather than face criminal trial American Sugar paid $2,000,000, and the others paid over $1,300,000. President Taft's brother was an American Sugar lawyer.

Lumber

William Vilas (Cleveland PG and Interior) was another big capitalist in Cleveland's cabinet. He died with an estate of almost $2,000,000 ($56,000,000 in 2109 buying power). Vilas and his old Albany Law School buddy John C. Knight were partners in timberland purchases. It was all public land, giving the two men an edge over competitors, as Knight was registrar of the land office for the area where they bought. Knight was accused of telling woodsmen that the tract they wanted was already taken. Then he allegedly would sign for it himself, with Knight and Vilas thereby avoiding the bother of personally scouting the area.[62] Knight and Vilas sold to customers large and small, ranging from Mississippi Logging Company to Weyerhaeuser.

In 1881 Knight and others organized Superior Lumber Company. Vilas was president in 1885, and Knight was general manager. Vilas also put money into Pacific Northwest pine lands and Wisconsin pulp and paper manufacturing.

After Vilas became Cleveland's postmaster general, Knight asked the Interior Department to be more cooperative in allowing logging on Indian land. Vilas had an associate, James T. Gregory, appointed as an Indian agent. Oshkosh lumberman Thomas Wall was appointed allotment agent. This job included transferring tribal lands to individual Indians, with whom logging contract could be made. Gregory ignored various regulations, such as having Indians do the logging, paying the Indians a specified wage as loggers, the basis of payment to Indians for timber, and the requirement to leave standing one-fourth of the timber on each tract. In addition to ignoring these factors Gregory also permitted logging under contracts unapproved by the Commissioner of Indian Affairs. Postmaster General Vilas then became Secretary of the Interior. He said it was proper to violate these regulations because they were impractical for timbermen to obey. He refused to fire Gregory, saying the Indian agent was doing a fine job.

After retiring from his cabinet job supervising usage of America's natural resources, Vilas said that Wisconsin timberland was ideal for cutting. Vilas maintained that this would clear the land for agriculture. He argued that even when game was driven out by cutting, hunters could fish, thereby preventing any loss to sportsmen.

Benjamin Harrison

Ca. 1861 President Benjamin Harrison's law income was good, supplemented by his publication of Indiana Supreme Court decisions. Then he bought a new house and nearly ruined his health through the effort needed to keep up payments. While a Civil War general he was deeply worried about money. He made good profits on publishing the Indiana Supreme Court decisions after the war, but the pace of work was draining. In 1873 his law practice yielded $12,000 ($250,000 in 2019 buying power), and rents from his properties brought in another $5,000 ($100,000 in 2019 buying power). Ca. 1875 he built a new $20,000 house ($460,000 in 2019 buying power). By 1886 he transferred all his Montana Cattle Co. investments to his son Russell. Russell lost at least fifteen percent by April 1887. William Miller (B. Harrison AG) blamed the son's ineptness. Miller's view was probably colored by the $15,000 of stock he owned in the enterprise. Russell may simply have been a victim of bad luck. The winter of 1886–1887 destroyed Theodore Roosevelt's cattle operation as well. In 1887 Harrison was hustling for money to pay his own debts and his son's. Harrison asked "robber baron, junior grade" Stephen Elkins (B. Harrison War, relative of 1904 Democratic Vice Presidential nominee) to save the Montana operation. Elkins promised cooperation, and Russell suddenly became more prosperous. The *Brooklyn Daily Eagle* credited the prosperity to Elkins and other capitalists, reporting that they were giving Russell insider advantages in their financial operations. Russell's wife also helped by getting a $5,000 salary federal job that didn't obstruct her social life.

Ex-President Harrison became lawyer for the Venezuelan government after President Cleveland declined the job. Harrison got a $20,000 retainer plus another $40,000 a year. He also had Venezuela hire Benjamin Tracy (B. Harrison Navy) for a $50,000 fee. Harrison got a total of $80,000 from his work for Venezuela. Harrison said, "I have given myself so absolutely and so constantly to the case of Venezuela since my employment that I have felt recently as if I was on the verge of a breakdown. For one year now I have taken no rest and have not even had the diversion that would come from other professional engagements. I hope Venezuela is satisfied with the work we have done."[63]

Former President Harrison's minimum law retainer was $500. His law income was almost $50,000 from 1894 to 1895 ($1,500,000 in 2019 buying power). Harrison left an estate of $375,000 ($12,000,000 in 2019 buying power).

Alaskan Seals

Elkins (B. Harrison War) was one of five stockholders in North American Commercial Co., which leased Alaska seal islands from the United States. While taking seal pelts the company didn't pay taxes and rentals to the federal government. The United States went to court and got a judgment against North American Commercial Co.[64] The company appealed. The longer they could drag out the appeal, the more money they could make before giving up the contract. Supposedly North American Commercial Co. killed only males, while operating in the wilderness without witnesses. The general situation of seal hunting in this area caused considerable tension with Britain, with some uneasiness about war. President McKinley became worried and appointed John Foster (B. Harrison State, grandfather of Eisenhower State) as commissioner to manage seal herds.

Closing the Frontier

People like Elkins helped close the Western frontier, ending the supply of public domain land which had provided homesteads for Americans since colonial times. As a lawyer in the 1870s Elkins charged fees of $10,000 and upwards in land cases, calling it among "the easiest money I ever earned."[65] He owned 100,000 acres in West Virginia, but his most spectacular land operation was in New Mexico Territory. Through a rigged sale Elkins became the main owner of the Maxwell Spanish land grant in 1877, one of the largest real estate holdings in America. The U.S. General Land Office ordered a survey. Elkins and another man posted bond for the two surveyors, one of whom was Elkins's brother. The General Land Office then granted a patent to 1,700,000 acres including towns, coal, timber, and minerals. Elkins mortgaged the grant to Dutch capitalists. The U.S. government then found evidence of fraud and brought court action to invalidate the grant. Elkins wasn't personally sued since he operated through the Maxwell Land Grant Co. As a member of Congress Elkins had gotten Congress to certify his claims. Since, while all was going on, future President Benjamin Harrison was a member of the U.S. Senate Committee on Territories, he probably knew all about it. Because of the Congressional action approving the land grant, the U.S. Supreme Court then upheld the 1,700,000-acre grant in 1887. Elkins's associates evicted settlers who had been turned into squatters by the court decision, and an armed rebellion broke out.

Elkins's conduct was nothing unusual. Many settlers were run off their property by big capitalists. Long before the great tracts of public land finally disappeared during the Benjamin Harrison administration, big capitalists had already made homesteading less and less practical.

Chapter 11

Department Stores and Mail Order Houses

While President, Benjamin Harrison's finances apparently improved. In 1889 he bought two Studebaker carriages for a total of $2,900 to $18,000 ($78,300 to $486,000 in 2019 buying power). As ex-President, Harrison's minimum law retainer was $500. His law income was almost $50,000 from 1894 to 1895 ($1,450,000 in 2109 buying power). Harrison left an estate of $375,000 ($12,000,000 in 2109 buying power). Gifts helped with this. John Wanamaker (B. Harrison PG) and some other Philadelphia citizens gave a wonderful seaside cottage to President Harrison's wife. A public outcry asked if this were a bribe. Harrison belatedly announced he had always intended to pay for it, and handed Wanamaker $10,000 in 1890 ($270,000 in 2109 buying power). Six years later, after things had quieted, Wanamaker returned the $10,000, saying he was purchasing the cottage from Harrison.

Wanamaker's Civil War clothing business has already been mentioned. This evolved into a large Philadelphia retail operation selling general merchandise. After his brother-in-law died Wanamaker had no partners, and for fifty years there were no stock offerings. Wanamaker's stores pioneered in special sales to move out slow merchandise. The stores were quick to use the innovations of electric lighting and electric ventilation, permitting multilevel and night operations. In 1887 Wanamaker bought the third largest wholesale dry goods in the United States—Hood, Bonbright & Co. of Philadelphia. Wanamaker's wholesale business soon reached $20,000,000 a year. A.T. Stewart (Grant Treasury nominee) died in 1876, and his New York firm dissolved in 1882. Its Ninth & Broadway business continued, however, under several names. Wanamaker bought it in 1896. Henry Morgenthau, Sr. (father of FDR Treasury) conducted the sale negotiations. President Taft spoke at the dedication of Wanamaker's new Philadelphia store in 1911. The next year Wanamaker seconded Taft's nomination at the GOP convention.

In urban areas the specialty shop began to face more competition from department stores such as Wanamaker's and Macy's. The father of Oscar

Straus (TR Commerce & Labor) opened a New York City crockery store in 1866. In 1874 the father opened a glassware and china department at Macy's. Similar deals were worked out with other stores. All Straus merchandise was imported. Since President Theodore Roosevelt's father was a major glassware importer in New York City at the same time, this suggests yet another link between the Roosevelt and Straus families (in addition to Old South ties). The china department at Macy's did so well that the Straus family eventually acquired ownership of Macy's. The father became a millionaire friend of President Cleveland. About the time Straus (TR Commerce & Labor) joined his father's firm it had four five-story buildings in New York City and operations in London, Paris, Limoges, Carlsbad, and other places. Reputedly this was the world's largest firm in its line of merchandise. In 1894 a brother of Straus was elected to Congress, where he pushed for lower tariffs. In 1933 FDR appointed Jesse Isidor Straus ambassador to France. James Mitchell (Eisenhower Labor) was director of personnel and industrial relations at Macy's 1945–1947.

President Carter's associate David Packard (Nixon Deputy Defense) owned Macy's stock. And Packard also had stock in Federated Department Stores, Inc., directed by President Carter's associates Lucy Benson and Peter Peterson (Nixon Commerce). A top Federated Department Stores executive directed Chase Manhattan Bank, run by President Carter's associate David Rockefeller (brother of Ford VP).

The latter 1800s also saw the growth of mail order houses such as Sears Roebuck and Montgomery Ward. The law partner of John Payne (Wilson Interior) was president of Montgomery Ward & Co. Robert Lamont (Hoover Commerce) was a Montgomery Ward director. Over Henry Stimson's (FDR War) opposition, FDR used Army troops to break a Montgomery Ward strike in the 1940s. Stimson seemed bewildered, as he felt the situation had no relation to the war effort. J.P. Morgan & Co., however had been involved with Ward, and the father of Edward Stettinius (FDR State) had been J.P. Morgan's partner. Did these involvements affect FDR's strikebreaking?

Telegraph and Telephone

During the Benjamin Harrison administration the use of telephones greatly expanded in the United States. The telephone originally supplemented the telegraph and later nearly replaced it. For instance, when W.T. Sherman (Grant War) was a San Francisco banker, often weeks and even months would elapse between the time he made a business commitment and the time he learned whether the St. Louis headquarters bank could stand behind the commitment. Businessmen had to operate ignorant of the resources available to them. Instantaneous electronic communication, however, allowed businessmen to coordinate business resources around the world. This helped contribute to the tremendous growth of capitalism in the nineteenth and twentieth centuries.

In 1843 John P. Kennedy (Fillmore Navy) was a key figure in getting federal funding of $30,000 ($1,000,000 in 2019 buying power) for telegraph experiments by Samuel F.B. Morse. Even though a demonstration telegraph was set up at the Capitol, members of Congress remained skeptical. Cave Johnson (Polk PG) ridiculed the telegraph by equating it with hypnotism. (One Congressman was unconvinced until Morse tapped out, "Tyler deserves to be hanged.") Future President Fillmore helped Kennedy get the floor of the House to propose the $30,000 expenditure, but Fillmore made Kennedy promise to drop the matter if debate arose. Richard Thompson (Hayes Navy) was among the majority in Congress who approved the money, and the experiments continued.

In 1845 Amos Kendall (Jackson and Van Buren PG) contracted with the proprietors of three-fourths of the Morse patents. Kendall got authority to manage or dispose of Morse's patent rights, with up to a fifty percent commission on sums that came in. This made both Morse and Kendall wealthy. Kendall became very busy creating and managing telegraph companies. This included negotiations with railroads. As noted earlier, Robert Walker (Polk Treasury) was prominent in transcontinental railway schemes, and around 1853 Kendall approached Walker on joining forces to build a telegraph line to California.

William Evarts (Andrew Johnson AG, Hayes State) was a Western Union Telegraph Co. lawyer. The brother of Elihu Washburne (Grant State) maintained that Western Union overcharged for its services. While a member of Congress the brother argued that the federal government should take over the Western Union system. As New York City Corporation Counsel, William Whitney (Cleveland Navy) ruled ca. 1879 that Western Union could lay underground wire without city permission. Around the 1880s Western Union Telegraph and Metropolitan Telephone Co. organized Consolidated Telegraph & Electrical Subway Co. Metropolitan Telephone Co. was later known as New York Telephone Co. About 1929 ex–President Taft declined to be board chairman of New York Telephone, a job that would have paid $50,000 a year to work three days a week ($700,000 in 2019 buying power).

In the later nineteenth century Western Union was run by Russell Sage and Jay Gould. John Wanamaker (B. Harrison PG) asked Gould to reduce charges to the Post Office Department. Gould's associates then tried to make Wanamaker back off by pressuring his Philadelphia store—calling loans, refusing credit, and the like. Philadelphia businessmen and bankers came to Wanamaker's aid, giving him access to millions of dollars. Wanamaker didn't have to draw on the fund, but he remembered the actions of his friends—and of Gould—for a long time.

Jay Gould had John Hay (Lincoln private secretary, McKinley State) elected to the Western Union board of directors after Hay's father-in-law (who was a director) died. Ca. 1890–1898 Elihu Root was a Western Union lawyer.

In alliance with Western Telegraphy Co., Ltd. (which had a monopoly on a telegraph cable on the eastern coast of South America) Western Union extended a cable from Buenos Aires to within three miles of Miami, Florida. Elihu Root's son was counsel for All-America Cables, Inc., which operated between the United States and Buenos Aires via South America's western coast. The younger Root found precedents forbidding foreign companies with monopolies to lay cables in the United States. President Wilson had a Navy ship prevent Western Telegraph from landing the cable. This generated a lawsuit which got a lower court ruling that Wilson had exceeded his authority. Before the case went to the Supreme Court, Congress gave the President that authority. When Wilson left office Charles Evans Hughes (Harding State), future President Hoover (Harding Commerce), and the companies agreed that the cable could be landed if monopoly rights were abandoned on both coasts. An arrangement along this line was worked out.

By the mid twentieth century the telephone industry in the United States was basically the American Telephone & Telegraph Company, which operated the Bell Telephone System. Theodore Vail ran the Bell Telephone Co. in its early years. Vail was David Key's (Hayes PG) assistant for railway mail. When Key's wife had $1,000 to invest while her husband was a cabinet member she was undecided between Bell Telephone or a western gold mine. Vail urged Mrs. Key to pick the telephone, but instead she went for the gold and lost everything.

In 1883, shortly before joining the Cleveland cabinet, Augustus Garland (Cleveland AG) became a lawyer for Pan-Electric Telephone Company, receiving $500,000 of stock for free. The company was essentially a group of men who owned the Rogers telephone patent claim. If Bell's patent could be overturned, this would mean big money for them. In 1885 Attorney General Garland's company asked him to start a Justice Department suit against the Bell patent. Ostensibly Garland declined due to the conflict of interest in holding ten percent of Pan-Electric's stock. Instead, the Solicitor General started the suit against Bell. Questions arose as to whether the Attorney General might have influenced his subordinate's action. President Cleveland announced an investigation of the matter, ordering Lucius

Lamar (Cleveland Interior) to determine if his cabinet colleague was a scoundrel. In 1886 Lamar announce that the suit was proper and should proceed.

American Telephone & Telegraph's influence in the executive branch may be inferred from the presence of AT&T directors in high government positions, including Richard Olney (Cleveland AG, State), the son of Root (McKinley War, TR War, State), David Houston (Wilson Agriculture, Treasury), John Davis (1924 Democratic presidential nominee, chief counsel J.P. Morgan & Co.), the father-in-law of Dwight Davis (Coolidge War), Charles Adams (Hoover Navy), Juanita Krebs (Carter Commerce), Archibald Davis (Carter associate), and William Hewitt (Carter associate). AT&T directors interlocked with Morgan Guaranty Trust, Chase Manhattan Bank (which controlled much AT&T stock), and Standard Oil of New Jersey.

At that time AT&T was close to Bell Telephone Company. The law partner of William Miller (B. Harrison AG) was a Bell Telephone attorney. William B. Schiller was director of a Mellon (Harding and Hoover Treasury) bank and was a Bell Telephone director. Robert Lamont (Hoover Commerce) directed Illinois Bell. Frederick Suits of the Dulles (IKE State) law firm was with AT&T's subsidiary Western Electric. Western Electric director William Batten had fellow Western Electric director Juanita Krebs (Carter Commerce) made a director of the J.C. Penny Company. This Krebs appointment illustrates how corporations lacking obvious connections among themselves nonetheless have the potential to informally coordinate policies via shared directorships.

Gas

The gas industry was to states and municipalities what the oil industry later was to unstable Third World governments. In 1884 a half dozen New York gaslight companies combined to form the Consolidated Gas Company. William Whitney (Cleveland Navy) and William Rockefeller became directors of Consolidated. George Cortelyou (TR Treasury) was president, and Root (McKinley and TR War) was a lawyer for the company.

In 1905 the New York legislature asked the brother of President Taft (TR War) to investigate the gas trust. Taft's brother instead recommended Charles Evans Hughes (Harding State). There was initial skepticism about Hughes, since he was a friend of John D. Rockefeller and ex-partner of utilities attorney Paul Cravath. Hughes nonetheless exposed corruption, overcharges, and unsafe conditions. Hughes concluded that the free market could no longer work to supervise this business, that a public regulatory commission was necessary. Many of Hughes's recommendations were enacted into law. In 1906 the New York legislature required Consolidated Gas to reduce its rate twenty percent, down to eighty cents per 1,000 cubic feet. The company went to court alleging that this would not allow a fair return on the company's investment. U.S. Supreme Court Justice Rufus W. Peckam wrote the decision. His brother was a corporation lawyer who helped get a bill aiding Consolidated Gas through the New York legislature. The Supreme Court nonetheless unanimously held that the eighty cents law was constitutional.

New York gas magnate E.C. Benedict was a close friend of President Cleveland. In 1893 Benedict's yacht *Oneida* was the locale for secret jaw cancer surgery received by President Cleveland. Benedict gave financial advice and handled securities trading for the President during the White House years. The two men had a joint bank account. Ex-President Cleveland wrote, "I like the joint account which has one careful father and an uncle who wishes it well for what he may make out of it. I as such an uncle am certainly much obliged to the Dad in this particular instance."[66]

Electricity

Thomas Edison (father of FDR Navy) perhaps did more than any other person to relieve the sheer drudgery of human labor in America. Packs of capitalist wolves are instantly attracted to successful inventions, driven to a frenzy by the scent of money. Edison was one of the few inventors who remained undevoured, who in fact beat back the man eaters and forced respect from them.

For instance, the electric light bulb itself meant nothing. Everyone was using natural gas. Millions, perhaps billions, of dollars were invested in a complex delivery system that permeated cities as thoroughly as arteries and capillaries in a human body. No one in his right mind would be willing to abandon that investment. Yet Edison was such an astute capitalist that he and his allies forced the gas industries to their knees. That astonishing story, alas, must be saved for another book.

Here we can mention a handful of Edison connections to Presidents and cabinet members. Robert Lincoln (Garfield and Arthur War) organized Western Edison Light Company. Hilborne Roosevelt (cousin of TR) was an important financial backer of Edison. Charles Edison (FDR Navy) was chairman of Edison Industries and president of Thomas A. Edison, Inc. An Edison lawyer was in Hughes's (Harding State) law firm. J.P. Morgan forces set up Edison Electric Illuminating Company, with Garret Hobart (McKinley VP) as a director and Henry Ford as chief engineer. George

Cortelyou (TR Treasury) and William Rockefeller (granduncle of Ford VP) became New York Edison directors. The Rockefellers controlled millions of dollars in Consolidated Edison stock, and Con Ed's credit source was Rockefeller's Chase Manhattan Bank. John Foster Dulles (Eisenhower State, and relative of Wilson State and of B. Harrison State) was a director of Detroit Edison, which his law partner helped organize. The Dulles law firm organized Potomac Edison Co. and Southern California Edison Co. President Hoover's son was director of the latter. Hoover himself was a friend of Thomas Edison, although this may have had less to do with electricity than with the inventor's rubber research. Hoover wanted to reduce American dependence on British Empire rubber. Wendell Willkie (1940 GOP Presidential nominee) was Ohio Edison's board chairman and directed Consumers Power Company, Southern Indiana Gas & Electric Co., and Central Illinois Light Co.

In 1892 a corporate consolidation of Edison interests created a company called General Electric. Richard Olney (Cleveland AG) and J.P. Morgan helped set up GE. Thomas Edison sold out to Morgan at this time and left the utility industry. Morgan's partner Edward Stettinius (father of Truman State) was a GE director, as were Charles Adams (Hoover Navy), Thomas Gates (Eisenhower Defense), Frederick Dent (Ford Commerce), and President Carter's associate J. Paul Austin.

Charles Evans Hughes (Harding and Coolidge State) was an attorney for GE, arguing in one case that the corporation owned a radio frequency and could not be restrained from using it. Nor could anyone else use it. GE simply staked out part of the electromagnetic spectrum, just as other corporations claimed forests, minerals, parts of rivers, and other natural phenomena. Yet in this case GE lost. Radio waves and the rest of the electromagnetic spectrum, including visible light, remained public property.

Earlier, ca. 1890, Hughes was a lawyer for two electric utilities, arguing that a law ordering power line repair or removal violated property rights. The court rejected this, saying, "When it is apparent, as in this case at bar, the condition of the wires is such that they are dangerous to human life, and that any passer-by, without negligence on his part, is liable to be struck dead in the street, can it be said for a moment that the public authorities have no power to abate this nuisance and protect the lives of its citizens?" The court also said the companies were "guilty of the willful violation of a manifest duty in allowing the wires to become dangerous. They are without excuse, and when they claim that the destruction of these instruments of death … is an invasion of the rights of property, such claim seems to proceed upon the assumption that nothing has a right to exist except themselves."

The Cross of Gold

The money supply was a big issue in the 1896 election. Democratic candidate William Jennings Bryan (Wilson State) wanted silver coinage increased. Republicans and Gold Democrats trembled at the specter of inflation that silver conjured, and they defeated Bryan. Inflation was only a side issue to silverites. Their concern was the same thing that shaped the banking policies of Andrew Jackson and George Washington—gold coinage alone couldn't provide enough money to pay debts, thus solvent persons were getting ruined. The scarcer money was, the lower prices got. Thus a person had to sell more and more assets (bank accounts, real estate, farm products, and the like) to pay off debts. Silverites wanted to inject an inflationary force into the deflationary trend and thus stabilize currency values.

Such an inflationary force came from an unexpected direction—the supply of gold itself was increased by gold discoveries in Australia. President Hoover (Harding and Coolidge Commerce) and his brother were active in Australian mining. During the silver currency controversy in America, Hoover discovered the fabulous Sons of Gwalia mine for his British employers Bewick, Moreing & Co. and supervised much of that firm's Australian operation. Hoover favored importation of Italians to work in the mines, finding them less troublesome than Australians. "I have a bunch of Italians coming up this week," Hoover wrote, "and will put them in the mine on contract work. If they are satisfactory I will secure enough of them to hold the property in case of a general strike, and with your permission will reduce wages."[67] Although the Italians' inability to understand English language warnings resulted in extra casualties, conditions in Hoover's mines were considered excellent for that era. The Hoover brothers' Zinc Corp. evolved into the gigantic Conzinc Riotinto. With the exception of Great Boulder Perseverance mine, in which Hoover said he lost $85,000 of his own money, Hoover's Australian work was usually quite profitable for his employers and himself.

Chapter 12

William McKinley

While he was a member of Congress in the 1870s, McKinley's annual law income was $10,000 (about $200,000 in 2019 buying power), and his Congressional salary was $5,000. His estate was then under $20,000, and much of that was mortgaged. Ca. 1880 McKinley seemed to have financial trouble due to Congressional expenses, living expenses, and his semi-invalid wife's medical bills. In addition his wife had expensive tastes, and McKinley was financially troubled for a decade. His wife's inheritance from her father in 1887 was helpful. McKinley declined a $25,000 a year job as a Western railway attorney, preferring to stay in Congress. His Ohio governor's salary was $8,000 ($224,000 in 2019 buying power). McKinley was always a soft touch for hard luck stories, which brought disaster after he became a Presidential hopeful. An old friend who had loaned money to him now asked McKinley to return the favor by endorsing notes, which McKinley did again and again. Ca. 1892 the friend (along with much of the country) had a financial collapse, and McKinley suddenly owed $130,000 ($3,500,000 in 2019 buying power). All of his property ($20,000) and all of his wife's ($70,000) were insufficient to cover the debt. McKinley went into seclusion, pondering the end of his Presidential dreams in an era when failure to pay debts was a terrible scandal. In these dark days McKinley stayed at the home of his friend Myron Herrick (American Bankers Association president). McKinley's friends rescued him. Philander Knox (McKinley AG) gave $300, John Hay (McKinley State) at least $2,000, Charles Taft (brother of future President Taft) $1,000, H.C. Frick (partner of Harding Treasury) $2,000, and Philip Armour (Chicago meatpacker) $5,000. Andrew Carnegie gave, and George Pullman was asked for $5,000. Corporations also chipped in—Illinois Steel Co. gave $10,000, and Ohio banks discounted McKinley's notes by ten percent. The $100,000 of gifts saved McKinley's Presidential hopes. "I have no words with which to adequately thank you," McKinley wrote to Hay. "How can I ever repay you and other dear friends?"[68] McKinley and his wife recovered all their property. He died with an estate of $215,000 ($6,880,000 in 2019 buying power).

Bellamy Storer was another person who came to McKinley's aid in 1893, with $10,000. Storer's wife was an old friend of McKinley and began using this financial assistance to get various favors from the President-elect. Theodore Roosevelt asked the woman to approach McKinley about appointing Roosevelt Assistant Secretary of the Navy. She agreed, with Roosevelt in turn consenting to use his influence to boom Mr. Storer for a full-fledged cabinet post. Storer's wife had more influence with McKinley than Roosevelt did. Storer lost out when cabinet positions were filled, but Roosevelt got exactly the job he wanted.

Private Clubs

Roosevelt immediately began to frequent the Metropolitan Club almost every day. There, in pleasant rooms, while dining on fine cuts of meat (double lamb chops for TR), Roosevelt began planning the Spanish-American War with various top military, political, and news media personalities. It was at the Metropolitan Club, not at the White House or in Congress, that the Spanish-American War was decided upon and its strategy developed—months before the *Maine* exploded in Cuba. Clubs such as the Metropolitan raise question not only about the value of twentieth century "open meeting" laws for government, but about the value of citizens' votes. Such clubs deserve further mention here.

Club life is so important that corporations rent space in club buildings. For instance, Duquesne Club suites were rented by U.S. Steel, Gulf Oil, Jones & Laughlin, Alcoa, and others. Duquesne Club suites included bedroom, living room, and dining room. "Pittsburgh would not be the production marvel it is without the exchange of information, techniques, and ideas that take place every noontime at the Duquesne,"[69] "the *ne plus ultra* of business clubs in the United States."[70] Clubs also contain apartments for men who wish to live literally in the center of business and economic life. A law partner of William Evarts (A. Johnson AG, Hayes State) wrote to his wife in 1895: "I have moved to the Union League where I have got for a wonder a big square room and am very comfortable indeed. I tried in vain for a room at the Metropolitan and the Union. I dine here at the Century [Association] where I almost always find some good fellow to sit with."[71] Charles Dawes (Coolidge VP) lived at Chicago's Union League in 1896. While a cabinet member, Henry Wallace (FDR VP, Truman Commerce) lived a while at the Cosmos Club.

In standard histories one finds little mention of club life, yet this was a crucial part in the lives of many Presidents and cabinet members. W.T. Sherman (Grant War, brother of McKinley State) spent several nights a week, hours at a time, visiting friends at New York's Union League. "For many years, the 'Bob Lincoln Corner' at the Metropolitan was a famous gathering place for good conversation and humor."[72] Bob Lincoln was Secretary of War for Garfield and Arthur, and the son of Abraham Lincoln. A University Club dinner and quiet conversation afterward with Charles M. Schwab gave J.P. Morgan the idea of buying out Andrew Carnegie and forming U.S Steel. Financiers used the Union League Club as headquarters while trying to stop the Panic of 1907. One day Clinton Anderson (Truman Agriculture) and former President Hoover lunched at the Metropolitan in Washington, D.C. That meal led to President Truman inviting Hoover to the White House, which promoted good relations, which allowed Anderson to recommend that Hoover be put in charge of the postwar international food supply program, a job Anderson couldn't quite handle. The Counsel to the President of the United States and a former Attorney General once sat together in a room at such a club, listening to a secret recording of a former White House consultant demanding money in return for keeping silent about Watergate.

Rough Rider cowboy Theodore Roosevelt once admitted, "The men I knew best were the men in the clubs of social pretension and the men of cultivated taste and easy life."[73] Elihu Root's (McKinley and TR War, law partner of FDR War) membership in the New York Union League was sponsored by J.P. Morgan's relative Charles Kirkwood. Root and President Arthur spent much time together there. In 1882 Root wrote to Frank Hatton (then First Assistant Postmaster General, later Postmaster General) recommending a postmaster appointment. Root closed on a light note: "If, after reading the foregoing, you are not satisfied that Mosher should be appointed, I beg you to seek further information from Col. George Bliss, who will tell you a Squibnocket fish story that will settle the question at once."[74] Squibnocket was an elite fishing club at Martha's Vineyard, comprised of ten Union League members.

Ca. 1911 Presidential hopeful Woodrow Wilson wrote to *Harper's Weekly* editor George Harvey: "Evert day I am confirmed in the judgment that my mind is a one-track road and can run only one train of thought at a time. A long time after that interview with you and Marse Henry at the Manhattan Club, it cane over me that when (at the close of the interview) you asked me that question about the *Weekly* I answered it simply as a matter of fact and of business, and said never a word of my sincere gratitude to you for all your generous support, or my hope that it might be continued. Forgive me, and forget my manners." Harvey answered, "Replying to your note from the University Club, I think it should go without saying that no purely personal issue could arise between you and me. Whatever anybody else may surmise, you surely must know that in trying to arouse and further your political aspirations during the past few years, I have been actuated solely by the belief that I was rendering a distinct public service.... Whatever little hurt I may have felt as a consequence of the unexpected peremptoriness of your attitude toward me is, of course, eliminated by your gracious words." Wilson replied: "Generous and cordial as was your letter written in reply to my note from the University Club, it has left me uneasy, because in its perfect frankness, it shows that I did hurt you by what I so tactlessly said at the Knickerbocker Club. I am very much ashamed of myself, for there is nothing I am more ashamed of than hurting a true friend, however unintentional the hurt may have been. I wanted very much to see you in Washington, but was absolutely captured by callers every minute I was in my rooms, and when I was not there was fulfilling public engagements. I saw you at the dinner but could not get at you, and, after the dinner, was surrounded and prevented from getting at you. I am in town to-day, to speak this evening, and came in early in the hope of catching you at your office."[75] This little exchange of correspondence is a rare documentation of club life.

Club life is important to non-politicians also. Conversing with a fellow diner at the Century Association, Nobel Prize winner Linus Pauling suddenly realized the molecular basis of sickle-cell anemia. President Cleveland enjoyed the Century Association, which was also Henry Stimson's (Taft and Truman War, law partner of McKinley War) favorite. Century Association luncheons were used for planning the 1961 Bay of Pigs invasion of Cuba. A dinner at the Alibi Club ("so exclusive that most Washingtonians had never heard of it") helped convince White House officials that the CIA could succeed with the Bay of Pigs invasion. While lunching at the Metropolitan Club officials from the CIA and a global corporation planned joint operations to attack the economy of Allende's Chile. The Soviet Union was well aware of the power of these clubs—in 1972 a Soviet representative clinched a big soybean deal over breakfast at the Links.

Such clubs are also important in other capitalist countries. During a golf game at the Hodogaya Club of Yokohama, Japan's World War II prime minister Fumimaro Konoye let Koichi Kido know that Emperor Hirohito wanted him to be secretary to the lord privy seal. Kido accepted the job, and the golf game resumed. Kido was later sentenced to life imprisonment for his war crimes.

If a cabinet officer belongs to a club, that gives all the club members access to all the cabinet officers. Members of different President's cabinets can keep in touch over the years via clubs. This contact is enhanced by the membership of various relatives, friends, and business associates of cabinet members. And of course such men are welcome guests at clubs where they don't hold memberships. Due to interlocking of memberships, a person who joins two or three prominent clubs has access to every business and political heavyweight.

At such clubs decisions are made which are ratified later in formal meetings of corporation boards or Presidential cabinets. Many of these clubs were notorious for their sexist, racist, and anti–Semitic rules. Oppression of women, non-whites, and Jews was official, if extra-legal, policy of American business and political leaders into the 1970s.

China

During the McKinley administration Secretary of State John Hay (Lincoln private secretary) proclaimed the "Open Door" policy for China, meaning the United States opposed exclusion of any business interest from China. In 1898 China granted the Canton–Hankow railroad concession to the American China Development Co., eventually controlled by J.P. Morgan, although Belgian capitalists also participated. After seven years no progress had been made, so the Chinese government exercised its right to terminate the concession. Morgan and the Belgians didn't like this and decided to get help from the U.S. government. King Leopold (chief Belgian stockholder) told Sen. Henry Cabot Lodge about the Belgian dissatisfaction with the Chinese government's attitude, and Lodge reported this to his friend and relative President Theodore Roosevelt, who in turn reported the Belgian view to his relative J.P. Morgan. This contact assured Morgan of U.S. government support in any effort to retain Morgan's ownership of the railroad concession. Lest the Chinese have any doubts on the matter, Morgan's lawyer in the controversy was Elihu Root (TR War, State). Moreover, Robert Bacon (TR State) was J.P. Morgan's business partner. Bacon's father and grandfather had built the family fortune via the China trade, and Secretary Bacon knew what strings to pull in China. The Chinese government found itself having to pay big money to the railroad company to avoid "possible diplomatic reclamation." Morgan then attempted to collect even more via arithmetical acrobatics, but this was foiled by China's powerful friend in Washington, John Foster (Benjamin Harrison State, relative of Wilson State and of Eisenhower State). Foster's adroit maneuvering carried the day, and Morgan sold out to the Chinese. This didn't mean the end of Morgan's interests in China. At one point Morgan was even the Chinese government's banker. By 1913 the political climate hand changed for Morgan. William Jennings Bryan (Wilson State) opposed use of U.S. military force to back the terms of a loan Morgan had made to the China government for Hu-kang Railway. Underscoring the change President Wilson supported Bryan's stand. Byran's eventual departure from the cabinet had grave portent for world peace, but signaled no change in White House hostility toward Morgan's China operations. Bryan's replacement was Robert Lansing, the son-in-law of Morgan's old nemesis John Foster. And Lansing himself was lawyer for the Chinese government.

The Harding cabinet was filled with old China hands who began getting their experience during the McKinley administration. Foremost among them was future President Herbert Hoover (Harding and Coolidge Commerce). Hoover did much mining work in China starting in 1898. He was chief engineer of the China government's Bureau of Mines (salary $20,000 a year), worked for the British Bewick Moreing enterprises, represented bondholders in the Ching Wang Tow harbor construction, and was director of Chinese Engineering & Mining Co. One of the suppliers to Chinese Engineering & Mining Co. was Curtis Wilbur (Hoover Interior, brother of Coolidge Navy). Hoover had an uneasy alliance with Belgian mining interests in China (and later switched to comfortable opposition). There was German involvement in Chinese Engineering & Mining, and the Russians followed the firm's activities with predatory interest. Hoover's firm became the biggest business corporation in China. Sometime after a British court case involving the company, Hoover allegedly got hold of the only full set of the proceeding's official minutes and destroyed them (although scholars have apparently unearthed those records). Because the time period of Hoover's China activities overlapped with the J.P. Morgan-Belgian railroad concession Hoover must have been aware of the controversy and perhaps was acquainted with participants even though he didn't participate. Hoover likely knew Edwin Denby, the brother of Charles Denby (Harding and Coolidge Navy). Charles was a senior executive of American China Development Co., and Edwin served as secretary to the U.S. legation at Peking from 1885 to 1897. Charles served in Chinese Imperial Marine Customs Service about the same time, and returned to the United States. Edwin stayed, however, and became a Tientsin businessman. Edwin was involved with Arnold, Karberg & Co. (international importers of Berlin, London, and New York, and therefore another possible Hoover contact with the German business community), with Tientsin Water Works, and helped organize Tientsin Land Co. Hoover operated from Tientsin while Edwin was there. Hoover was a leader of defense efforts against the Boxer siege at Tientsin. After the Boxer Rebellion, Edwin was secretary-general of the provisional government imposed upon Tientsin and North China by the European forces. He was later foreign adviser to the viceroy of Chihli province in North China. The law firm of Charles Evans Hughes's (Harding and Coolidge State) old partner Cravath represented the Chinese government.

At a cabinet meeting President Harding jokingly asked Andrew Mellon (Harding, Coolidge, and Hoover Treasury) if he had any interest in Chinese Eastern Railway. Mellon astounded Harding by replying, "Oh, yes. We had a million or a million and a half of the bonds."[76] In the 1970s the Bank of England was still handling the Chinese Imperial Government's Gold Loan of 1898.

Chapter 13

Theodore Roosevelt

President Theodore Roosevelt (McKinley VP) was from a prominent New York family. His father was cordial with President Lincoln and accompanied Lincoln's wife on shopping sprees. The father also knew Lincoln's private secretary John Hay (T. Roosevelt State). Young Roosevelt's tutor also taught J.P. Morgan, John D. Rockefeller (grandfather of Ford VP), and Harry Payne Whitney (relative of Cleveland Navy). The family was on excellent terms with Mrs. William Astor, the ruler of New York's high society, and TR moved comfortably among British high society. TR himself was a long time friend of FDR's mother.

His family's wealth may have encouraged TR's financial recklessness. TR believed that anyone without wealth was a failure in life. In 1871 his father inherited $2,500,000 ($50,000,000 in 2019 buying power). TR's annual income while a Harvard student was $8,000, far more than the university president was paid. TR was a big spender at Harvard, the only student with a dog-cart (a flashy horse drawn vehicle). At this time, most Harvard students spent $650 to $850 a year, rarely as much as $1,500. In his first year at Harvard Roosevelt spent over $1,700 ($40,800 in 2019 buying power), the next year over $2,000, and the next year over $4,000. His big Harvard expense was clothing. He soon inherited about $200,000 from his parents. In 1880 he spent about half of his $8,000 income on presents. Three years later his income was $13,920 ($348,000 in 2019 buying power) including his salary as a New York legislator. One check he wrote that autumn exceeded his entire year's income and still cleared at the bank. Thus TR may have been expending his inherited capital, or perhaps was dipping into some other money source such as his uncle. About this time the uncle loaned him $10,000 to cover a $20,000 check which TR had bounced. (The check bought him a limited partnership in the Putnam book publishing company, a decided advantage in furthering his literary career.) In 1884 Roosevelt spent about $45,000 ($1,170,000 in 2019 buying power) on his

Oyster Bay mansion and grounds. In 1887, after losing $52,000 ($1,400,000 in 2019 buying power), Roosevelt realized he had to start living within his income. In 1888 he felt he should make at least $4000 ($100,000 in 2019 buying power) to avoid financial inconvenience. His writing produced only $700 to $800 that year, however. About this time President Benjamin Harrison appointed Roosevelt as U.S. Civil Service Commissioner, which paid $3,500 a year. He moved to Washington where he mooched free rent and food from his relative Henry Cabot Lodge. (Roosevelt was well connected with Boston's elite.) This mooching off Lodge offended President John Quincy Adams's grandson, who wanted his relative Roosevelt to live with him. In 1893 Roosevelt ran $2,500 ($70,000 in 2019 buying power) to $3,000 in the red. The next year things were so tight that TR was uneasy about accepting postage due letters. He was perturbed but not anguished by such financial difficulties. His salary as Assistant Secretary of the Navy was $4,500 ($135,000 in 2019 buying power).

Roosevelt then got in trouble by reducing expenses through tax trickery. He told the New York City tax man that he lived in Oyster Bay, and told the Oyster Bay tax man that he lived in Washington, D.C. In the middle of his 1898 campaign for governor, people suddenly realized that Roosevelt had thus declared that he wasn't a resident of New York state. Thus he couldn't be governor. Elihu Root (TR State) and the law partner of William Evarts (A. Johnson AG) were hired to provide legal briefs alleging that Roosevelt met the New York residency requirement anyway. The two lawyers were unsure if TR really was a New York resident, but their arguments were accepted. Roosevelt declared his domicile was New York City and paid the city taxes of $1,000. In late 1898 Roosevelt gave eight lectures at Harvard for $200 apiece (total $48,000 in 2019 buying power). His governor's salary was $10,000 ($300,000 in 2019 buying power).

Steel

Andrew Carnegie's steel business got its start in the Civil War, lubricated by Carnegie's profits from Columbia Oil Co. Philander Knox (McKinley & TR AG, Taft State) helped organize Carnegie Steel Co. and was counsel for the firm. Reportedly his retainer was $50,000 a year. H.C. Frick, Carnegie, and J.P. Morgan all personally urged President McKinley to appoint Knox as Attorney General. Perhaps little persuading was needed, for Knox was one of the fat cats who helped save McKinley from personal financial disaster in 1893. Another McKinley cabinet member, Elihu Root (McKinley & TR War, TR State), was a Carnegie Steel Co. attorney. Benjamin Bristow (Grant Treasury) advised his friend Carnegie on claims of Carnegie

Steel Co. against Louisville & Nashville Railroad. Possibly this gave Carnegie an edge, as Bristow was Louisville & Nashville Railroad's lawyer. Bristow became a Carnegie Steel lawyer.

Andrew Mellon's (Harding, Coolidge, Hoover Treasury) business associate H.C. Frick was chairman of the board of managers. For twenty year's Frick's *Who's Who* biography incorrectly stated: "Came into pub. notice by his vigorous management during the famous strike at Homestead, 1892, when he was several times shot and stabbed by one of the strikers." The assailant wasn't a striker, but Frick apparently wanted the public to think the workers were to blame. Andrew Carnegie credited Oscar Straus (future TR Commerce & Labor) with soothing labor after the strike.

One Homestead Strike complication was that the Navy Department had an urgent armor plating order that the strike was hindering. Carnegie Co. admitted falsifying test data and supplying the Navy with inferior armor plate in the 1890s. The company was fined $288,000. President Cleveland said this was too severe, and the fine was reduced to $140,484.94. Knox (McKinley & TR AG, Taft State) was the lawyer defending the company in these armor plate frauds. About the time he was Attorney General, Knox asked Frick to make big investments for him in Pittsburgh banks. Andrew Mellon (Harding, Coolidge, Hoover Treasury) was king of the Pittsburgh banking community.

Carnegie decided to retire, and that decision inspired J.P. Morgan to create United States Steel Corp. Morgan was encouraged by the hospitality of Theodore Roosevelt in TR's Vice Presidential days. William Cromwell (law partner of Eisenhower State) also helped organize U.S. Steel, and William Curtis (law partner of Eisenhower State) was the corporation's first president. Directors over the years included Robert Bacon (TR State), David Houston (Wilson Treasury), Edward Stettinius (Truman State), various Rockefellers (family of Ford VP), and President Carter's associate David Packard (Nixon Deputy Defense). Truman Newberry (TR Navy) was president of a U.S. Steel subsidiary. Attorneys for U.S. Steel included Frank Kellogg (Coolidge State), and Charles MacVeagh (son of Garfield Treasury, nephew of Taft Treasury). Ex-President Taft had $200,000 of U.S. Steel mortgage bonds given to him free by Andrew Carnegie.

In 1919 striking U.S. Steel workers protested 69-hour work weeks, a 30 percent wage cut, and oppressive labor relations. The great men who ruled U.S. Steel responded by sending in troops and strikebreakers.

Panic of 1907

John D. Rockefeller started Tennessee Coal & Iron Co. In 1907 it owned 500 to 700 million tons of iron ore and two billion tons of coal. In the financial panic of 1907 E.H. Gary and H.C. Frick lied to President Theodore Roosevelt about the necessity of J.P. Morgan acquiring Tennessee Coal & Iron Co. to help stem the crisis. On the basis of these falsehoods President Roosevelt agreed to refrain from antitrust prosecution. TR clearly felt uneasy in agreeing to this criminal act, for he removed information about it from the Bureau of Corporations and hid it at the White House where Senate investigators were unable to get at it. Rather than admit he had been fooled, Roosevelt gave an outraged defense of U.S. Steel when the Taft administration decided to prosecute over the acquisition of Tennessee Coal & Iron. This prosecution had much to do with TR's decision to run against Taft in 1912. Indeed, President Taft felt U.S. Steel was bankrolling TR's 1912 Republican nomination fight. In this regard it is of some interest that Elihu Root (TR State and War) was attorney for J.S. Morgan and Co. (affiliate of J.P. Morgan and Co.). Bacon (TR State) was a J.P. Morgan & Co. partner in 1894. Morgan himself was fond of Bacon, and they had known each other for years. Bacon was particularly involved with Federal Steel Corp. on Morgan's behalf. George von L. Meyer (TR PG, Taft Navy) was a Morgan agent.

Northern Securities

Northern Securities Co. was an illegal holding company owning Great Northern and Northern Pacific railroad stock formerly held by the father of W. Averell Harriman (Truman Commerce), and others. In evaluating President Theodore Roosevelt's "vigorous" action against this illegal business operation, we should keep in mind that TR's Secretary of State Bacon was a key figure in setting up the operation, in which Daniel Lamont (Cleveland War) was also involved. TR's "smashing victory" altered the form of the monopolistic arrangement, but the new arrangement was just as effective for participants. Moreover, a U.S. Supreme Court decision let the company add another $100,000,000 to the capital stock. Elihu Root (TR State) was (for a fee of $75,000) lawyer for the J.P. Morgan and James J. Hill interests and against railroad man Harriman and financiers Kuhn, Loeb as Northern Securities affairs ended under Supreme Court order. President Wilson's law partner Bainbridge Colby was a lawyer in the matter, too. Several persons around TR were relatives of Kuhn, Loeb figures.

Santa Fe Railroad

Richard Olney (Cleveland AG & State) was an Atchison, Topeka, and Santa Fe Railroad lawyer and may have received a salary from ATSF while Attorney General, just as he did from CB&Q railroad. Julius Morton (Cleveland Agriculture and father of TR Navy) was an ATSF lobbyist and scouted mineral land in the Southwest for the railway. ATSF president Joseph Reinhart was a close personal friend of President Cleveland and of John Carlisle (Cleveland Treasury). In 1891 Stephen Elkins (B. Harrison War) sold his Carillos Coal & Iron Co. to ATSF for $1,000,000 ($27,700,000 in 2019 buying power). Paul Morton (TR Navy, son of Cleveland Agriculture) was an ATSF vice president about that time. In 1901 the Interstate Commerce Commission questioned Paul Morton about illegal rebates. He didn't deny committing those crimes. President Theodore Roosevelt ordered the Justice Department to limit its investigation. In 1904 illegal ATSF rebates to Colorado Fuel & Iron Co. were discovered, a direct violation of a court injunction. Morton had been vice president of Colorado Fuel & Iron. Judson Harmon (Cleveland AG) was made a special investigator of ATSF rebates. In 1905 Harmon traced over $1,000,000 of rebates to Morton. President Roosevelt had roundly condemned such practices. Confronted with this evidence of Secretary Morton's illegal conduct, Roosevelt did nothing. Secretary Morton later resigned. H.H. Rogers of Standard Oil was an ATSF director, as were H.C. Frick (associate of Harding Treasury), Ogden Mills (Hoover Treasury and relative of 1892 GOP VP nominee), and assorted J.P. Morgan men. The father of W. Averell Harriman (Truman Commerce) was influential in ATSF.

Meat

Meat packers profited from wars. In addition, during the Spanish-American War of the 1890s, Armour & Co. generated much business for the tin-plate manufacturers, an important relationship between two seemingly diverse industries. Railroads were also linked to meat production. In 1855 over half the cattle slaughtered in Boston, New York, Baltimore, and Philadelphia had come in by rail from the Midwest. Some railroad presidents had big cattle ranches and made sure that shipping prices for cattle were kept low. Eastern rates for meat were kept high to encourage Eastern markets to use Western cattle. Meat companies, in turn, made money from shipping rate rebates. At the turn of the century the biggest Chicago packers based their prosperity on railway rebates. At that time, too, contrary to popular belief, big packers supported federal meat inspection and grading. The federal government passed such laws in the 1890s at packer request. The new laws ca. 1906 resulted as much from continued packer pressure as from Upton Sinclair's "fictional" exposé *The Jungle.* During World War I big meat companies made incredible profits, although this was disguised by creative financing. Public health was a secondary concern to meat companies. The laws were intended to satisfy European health restrictions on export of American meat to that continent. Foreign profits were the motive.

One of the great centers of meat packing was Chicago's Union Stockyards. Ca. 1890 Richard Olney (Cleveland AG, State) was involved in financial manipulations by British capitalists affecting the stockyards. Olney helped reorganize Union Stock Yards from 1890 to 1893. The law partner of John Payne (Wilson Interior) was president of Union Stock Yards Co. Payne's law firm was general counsel of Union Stock Yards & Transit Co.

After the Civil War Jeremiah Black (Buchanan AG, State) was a lawyer for Louisiana in litigation known to jurisprudence as the Slaughterhouse Cases. The carpetbagger government had given a monopoly to a slaughterhouse. Opponents lost in the Louisiana Supreme Court and appealed to the U.S. Supreme Court under the Fourteenth Amendment, among other bases. The U.S. Supreme Court ruled that states have supreme control over civil rights, and thus the Fourteenth Amendment didn't provide standing for federal jurisdiction. This crucial ruling extinguished the civil rights of many American citizens for years. Note how the decision was based not on a consideration of human liberty, but on corporation rights.

Kuhn, Loeb Bank

Theodore Roosevelt won the Nobel Peace Prize for his reluctant diplomacy that ended the Russo-Japanese War. The Kuhn, Loeb bank helped finance the successful Japanese war against Russia. Kuhn, Loeb's Jacob Schiff sent over $250,000,000 to Japan from ca. 1901 to ca. 1910. Schiff's aid to Japan was a direct reaction to Russian anti-Semitism—an example of how bigotry can harm bigots. Schiff, who was a relative of Oscar Straus (TR Commerce & Labor) and of Paul Morton (TR Navy) was one of President Theodore Roosevelt's top advisers. This relationship gave TR leverage in the peace treaty negotiations.

For many years Kuhn, Loeb was chiefly a railroad securities operation, no doubt one reason that Schiff became close to railroad magnate E.H. Harriman (father of Truman Commerce). Kuhn, Loeb helped J.P. Morgan start U.S. Steel, and Kuhn, Loeb helped arrange the merger of Chase National Bank with Manhattan Bank. Schiff was a key figure in Wilson's 1912 nomination fight. At the Versailles Peace Conference Schiff's son invited Lewis Strauss (Hoover Pvt. secretary, Eisenhower Commerce) to join the firm. While at the peace conference Strauss was living in Paris with another

Versailles participant, Oscar Straus (TR Commerce & Labor). The former cabinet member Straus urged the future cabinet member Strauss to accept. Strauss did so, declining a $10,000 salary job with the League of Nations ($135,000 in 2019 buying power).

Panama Canal

While they were members of the Andrew Johnson cabinet, William Seward and William Evarts went to New York to organize a transoceanic canal company. The route was to cross the isthmus of Panama. Seward and Evarts waxed enthusiastic to stockholders, but the project failed.

Nicaragua was a long time competitor against Panama (Colombia) for a canal. President Grant was offered the presidency of Nicaraguan Interoceanic Canal Co. The Grant & Ward bank supported Maritime Canal Co. of Nicaragua, but the bank's collapse wrecked the canal company. President Arthur's (Garfield VP) administration tried to reopen a Nicaraguan canal project, with no luck. President Franklin Roosevelt's father helped found a Nicaraguan canal company. FDR's father raised $6,000,000, but the company flopped in 1893. By then interest was turning more toward the isthmus of Panama in Colombia. Indeed one factor in the Spanish-American War was the strategic location of Cuba and Puerto Rico in relation to Panama.

The French DeLessups canal company was looking for U.S. support in the 1870s and formed American Committee of the Panama Canal Co., comprised of bankers from J.&W. Seligman, Drexel Morgan & Co., and Winslow Lanier & Co. Congressional investigation showed these banks got $400,000 to $1,200,000 each to act as fronts for DeLessups. President Grant was invited to be chairman of the committee, but declined since he was promoting a rival Nicaraguan canal. Instead Richard Thompson (Hayes Navy) became chairman. Thompson had been involved with the Panama isthmus for years as lawyer for Chiriqui Improvement Co.—a brutal scheme for shipping free blacks out of the United States and making them laborers in Colombia. That company was still operating after a fashion in the 1870s. President Hayes told Thompson to set up Navy coaling stations in the isthmus area. This work was covered by a federal contract with Chiriqui Improvement Co. Thereby Thompson was well known to the French DeLessups Co. Since Thompson was outspending his cabinet salary in an alarming way he welcomed the additional $25,000 a year from the French ($625,000 in 2019 buying power). He intended to hold both jobs, ignoring the awkwardness of the Navy Secretary being in the pay of a French operation whose interests were not always the same as those of the

United States. President Hayes refused to ignore the situation and forced Thompson from the cabinet. Regarding the canal job another ex-cabinet member, George McCrary (Hayes War), wrote to Thompson, "For my part I am glad for the country's sake as well as your own that you have taken the place" in the DeLessups company.[77] Thompson spent nine years working hard for the French company which reeked of bribery and corruption. The company busted in 1889.

DeLessups's Panama Canal Co. had controlling interest in Panama RR Co. Thompson (Hayes Navy) was president of the railway for a while, and so was the father-in-law of President Cleveland's relative William E. Dodge. Reportedly William Evarts (A. Johnson AG, Hayes State) was a Panama RR lawyer, but for sure Benjamin Bristow (Grant Treasury) and William Cromwell were lawyers for the railroad line. Cromwell was a law partner of John Foster Dulles (Eisenhower State). In 1896 Cromwell represented a new Panama Canal Co. which replaced the defunct one of DeLessup. Another Dulles partner William J. Curtis (U.S. Steel president) was also involved with the new canal company. In 1899 the new company's assets were transferred to a New Jersey corporation which Cromwell organized, the Panama Canal Co. of America. Founders included August Belmont, Levi Morton (B. Harrison VP), and clerks from the Dulles law firm. Such use of clerks suggested that someone else had a hidden participation. Kuhn, Loeb helped finance the company, but major funding was from J.P. Morgan. This was a joint United States–French operation. The French suddenly pulled out, and the company collapsed. Cromwell, who was Fiscal Agent of the Republic of Panama, then worked to have the U.S. government buy the company's assets.

Andrew Mellon's (Harding, Coolidge, Hoover Treasury) McClintic-Marshall Construction Co. built the Panama Canal locks. Future President Franklin Roosevelt was on the national committee of the Panama Pacific International Exposition, a World's Fair celebrating the canal. Exposition officials sent future President Hoover (Harding & Coolidge Commerce) overseas to help arrange European participation. World War I broke out while Hoover was doing advance work in London for the Exposition. As a mere patriotic favor Hoover began helping U.S. citizens stranded by the initial panic, and the job snowballed into a massive supply operation to feed millions of Europeans and later to rebuild the postwar continent. This work made Hoover a Presidential candidate. Hoover's involvement with FDR's Exposition made it all possible.

In 1917 President Wilson needed a confidential agent to go to Central America and seek support for the United States if it entered the European war. Wilson's dispatch of U.S. troops to fight in the Mexican civil war had done nothing to win Latin American friends. Robert Lansing

(Wilson State) picked his nephew John Foster Dulles (Eisenhower State) to be the secret agent. The Dulles law firm represented the government of Panama, so the journey was easily disguised as a normal business trip. Using his law firm's Central American contacts, Dulles succeeded in his mission.

Chapter 14

William Howard Taft

President Taft (TR War) and his brothers inherited probably $100,000 from their grandfather. By 1879 young Taft didn't have to worry about working. He made good money as a collector of federal internal revenue in Cincinnati under President Arthur (Garfield VP). With a $7,000 salary as U.S. Solicitor General ($194,000 in 2019 buying power) Taft paid $1,200 a year in house rent. In May 1890 Taft asked his brother Charles for $250. Charles was always willing to bail out William, sending money throughout Taft's White House years. Although both President Taft and his father (Grant War) were corporation lawyers, President Taft's main legal career was as a judge. Taft's salary as a federal district judge was $6,000 ($166,200 in 2019 buying power), $1,000 less than the salary he found inadequate as Solicitor General. Judge Taft first paid $300 a month in house rent in Cincinnati, later moving to a $60 a month place. He barely paid his household bills. His Philippines governor salary was $20,000 ($600,000 in 2019 buying power). He paid $2,750 for servants, $1,200 for horse feed, and perhaps $3,600 for electricity. About this time his life insurance premiums were $2,000 a year. "I do not expect to have a cent left out of the salary," Governor Taft said.[78] Secretary of War Taft had an $8,000 salary ($226,000 in 2019 buying power) supplemented by a shower of gold from his brother Charles, who had many contacts in the business world. Charles urged Taft to live in a fine house and entertain generously, promising $10,000 a year for the purpose. Taft saved $100,000 as President ($2,550,000 in 2019 buying power) and assured President-Elect Wilson that the Presidency was no financial drain, quite the opposite—a $75,000 salary and $25,000 travel account plus many perquisites. Wilson thanked Taft for the advice and said he had needed the information. Ca. 1912 Taft had about a $175,000 estate ($4,427,500 in 2019 buying power) plus $60,000 in life insurance ($1,500,000 in 2019 buying power). Yale paid ex-President Taft $5,000 in 1913 for four hours of lectures per week. In 1915 he was looking forward to $10,000 from investments and a $250,000 estate including life insurance ($6,250,000 in 2019 buying power). In 1919 his estate including life insurance was $300,000 ($4,050,000 in 2019 buying power). Thus we see an impact of wartime inflation. In 1919 he accepted $200,000 in United States Steel mortgage bonds willed to him by Andrew Carnegie ($2,700,000 in 2019 buying power). As President, Taft had refused Carnegie's offer of a $25,000 pension, saying it would look bad. Elihu Root (TR State), George Wickersham (Taft AG), and Taft's wife (who would receive the $10,000 annual income from the bonds if she survived him) all urged Taft to take the 1919 legacy, which he did. This almost doubled his estate. Taft was highly embarrassed when the bonds were publicized years later, and assigned the income to Yale University after the public learned of the bonds. Chief Justice Taft said the U.S. Steel securities didn't influence his judicial decisions. He bought a $75,000 Washington house when he became Chief Justice ($1,102,500 in 2019 buying power). His died with an estate of $475,000 ($7,505,000 in 2019 buying power).

Taft's brother was a member of Cadwalader, Wickersham & Taft. The law firm was organized in 1796, and in 1920 had clients dating from 1820 and earlier. One of the founding partners prepared a will for the widow of Alexander Hamilton (Washington Treasury). Wickersham was President Taft's Attorney General. Under questioning by Senate Appropriations Committee chairman William Windom (Garfield, Arthur, B. Harrison Treasury) John Lambert Cadwalader (Grant Asst State) kept quiet about a money claim he believed unjust, involving Jay Cooke and Henry Cooke. Hamilton Fish (Grant State) was an intimate associate of Cadwalader. Charles Evans Hughes (Harding & Coolidge State) declined an offer to take Cadwalader's place when that partner died. William Rogers (Ike AG, Nixon State) was with this firm.

Henry L. Stimson (Taft War, Hoover State, FDR and Truman War) joined Root's (McKinley & TR War, TR State) law firm after Stimson's father mentioned to his own Yale classmate George Dimmock that young Stimson was frustrated. Dimmock was intimate with William Whitney (Cleveland Navy) whose streetcar operation was Root's personal client. Whitney felt Root needed an assistant, and Root hired Stimson in 1891. When Root went to Washington, D.C., Stimson had to struggle to hold clients safe from enticements of competing Wall Street law firms. Stimson's firm was known for its low key practice. In stark contrast to other firms, Stimson's colleagues only worked 9:30 to 5:30 (except when in court) and refused to discuss business after hours. The big part of its business in the 1920s was corporation finance and public utility companies. Stimson's annual law income was over $22,000 a year ca. 1905 ($620,000 in 2019 buying power) and about $50,000 from 1919 to 1928 ($725,000 n 2019 buying power). Sargent Shriver (1972 Democratic VP nominee and brother-in-law of JFK) was with Stimson's firm in the 1940s. J. Edward Day (JFK PG) was also in the firm. Stimson's grandfather was senior partner of Henry C. Stimson & Son. In his prime the grandfather was regarded as a top Wall Street operator working for Vanderbilt, Jay Gould, and Leonard Jerome (grandfather of British prime minister Winston Churchill). The uncle of W. Averell Harriman (Truman Commerce, Carter SALT II spokesman) worked in the office of Churchill's grandfather.

Stimson's law partner Root (McKinley & TR War) had an annual income of about $5,000 in 1869 ($90,000 in 2019 buying power). In 1887 he received a $17,000 ($454,000 in 2019 buying power) *installment* on *one fee*. In the few months between cabinet posts in the Theodore Roosevelt administration Root's fees totaled somewhere between $100,000 and $200,000 ($2,800,000 to $5,600,000 in 2019 buying power). His law income was twenty-five times the government salary he received as Secretary of State.[79]

Root's clients included James H. Ingersoll, "Boss" Tweed, Samuel Tilden, William Whitney (Cleveland Navy), President Theodore Roosevelt, Frederick W. Vanderbilt, August Belmont, and Thomas Fortune Ryan.

Philippines

These islands were a Pacific outpost of American capitalism for years. The law firm of Paul Cravath (law partner of Harding & Coolidge State) represented various Philippine companies. U.S. governors of the Philippines invariably had close contact with U.S. corporations that were interested in Asia, either as a market or as a source of raw materials. Such governors included Luke Wright (TR War), future President Taft (TR War), Henry L. Stimson (Taft War, Hoover State, FDR & Truman War), Dwight Davis (Coolidge War), Homer Cummings (FDR AG), Frank Murphy (FDR AG), and Theodore Roosevelt, Jr.

Governor Stimson was initially unsympathetic about Filipino hostility toward big corporations gaining large amounts of real estate. Stimson was also initially unsympathetic about the way tenant farmers and hired hands were exploited. Stimson viewed these conditions as encouraging to business investment and economic development. Stimson gradually converted to the Philippine view, however. He even openly worked against a big U.S. rubber corporation's proposed real estate acquisitions. Stimson saw an opportunistic angle to U.S. corporation agitation for Philippine independence. Once independence was granted, U.S. tariffs would apply to Philippine products. This was especially important to the sugar industry. Stimson's successor as Philippines governor was Dwight Davis (Coolidge

War), who married the widow of a Cuba Cane Sugar Corp. director. Cuban sugar would benefit from tariffs against Philippine sugar.

Bull Moose Campaign

The Guggenheim family was prominent in mining. William Whitney (Cleveland Navy) was director of Guggenheim Exploration Co. and owned $1,600,000 in shares. Richard Ballinger (Taft Interior) was a Guggenheim attorney and was accused of favoritism in opening up federal coal land in Alaska. Supposedly Taft's firing of Ballinger's accuser Gifford Pinchot was a key factor in former President Theodore Roosevelt's decision to challenge Taft for the Presidency in 1912, an election known to history as the Bull Moose campaign. In this regard we should remember that William Loeb, Jr. (TR private secretary) was with Guggenheim's American Smelting & Refining Co.; the son of Root (TR State) was a director; the son of Oscar Straus (TR Commerce & Labor) was president, and the grandson of Straus was vice president. Paul Morton (TR Navy) and Straus were Guggenheim relatives. In World War I Straus was on future President Hoover's New York committee for Belgian relief work, and Hoover declined a handsome offer to work for the Guggenheims. Hoover made Pinchot an aide in World War I, which may have influenced Taft's sour disposition toward Hoover. Another of Ballinger's accusers, Louis Glavis, re-entered the Interior Department under TR's protégé Harold Ickes (FDR & Truman Interior).

Prosecution of U.S. Steel for its acquisition of Tennessee Coal & Iron has already been mentioned as another factor in TR's decision to wage the Bull Moose campaign. The prosecution meant Taft was implying that TR approved of criminal activity. TR was not the sort of person to ignore such implication, and this helped turn the election of 1912 into a grudge match.

There was yet another factor in the Bull Moose fight. International Harvester Co. was established under the control of J.P. Morgan interests, with help from Paul Cravath (law partner of Harding State). Company president was Cyrus McCormick (son of the inventor). International Harvester finance committee chairman George Perkins was also vice president and finance committee chairman of New York Life Insurance Co. New York governor Theodore Roosevelt had helped Perkins wreck a bill that would have limited how much insurance a New York–chartered corporation could carry. Perkins then worked industriously to make Roosevelt the 1900 GOP Vice Presidential nominee, which brought TR to the White House. An anti-trust investigation began in 1907. Herbert Knox Smith (TR Commissioner of Corporations) said the government should do nothing to offend J.P. Morgan, and Straus (TR Commerce & Labor) endorsed that attitude in a letter to President Theodore Roosevelt. Straus treated International Harvester in a kindly manner during the investigation. He and George Perkins were associates in New York Life Insurance Co. The federal government's "investigation" was based on information provided by International Harvester. This information was then sent to President Roosevelt who could, by agreement with International Harvester, publicize the information. If International Harvester furnished any evidence of criminal conduct, the U.S. Bureau of Corporations specified that it retained the option to refer the evidence to Charles Bonaparte (TR AG). The Bureau of Corporations slowed the "investigation." Straus urged that no speed-up be attempted, citing International Harvester's cooperation. In 1912 President Taft lost patience, having yet to receive the Bureau of Corporations report. The Taft administration filed an anti-trust suit anyway. International Harvester director Perkins helped bankroll TR's 1912 nomination fight. Perkins, Herbert Smith (TR Commissioner of Corporations), Straus (TR Commerce and Labor), and Bonaparte (TR AG) all left the Republican Party when Taft won the GOP presidential nomination. They all joined TR's "Bull Moose" Progressive Party.

International Harvester executives also threw support to Woodrow Wilson, as if the important thing were to defeat Taft. This way, too, the corporation might have a friend in the White House regardless of whether Roosevelt or Wilson won. Cyrus H. McCormick raised $53,000 for Wilson's 1912 Democratic nomination battle ($1,341,000 in 2019 buying power). They were old friends, classmates at Princeton. As a Princeton trustee, McCormick was a key in Wilson's appointment as president of the university. McCormick was one of several corporation executives who personally funded Wilson's lifestyle over the years, as will be seen shortly. International Harvester director Thomas Jones was a close friend of Wilson. Jones donated $10,000 to Wilson's 1912 nomination campaign ($253,000 in 2019 buying power). Wilson appointed Jones to the Federal Reserve Board while the anti-trust suit was still active, but the nomination wasn't confirmed by the Senate.

Woodrow Wilson

President Woodrow Wilson came from a well-known Southern family. His relatives served in the cabinets of Presidents Jefferson, Zachary Taylor, Buchanan, and Lincoln. Although the family's national prominence declined with the South's defeat, it remained prominent regionally. President Wilson's uncle, for instance, was president of Central National Bank of Columbia, SC, and directed several industrial and financial businesses.

The uncle knew David Houston (Wilson Treasury). Houston, in turn, knew Albert Burleson (Wilson PG) and Thomas Gregory (Wilson AG); the three wives were also well acquainted, all born in Austin, TX. Burleson and Gregory attended University of Texas together. While teaching there a few years later Houston lived just a few blocks from Col. Edward House (Wilson adviser), and the two men got to know each other.

Wilson needed more than the $2,000 Bryn Mawr was paying him to teach in 1888 ($53,400 in 2019 buying power). Wesleyan University in Middletown, CT, offered him $2,500 for less work ($66,750 in 2019 buying power). Wilson told Bryn Mawr he was willing to stay for $3,000 ($80,000 in 2019 buying power) and the freedom to leave whenever he wanted. Bryn Mawr refused; Wilson broke his contract, and left for Wesleyan. After going to Princeton, Wilson got a $6,000 ($175,000 in 2019 buying power) offer to become president of the University of Illinois. He used that offer to wring an assistant and a $3,500 ($105,000 in 2019 buying power) salary while a Princeton professor; this was more money than any other faculty member got. Only the school president received more. Wilson used an offer of the University of Virginia presidency to extract another $2,500 a year beginning in 1898 ($75,000 in 2019 buying power). This additional salary was furnished by certain Princeton trustees from their own pockets. These were the men who personally bankrolled Wilson for years: Cyrus H. McCormick (International Harvester), Cleveland H. Dodge (National City Bank), Moses Taylor Pyne, and Percy R. Pyne (whose family started National City Bank). Wilson badly needed money in the 1890s. There were family expenses, and he built a $9,000 house ($270,000 in 2019 buying power) that burdened him. He got a mortgage and sold at least some of his real estate and also about $1,000 of his stock in Charlotte, Columbia, & Augusta Railroad. Already a fulltime Princeton faculty member, he took on a heavy schedule of off-campus lectures to raise money, and worked himself into illness. He suffered a moderate stroke in 1896 and a severe one in 1906. His medical disabilities were unapparent to observers after each convalescence, and the nature of the ailment was kept secret. Wilson's salary as Princeton's president was $10,000 ($282,000 in 2019 buying power).

While President of the United States Wilson got Dodge to fund Walter Hines Page (Wilson ambassador to Britain) with $25,000 a year ($500,000 in 2019 buying power). A trust fund set up in 1923 helped relieve ex–President Wilson from financial trouble, providing a $10,000 annual income ($150,000 in 2019 buying power). Four men set it up: Cyrus McCormick, Cleveland H. Dodge, Thomas Jones, and Jesse Jones (FDR Commerce). All but Jesse Jones were in the Princeton class of 1879 with Wilson. Wilson's final estate was estimated at $600,000 ($8,820,000 in 2019 buying power).

National City Bank

National City bank was the gray eminence of the Wilson administration. Incorporated in 1812, National City may have lent money to the U.S. government to fight the War of 1812, loans personally guaranteed by New York governor Daniel Tompkins (Monroe VP), who was ruined when the U.S. government refused to repay the loans. Moses Taylor and City Bank (as the firm was known in the 1800s) were almost one entity. Moses Taylor became a power in mid-nineteenth century national politics. His bank had many ties to the South when the Civil War broke out—cotton traders, sugar traders, and Cuban traders did their banking with Moses Taylor. Metal and coal men became attracted to National City.

Frank Vanderlip (McKinley Asst. Treasury) was a National City man. The Rockefeller and Dodge families ran National City for a long time. Henry Ford was associated with National City. Such an alliance of automobile and oil executives was natural. As World War I approached, National City was the largest U.S. bank. National City had seventy-five foreign branches at a time when no other U.S. bank had more than four.

Cleveland H. Dodge of this bank was the key money man for Wilson's 1912 nomination. Dodge was very influential in Wilson policies. In 1907 Dodge was indicted for his mining activities involving federal lands in New Mexico Territory. Albert Fall (Harding Interior) was one of Dodge's attorneys. Dodge was then indicted in Arizona on a similar charge. Upon Wilson's election to the presidency, James McReynolds (Wilson AG) ordered the two cases dropped.[80] Wilson's son-in-law William McAdoo (Wilson Treasury) was strongly influenced by the Rockefellers and Thomas Fortune Ryan via National City. Anaconda Copper Mining president John D. Ryan (Wilson Asst. War) was involved with National City.

With President Wilson's assent, William Jennings Bryan (Wilson State) informed J.P. Morgan & Co. that money was a contraband of war—in Bryan's words, "the worst of all contrabands because it commands everything else."[81] Therefore loans to warring nations would be unneutral. Then, while Bryan was speechmaking out of town, National City vice president Samuel McRoberts got to diplomat Robert Lansing (who ran the State Department in Bryan's absence) and convinced him (who in turn convinced Wilson) that extension of credit wasn't a loan and therefore not violate American neutrality in the European war. Bryan decided to go along, perhaps because he realized a ban would hurt the Allies more than the German powers, and would therefore be unneutral after a fashion. Or perhaps Bryan wanted to help the American economy. Or perhaps he realized there was nothing he could do about it anyway, since Wilson had approved the policy.

Mexico

President Wilson's aggression against Mexico is regarded as uncharacteristic of the man, yet in examining that war we find the presence of Wilson's gray eminence—National City Bank. National City's Cleveland H. Dodge owned large properties in Mexico. Standard Oil got into a big struggle against Britain's Mexican Eagle oil operation. England had support from Mexico's ruler Porfirio Diaz. In 1911 Diaz was overthrown at the instigation of Standard Oil and Ed Doheny (Teapot Dome). Shortly thereafter Andrew Mellon's (Harding, Coolidge, & Hoover Treasury) Gulf Oil began Mexican operations.

Standard Oil put in Francisco Madero as Mexico's ruler, who was soon overthrown by the British in the personification of Victoriano Huerta (who killed Madero). Cleveland Dodge decided the United States should then back Venustiano Carranza against Huerta. Ed Doheny declared, "Every American corporation doing business in Mexico extended sympathy or aid, or both—and we extended both—to Carranza." Doheny's help to Carranza included $100,000 cash and credits of $685,000. Cleveland Dodge was vice president of Phelps, Dodge & Co. which was accused of illegally sending ammunition to Carranza forces in 1913. James McReynolds (Wilson AG) ordered a U.S. Attorney not to indict Winchester Arms (directed by Cleveland Dodge) for its alleged involvement. The U.S. Attorney then indicted two Phelps, Dodge officers, and McReynolds then fired the U.S. Attorney. President Wilson appointed the judge who dismissed the case. While the case was going on Wilson lifted the arms embargo. This tended to moot the case since the alleged conduct which led to charges against Phelps, Dodge was no longer a crime. Remington Arms and Winchester Arms then legally supplied Carranza. Huerta put up such a good fight that Cleveland Dodge decided the United States should consider an accommodation with Huerta. Huerta, however, was rather uninterested in the U.S. terms. He had powerful support from the British, who helped finance his government, complicating English efforts to get the United States into the European war. President Wilson then sent the U.S. military into Mexico. With arrival of the Yankee military, Carranza defeated Huerta.

Pancho Villa was an opponent of Carranza, so Carranza welcomed a U.S. military expedition into Mexico to hunt down Villa, in response to his attacks on American border towns. Carranza quickly became alarmed at the size of the U.S. Army expedition and its ever-expanding penetration into Mexico. His alarm increased when the United States rejected his protests about the growing presence of the U.S. Army in Mexico. Carranza decided to eject the Yankees by force. So now the U.S. Army was fighting both Mexican rebels and the Mexican government. On the eve of United

States entry into World War I eighty percent of the entire regular U.S. Army was battling Mexicans and getting nowhere fast.

Revelation of a German offer to become Mexico's ally was thus stunning, since this would bring the European war on to U.S. territory and cripple U.S. aid to the Allies. The German offer backfired. For the first time many Americans now viewed the Kaiser as a direct threat to the United States. This generated much popular support for U.S. entry into the European war.

Germany's offer of alliance with Mexico didn't arise from a vacuum. The law firm of Charles Evans Hughes's (Harding State) old partner Paul Cravath was involved with Mexican railroads on behalf of U.S. and German banks. German banks were active supporters of Carranza, and Germans were able to buy up mining properties owned by Americans who had fled Mexico during the turmoil.

Albert Fall (Harding Interior) was very interested in Mexican land titles, and his Mexican mining activities dated to 1883. He and Ed Doheny were mining associates there ca. 1890. Fall started a Mexican law practice in 1891 and dealt with railroads, coal, and lumber. Ca. 1900 Fall hooked up with William C. Greene, who was a multimillionaire with big Mexican mining operations. Fall ran a staff of lawyers and Mexican laborers for Greene, acting as Greene's general counsel and as manager of Greene's operations. Fall eventually acquired some of Greene's gold and silver mines. Fall was President Harding's adviser on Mexican matters and advocated a U.S. invasion of the country. Harding (a former president of Tri-Metallic Mining, Refining & Smelting Co. which operated in Mexico) was sympathetic to Fall's viewpoint, having called for United States annexation of Mexico during the Wilson presidency. The Wilson era turmoil in Mexico hurt American businessmen large and small—from the Guggenheim's American Smelting & Refining Co., which found itself outstripped by Germany's Companía Metallurgies de Terreón, to Romney's (Nixon HUD) father whose prosperous building business in Mexico was ruined.

World War I

The Navy League of the United States promoted a strong navy for national security. Such a navy would also protect American commerce and investments around the world, and require large amounts of steel to construct it. The Navy League was organized in 1902 by members of the New York Yacht Club. The club was no mere social organization. It was involved with various business operations over the years. The Navy League president was Benjamin Tracy (B. Harrison Navy). Vice president was William

McAdoo (Wilson Treasury). General counsel was Herbert Satterlee (TR Asst. Navy, Pvt. secretary to Hayes State, aide to B. Harrison VP, son-in-law of J.P. Morgan). Morgan himself was an honorary vice president, as was John Weeks (Harding and Coolidge War, father of Eisenhower Commerce). Satterlee's brother represented Germany's Krupp-Bruson iron works. John Long (McKinley Navy) had the U.S. Navy buy about 37,000 tons of Harveyized steel armor from Krupp ca. 1900. Navy League founders included George Westinghouse, Charles M. Schwab (Bethlehem Steel), and William Whitney's (Cleveland Navy) son. Midvale Steel Co. was also listed as a founder. Officers as World War I approached included president Robert M. Thompson (International Nickel Co. chairman), vice president H.C. Frick (associate of Harding Treasury), director Robert Bacon (TR State & U.S. Steel director). Members were involved with U.S. Steel, Bethlehem Steel, Carnegie Steel, Harvey Steel, Lackawanna Steel, Cambria Steel, Midvale Steel, Eastern Steel, Pennsylvania Steel, Pacific Hardware & Steel, Federal Steel, Illinois Steel, Minnesota Steel, Union Steel, American Steel & Wire, Phelps Dodge & Co., Amalgamated Copper (Anaconda), American Brass Co., New Jersey Zinc, International Nickel, et al.

William Jennings Bryan's enemies called him a failure as Wilson's Secretary of State. For example, he objected to Britain's practice of flying U.S. flags on their vessels. After all, Bryan's critics said, this protected them from German submarine attack. From this viewpoint, Bryan would have been "paranoid" to imagine that the British could hope that a German sub might thereby attack a real American ship and bring America into the war. Persons disputing his world view argued that he was heartless to say Americans who sailed on British ships would have to accept some responsibility for taking such a risk. So what if the Germans published a warning that the *Lusitania* would be sunk. After all it was a "peaceful" passenger liner with orders to ram or fire on any German sub in sight. Bryan's opponents argued that if Bryan felt that the *Lusitania*'s cargo of thousands of cases of ammunition (manufactured in part by Winchester Arms Co., Remington Arms Co., and Union Metallic Cartridge Co.) was relevant, that just showed how little respect he had for innocent lives lost. The British government showed its respect by vowing revenge. President Wilson found it necessary to turn toward such advisers as Cleveland H. Dodge (National City Bank) who was chairman of "Survivors of the Victims of the Lusitania Fund." Dodge was also director of Winchester Arms Co., Remington Arms Co., and Union Metallic Cartridge Co.

Bethlehem Steel's president Charles Schwab wanted to build submarines in sections and ship the unassembled vessels to Britain in 1914. He got State Department official Robert Lansing to agree one day while Bryan was absent from Washington. On his return Bryan immediately informed

President Wilson, saying that while the Schwab–Lansing agreement was technically consistent with neutrality, there was little practical difference from sending completed subs—which would violate neutrality. Wilson ordered Lansing to prevent subs or submarine sections from leaving the country. Lansing disobeyed and allowed Schwab to send the unassembled vessels to Canada. The Austrian ambassador protested. Bryan inquired, was deceived by Schwab, and told the Austrian ambassador that his assertions were wrong.

Ca. World War I Bethlehem's chief counsel was Paul Cravath (law partner of Harding State). Schwab was chairman of the federal government's Emergency Fleet Corp. Hog Island Shipyard near Philadelphia, one of the world's largest, was constructed at this time with the vital assistance of future President Kennedy's father and of Franklin D. Roosevelt (Wilson Asst. Navy). Kennedy's father managed Bethlehem's Fore River Yard in World War I. FDR often had battleships constructed merely on his own authority. "We made millions of dollars worth of supplies for the government with no more authority than a telephone call from him," JFK's father recalled.

Aviation presented a new opportunity for wartime money making. In April 1915 Harold Talbott (Eisenhower Air Force) and his father, along with Charles Kettering (General Motors), and Colonel E.A. Deeds (vice president of National Cash Register) organized Dayton Metal Products Co., which primarily made fuses for the British government. Two days after Congress declared war in April 1917 Dayton Wright Aircraft was incorporated by the founders of Dayton Metal Products with the addition of Orville Wright. Deeds became chairman of the government's airplane production board. He had no aviation experience but was director of National City Bank, a pedigree with influence in the Wilson Administration. Newton Baker (Wilson War) publicly praised Deeds when questions arose about his conduct. William Redfield's (Wilson Commerce) memoirs vigorously defended Deeds, so vigorously that criticism of Deeds seems to be treated as criticism of Redfield.

Dayton Wright's DH-4 airplane was called "the flaming coffin," and the situation under Deeds became so murky that question arose about whether any Dayton Wright aircraft were actually delivered for combat. President Wilson turned to his 1916 election opponent Charles Evans Hughes to investigate and report. Hughes found no crime but did find conduct which he believed merited court martialing of Colonel Deeds. Thomas Gregory (Wilson AG) told the President that the Justice Department agreed with Hughes's findings. Newton Baker (Wilson War) declined to accept the Hughes recommendation. Deeds returned to Ohio where he remained a prominent industrialist. At his nomination hearing Harold Talbott was asked about the Hughes inquiry and replied, "I wish I could say definitely, but I don't remember." Charles Wilson (Eisenhower Defense) said the Hughes report cleared Talbott, although Charles Wilson acknowledged that he had never read it, or the report issued by a congressional investigation of the matter. Under President Harding the Justice Department claimed that Dayton Wright had received $3,000,000 that was not owed, and filed suit to recover, but Dayton Wright won the case. John Weeks (Harding War) received a letter from Charles Hayden (associate of JFK's father) asking for help in a lawsuit in which the government was trying to recover $5,270,000 from Dayton Wright. Weeks got the Justice Department to drop the case, and the investigator's report disappeared from Justice Department files.

World War I Finance

As the war opened foreigners owned many shares of U.S. corporations. All European stock exchanges closed lest enemy countries raise capital by selling stocks in one another's exchanges. At the war's outbreak the New York Stock Exchange temporarily closed to avoid a disastrous break in prices as all European sell orders headed toward New York. In January 1915, after the New York exchange had reopened, Britain's Exchequer forbade loans "for undertakings outside the Empire." This transferred the international financial headquarters from London to New York. Immense capital that once flowed through London now went through New York. As the war progressed, Europeans needed more money for military operations and thus began selling stock in American corporations to raise cash. In a 1915 speech J.P. Morgan partner Thomas Lamont said the longer the European war continued, the more U.S. securities could be bought back by American investors. Moreover, the United States could become a creditor nation rather than a debtor. Lamont said if the war went on long enough the American dollar would replace the British pound as the world's premier currency. William McAdoo (Wilson Treasury) and Robert Lansing (Wilson State, uncle of Eisenhower State) maintained secret contact with Morgan partners about the status of war loans to Britain (many of which were made by U.S. corporations), and the Morgan partners kept the British abreast of Wilson administration thinking. The official British representative to J.P. Morgan & Co. for war purchases was a friend of Col. Edward House (Wilson adviser). One month before President Wilson asked Congress for a declaration of war, U.S. ambassador to Britain Walter Hines Page warned Wilson that the Allies' financial needs now exceeded J.P. Morgan resources. This meant a U.S. domestic financial collapse was possible unless the U.S. government guaranteed or outright granted loans to the

Allies. The only way this could be done was if war was declared. The first Liberty Loan paid over $400,000,000 to J.P. Morgan & Co. to satisfy debts of the British government. John Foster Dulles (Eisenhower State, nephew of Wilson State) was lawyer for J.P. Morgan & Co. regarding World War reparations.

Chapter 15

Herbert Hoover

Future President Herbert Hoover (Harding and Coolidge Commerce) began his adult career in mining. The mining world abounded with rascals, daredevils, and wheeler-dealers. A survey was taken of deans of mining and technical schools to learn which mining engineers were highly regarded. The fifth engineer on that list owned a 2,500 ton 300-foot steam-driven yacht carrying fifty crew members, thirty guests, a miniature golf course, motion picture theatre, and two brass guns to ward off pirates. That was the fifth man on the list. The top man on the list was Herbert Hoover.

Hoover began professional mine engineering with California's Janin firm. The Janin family was prominent in Western mining for years. A Janin was Robert Walker's (Polk Treasury) California agent for mining ca. 1855. In addition to engineering Hoover also assisted Louis Janin's attorney Curtis Lindley. Janin paid Hoover $200 a month for engineering work in 1896 ($6,000 a month in 2019 buying power). Around 1898 Hoover joined the British mining firm of Bewick, Moreing & Co. Hoover's Bewick, Moreing salary in 1898 was $12,500 ($375,000 in 2019 buying power). The next year Hoover got $7,500 salary plus ten percent of the company's profits.

He prospered in that company, becoming a partner. His partner Moreing was a Conservative Member of Parliament. Hoover's work in the British mining industry earned him lifelong suspicion from American Anglophobes. The British ambassador to the United States was one of Hoover's confidential advisers on whether to seek the Presidency in 1920.

Hoover traveled the globe as a field man for Bewick, Moreing. He worked in South Africa, where American mining engineers had helped start the Boer War. J.P. Morgan's partner Edward Stettinius (father of FDR State) was associated with William Boyce Thompson in South African gold, platinum, and diamond interests. Thompson was a partner in the Hayden, Stone banking operation of future President Kennedy's father. Chinese Engineering & Mining Co. sent coolie labor to South Africa. Hoover directed Chinese Engineering & Mining and owned $250,000 of the company's stock. Émile Francqui (Hoover World War I associate) and the king of the Belgians were important figures in that company. Hoover recommended against the use of Chinese coolie labor in South Africa. Belgium's Katanga Company had a contract with the Phelps Dodge subsidiary Nichols Copper Company. Phelps Dodge, of course, had influence with President Wilson.

Ca. 1939 former President Hoover, Lewis Strauss (Hoover Pvt. secretary, Eisenhower Commerce), and others supported a project to create a new African country of white settlers, mainly European refugees from Hitler, in the uplands of central–east Africa (Northern Rhodesia, Tanganyika, Kenya, Congo). Hoover offered to go to Africa and organize communications, transportation, and resource development of the new country. Strauss figured on a white population of 10,000,000 to 20,000,000. Britain, however, refused to cooperate. Since Britain had sovereignty over much of the territory in question, that circumstance scuttled the proposal. Feelings of native populations were apparently considered irrelevant all along.

In 1900 Hoover's Bewick, Moreing partnership brought him a $12,500 salary ($375,000 in 2019 buying power), plus twenty percent of the firm's profits, plus $250,000 in stock ($7,500,000 in 2019 buying power). A few years later he lost $127,000 when Bewick, Moreing was victimized by an embezzler. Reportedly Hoover eventually drew a $100,000 salary, with $5,000 for engineering services and $95,000 for Bewick, Moreing stock market work. Hoover, however, later vehemently declared that he dealt mainly in engineering in those days. In 1908 Hoover sold his interest in Bewick, Moreing for $169,000 ($4,783,000 in 2019 buying power) and left the partnership. He agreed not to compete with Bewick, Moreing when he set up his own firm. Bewick, Moreing then sued, alleging that Hoover violated that agreement through his oil operations in Peru, Mexico, California, Russia, and Galicia. In 1911 Hoover paid Bewick, Moreing $125,000 to settle out of court ($3,537,000 in 2019 buying power). Hoover was already a millionaire, perhaps having $3,000,000 ($69,000,000 in 2019 buying power). By 1918 he had $4,000,000 ($62,000,000 in 2019 buying power). Hoover was considered the world's greatest mining engineer. He wrote the standard textbook and was offered the deanship of the Columbia School of Mines.

Hoover and his brother were active in Russian mining. This was one place Hoover thought he could work without fear of violating his agreement to avoid competing against his old Bewick, Moreing firm. Hoover was in Russia by 1908. He was chairman of Inter-Russian Syndicate and director of Kyshtim Corp., Irtysh Corp. and Russo–Asiatic Corp. The latter was linked to St. Petersburg banks. Hoover was also involved with oilfields. At one point in his Russian days Hoover worked for the Tsar's family. All of

Hoover's Russian properties went into decline during the turmoil of revolution and civil war. Irked, Hoover sold most of his Russian holdings.

Hoover was chairman of Burma Corporation, and owned eighteen percent of the company. The firm's Bawdwin mine on the road to Mandalay was the basis of Hoover's personal fortune. German industrialists were involved with the running and financing of Hoover's company. Such links with the German business community surely helped Hoover in his World War I relief work. From 1915 to 1918 he sold most of his interest in Burma Corp. for $2,500,000.

As a Bewick, Moreing mining partner Hoover worked with Morgan-associated British banks. In 1909 Hoover became involved with William Boyce Thompson in London. Thompson was a Hayden, Stone & Co. investment bank partner (firm of JFK's father) and sponsored Hoover's entry into Hayden, Stone operations. Thompson also conducted stock market operations with Morgan partner Thomas W. Lamont. This relationship helped Hoover's rise in London and New York financial circles. David Houston (Wilson Treasury and Agriculture) directed International Acceptance Bank, an institution involved with American financing of war-related reconstruction in Europe. International Acceptance was actually a Warburg (Kuhn, Loeb bank) operation. Paul Warburg offered to let Hoover join International Acceptance in 1920, when it was being organized, but Hoover declined. Presumably he maintained ties with the Warburgs over the years via Kuhn, Loeb partner Lewis Strauss (Hoover Pvt. secretary, Eisenhower Commerce). International Acceptance merged with Manhattan Bank. On behalf of the Rockefellers, Strauss and other Kuhn, Loeb bank partners assisted the merger of Manhattan Bank with Chase National Bank. Hoover cultivated the Rockefellers as a funding source for his Belgian relief work in World War I, work we shall hear more about.

Twenty-five-year-old Joseph Kennedy (JFK's father) was president of Columbia Trust Co. (Boston). As noted earlier, in World War I Joseph Kennedy ran a shipbuilding operation for Bethlehem Steel. Afterward he contacted shipping company executive Galen Stone about building ships. Kennedy apparently impressed Stone, who made Kennedy manager of Hayden, Stone & Co.'s Boston office at a salary of $10,000. Thus Kennedy was willing to take a salary cut (he made $20,000 at Bethlehem) for a chance to make his fortune. Hayden, Stone was active with Latin American operations and was involved with National City Bank and Chase National Bank. Hayden, Stone partner William Boyce Thompson loaned $1,000,000 to the GOP in 1916 ($22,000,000 in 2019 buying power), which was repaid. He donated $300,000 to the 1918 GOP campaign ($4,650,000 in 2019 buying power). Thompson directed the New York Federal Reserve Bank and was a large stockholder in Chase National Bank and Sinclair Oil. The 1916

GOP campaign manager Will Hays (Harding PG) was Sinclair Oil's chief counsel. Thompson worked for the Guggenheim mining family and dealt with future President Hoover (Harding Commerce) in London during Hoover's mining days. Hoover received a fabulous offer from the Guggenheims to join their operation, but he declined. Thompson cut Hoover in on several Hayden, Stone operations. Through Thompson, Hoover made contact with top U.S. financiers and politicians. These contacts, in particular Thompson's close relations with copper interests who were influential with President Wilson, had much to do with Hoover's joining Wilson's War Council as Food Administrator. In 1920 Thompson helped solidify Hoover's links with the GOP, with special attention to Republicans in New York, California, and Colorado. Through Thompson, Hoover developed close relations with Rockefeller ally Charles Hayden, Chase National Bank president Albert Wiggins, Teapot Dome figures Harry Sinclair and E.L. Doheny, and J.P. Morgan partner Thomas Lamont. Hayden headed the 1928 Hoover election finances. In 1932 JFK's father was prominent in the FDR campaign. Aid to Roosevelt normally soured anyone's relations with Hoover, but Hoover remained close to the Kennedy family. Ex-President Hoover and JFK's father worked together on government commissions. Robert Kennedy (JFK and LBJ AG) began his public career as a personal assistant to former President Hoover.

Hoover knew Charles Hayden and Daniel Jackling from the mining industry in addition to banking. Hayden and Jackling were involved in Consolidated Mercur Gold Mines where George Dern (FDR War) was general manager.

In 1914 future President Hoover was in his familiar London surroundings promoting FDR's Panama–Pacific Exposition (a world's fair). While there he was approached by representatives of the Belgian government. The German invasion had devastated Belgium's food supply. Hoover was asked to direct food relief operations there. The Belgians were familiar with his ability to coordinate logistics problems of the mining industry on a worldwide scale. As noted earlier, King Leopold and Émile Francqui were important figures in Hoover's Chinese Engineering & Mining Co. Francqui was to become a top official in Hoover's Belgian relief organization. Also Hoover worked closely in London with J.P. Morgan banks, and the Belgian government banked with Morgan. Hoover had been hoping to enter some sort of public service career. Upon accepting the Belgian assignment he suddenly left the room full of dignitaries and returned a few minutes later. He explained that he had just ordered 10,000,000 bushels of wheat from Chicago. That little scene illustrated two things in addition to Hoover's efficiency. Rather few business executives have the foggiest notion of how to order 10,000,000 bushels of wheat. Thus Hoover already knew something about the grain trade. Also rather few grain brokers would accept an ordinary businessman's pledge of payment for 10,000,000 bushels of wheat. We may therefore conclude that Hoover was already well known in international business circles.

Hoover and his organization, Commission for Relief in Belgium, became world famous. Edouard Bunge (Hoover associate) was King Leopold's right hand man in business, and was particularly active in exploiting the Congo's rubber and ivory. Bunge's grain company was considered one of the globe's Big Five. The Phelps Dodge company was involved with Belgian mining operations in Africa. Cleveland Dodge was one of the most influential persons around President Wilson, and Hoover consulted with Dodge about obtaining the 1920 Democratic presidential nomination.

Hoover's mastery of European food logistics led to his appointment as U.S. Food Administrator after America entered the war, a post that was crucial in the war leadership. He was responsible for providing adequate food supplies to all Americans, all European allies, and to civilians in specified enemy occupied territory. At least fifteen top grain dealers worked in the Food Administration under Hoover, giving him daily involvement with an industry famed for its profits and secrecy.

During World War I Hoover's mentor William Boyce Thompson (associate of JFK's father) headed the Red Cross in Russia. This was a cover for his secret War Department work trying to prevent a separate Russian–German peace. Thompson spent $1,000,000 bribing the All–Russian Democratic Congress to keep Alexander Kerensky in power. Thompson was in contact with J.P. Morgan & Co. throughout this period. On the side, Thompson got a big personal mining concession from the Kerensky government. After the separate peace occurred Thompson worked to keep Germany from getting Russian war supplies. Under Thompson the Red Cross aided anti–German elements and refused to aid pro–German elements in Russia. Another War Department secret agent in wartime Russia was ostensibly a Commerce Department trade commissioner, traveling the country as a Red Cross worker. As World War I ended President Wilson sent American troops on an ill-fated invasion to overthrow the Russian Communist government.

This is the context in which Secretary of Commerce Hoover, who had already smashed Communist governments in Europe, offered to send hundreds of Americans to direct famine relief efforts throughout Russia in the 1920s. The Communists kept close tabs on top American capitalists and could hardly have been unaware of the relationship between Hoover and William Boyce Thompson. The Soviets were certainly aware of the anti–Communist work of both men, some of it indistinguishable from ostensibly humanitarian relief efforts. Ca. 1921, however, the Russian famine was so bad that the government was teetering with anarchy looming. Communists and capitalists share a hatred of anarchists, so with much trepidation the Communists gave Hoover permission to send in the American food experts. Hoover's men ended the famine in a couple of years. This was much to the Communists' surprise—fifty years later they were still suspicious that the Americans had been spies. The Russians nonetheless officially thanked Hoover for helping to save the Soviet state. The irony wasn't lost on Hoover, but he angrily replied to a critic, "Twenty million people are starving. Whatever their politics, they shall be fed!"[82] Hoover's relief program did much to brighten U.S.–Russian relations previously ruined by President Wilson's hamhandedness.

Election of 1920

Hoover became a war hero, an accolade usually reserved for generals rather than humanitarians. He won the Michigan Democratic Presidential primary without even campaigning, and seemed in a good position to get the Presidential nomination. The eventual Vice Presidential nominee, Franklin Roosevelt, boosted Hoover, telling one and all, "Herbert Hoover is certainly a wonder, and I wish we could make him President of the United States. There could not be a better one." Hoover halted such Democrat dreams by announcing he was a Republican.

President Wilson's son-in-law William McAdoo (Wilson Treasury) was another possibility for the 1920 Democratic nomination. In 1899 McAdoo bought Knoxville Street Railway Co. with $25,000 of his own money ($750,000 in 2019 buying power) and a $50,000 loan from Union Trust Company of Philadelphia. The line went to a public park, and McAdoo led a campaign to keep admission to the park free, and thereby maintain the volume of streetcar fares. The company went into receivership in 1892, and McAdoo then reorganized it. McAdoo, an ambitious man who fancied himself a tough operator, also started Citizens Street Railway Co. which competed with Knoxville Street Railway Co. while the latter was in receivership. The competition got bitter. When things reached the stage of riot, gunplay, and death, "tough operator" McAdoo decided to leave town. He mortgaged his first wife's $10,000 house, and they went to New York City, hoping to thereby pay off streetcar debts.

Ca. 1903 McAdoo hooked up with Walter Oakman (Guaranty Trust president) and E.H. Gary (U.S. Steel) in forming Hudson & Manhattan RR Co. Walter Brown (Hoover PG) was board chairman and Lewis Strauss (Hoover Pvt. secretary, Eisenhower Commerce) was a director. McAdoo organized New York & New Jersey RR to tunnel under the Hudson River at New York City. McAdoo's salary as New York & New Jersey RR president was $15,000. After losing a financial clash with Thomas Fortune Ryan, McAdoo decided to devote his restless energy to politics instead. He had already met Woodrow Wilson through discussion of New Jersey regulations affecting Hudson & Manhattan RR.

McAdoo declined receivership of Brooklyn Rapid Transit Co. about the time he left Wilson's cabinet, and hooked up with oil operations of Teapot Dome figure Ed Doheny. Lindley Garrison (Wilson War) took the Brooklyn Rapid Transit receivership that McAdoo had turned down. William Redfield (Wilson Commerce) was New York City Commissioner of Public Works in 1901 and regulated streetcar companies while McAdoo was active in New York City.

Warren G. Harding

The winner of the 1920 election was Ohio newspaperman Warren Harding. Some years earlier he had signed notes for Marion Manufacturing Co. which made tractors. It failed in the Panic of 1907. Harding lost a lot but wasn't ruined. Harding's father-in-law hated him and had enough money to make Harding's life miserable. The father-in-law even started a newspaper to compete with Harding's, helped a man buy up Harding's notes and force immediate payment in hopes of bringing Harding down, and recruited a candidate to run against Harding in a state senate race. Nonetheless ca. 1915 Harding was making $20,000 a year ($500,000 in 2019 buying power) from his newspaper plus U.S. Senate pay and benefits. In 1919 one month's liquor bill was $529 ($7,100 in 2019 buying power). Harding got liquor at a ten percent discount from a dealer friend in Columbus, Ohio. That year Harding was looking for a good oil investment, saying, "I need somehow to make some easy money."[83]

President Harding's poker buddies included William Wrigley (of chewing gum notoriety), Harry Sinclair (Teapot Dome), and Charles Schwab (Bethlehem Steel, associate of JFK's father). Harding was occasionally given side bets of 50 to 1. This could have been a form of bribery. Indeed, espionage agents are told to bribe people by letting them win card games. Harding once played poker with Louise Brooks (future wife of Gen. Douglas MacArthur), winner name stakes. Harding probably wanted sexual favors from her, but she won. She demanded a set of White House dishes, and Harding sent her a barrel of Benjamin Harrison china.

Nan Britton said that President Harding told her at their last meeting that he was $50,000 in debt ($740,000 in 2019 buying power). Britton's general veracity has been strongly supported by scholarly research.

Harding died in debt to Washington, D.C., stockbroker Sam Ungerleider. Harding had two secret accounts with Ungerleider, including one in the name of Secret Service agent Walter Ferguson. Another Secret Service agent, who was Harding's go-between with Nan Britton, was slated to become Ungerleider's manager. Trying to recoup earlier losses, before leaving on his fatal Alaska trip Harding bought $500,000 of stock on margin ($7,400,000 in 2019 buying power)—including Pure Oil (company of Coolidge VP's brother), Bethlehem Steel (on advice of Charles Schwab), and Mexican Seaboard (on advice of Commerce Secretary Hoover's associate John Hays Hammond). Harding's death put Ungerleider in a tight spot. He had allowed Harding to buy the stock with insufficient margin, in violation of stock exchange rules. Plus prices had dropped $200,000 (so much for the inside tips that Harding received). Plus Ungerleider had no authorization to sell the stock and cut his losses. Ungerleider's lawyer Newton Baker (Wilson War) explained the situation to Attorney General Harry Daugherty, and Ungerleider got permission to sell. Losses on the "Ferguson" account ($30,000) were covered. Ungerleider took the other $170,000 as a tax deductible loss.

Harding left an estate of $930,000 ($13,764,000 in 2019 buying power).

Newspapers

President Harding was an old hand at the newspaper trade. In 1875 he was an errand boy, printer's devil, and typesetter at his father's *Caledonia Argus*. At college Harding worked in the *Union Register* print shop. He and a college chum started their own paper in 1882, *Iberia Spectator*, using the *Register*'s press. The *Spectator* folded when the two students graduated. Harding's father then got half interest in the *Marion* [OH] *Star*. Under the father's uninterested management the *Star* appeared so sporadically that locals jokingly called it the *Comet*. Harding himself and two friends finally bought the *Star* for $100 each. A rival editor loaned Harding $100 for the purchase to spite the town's third paper. Harding won one partner's interest in a poker game. (The two men remained on good terms.) In 1885 the remaining partner sold out, giving Harding complete ownership. Harding often went into debt because he liked to buy new equipment for the *Star*. He acquired AP wire service in the 1880s. The paper printed much government advertising. Such advertising can be a lucrative reward of the political spoils system. The *Star* opposed a scheme of the Canton Shale Brick Co. to get a municipal paving contract. Harding's hated father-in-law was a large Canton Shale Brick Co. stockholder. Harding introduced a bill in the Ohio senate to protect publishers who print statements they believe to be true. The *Star* was doing well when Harding became a U.S. Senator, and afterwards Harding did nothing with his position to aid his paper. Harding's wife got involved with the *Star* in 1894. Often she is wrongly credited as the true manager of the enterprise because she made her presence so obvious. For example, when the staff greeted her after a banquet celebrating a Harding political victory, "She eyed them coldly .... 'You needn't look for a raise this time,' she rasped at them. 'That little show cost us 1,300'" ($36,800 in 2019 buying power).[84] In 1909 Harding reorganized the *Star* as Harding Publishing Co. Harding kept three-fourths of the $80,000 capital stock ($2,264,000 in 2019 buying power). He offered the rest to his employees, on installment if they liked, with installment payments to come from dividends. In other words, employees could get stock without paying anything from wages or savings. In 1910 Harding supported unionization of his employees. Ca. 1918 Harding offered to sell the *Star* for $140,000 ($2,170,000 in 2019 buying power). While President he eventually sold it for $550,000 ($8,250,000 in 2019 buying power).

Harding's involvement with the news media was part of an American tradition. Presidents and cabinet members controlled or managed newspapers such as *Aurora, U.S. Telegraph, Washington Globe, New York Herald Tribune, Omaha World-Herald, Indianapolis Journal, Manchester Union & Leader, Chicago Daily News, Chicago Sun-Times, Houston Post, Los Angeles Times, New York Post, Washington Post*, and *New York Times*. The same goes for magazines such as *North American Review, Harper's Weekly, New Republic, Better Homes & Gardens, Wallace's Farmer, Newsweek*, and *Time*. Later we shall see the same kind of involvement in radio and television. These business interests of Presidents and cabinet members are one reason why U.S. news media concern themselves so much with information on rivalries among politicians. For the same reason news media of that era contained little thoughtful criticism of the basis of American government and basis of our economic system.

Insurance

President Harding was Marion, OH, agent for three companies. His insurance career ended when he wrote a big policy for Hotel Marion at less than the company's rate and then took several hundred dollars as a commission. This of course was a mere interlude in Harding's business activity.

The insurance industry, however, first brought to public attention one of the ablest members of the Harding cabinet—Charles Evans Hughes (1916 GOP Presidential nominee, Harding & Coolidge State, U.S. Sup. Court CJ). The industry would have been content for Hughes to remain in obscurity because he rose to fame by exposing fraud and corruption in some of the nation's most respected insurance companies.

Insurance policyholders often don't realize they are participating in a banking venture, but insurance companies make profits and generate capital in much the way that banks do. A small business operator may turn to a bank to finance an expansion of the business. A big businessman would likely turn to an insurance company. Insurance companies can make long-term loans to corporations and governments more easily than banks can. This is because insurance companies don't have to worry about liquidity as much; policyholders generally can't withdraw much capital from an insurance company, and there is no such thing as a run.

Insurance corporations can be structured as a joint stock company or as a mutual society. In a joint stock company the stockholders elect the corporation directors. In a mutual society the directors are supposedly elected by the policyholders. The mutual society may sound more democratic, but in practice mutual society executives stay in power more easily since it's nearly impossible to organize the policyholders or buy out their policies.

The father of William Whitney's (Cleveland Navy) streetcar associate James Hazen Hyde founded Equitable Life Assurance Society. Young Hyde served as vice president for five years after graduating from college. Hyde was considered incompetent, but he couldn't be fired since he owned a majority of Equitable's stock. Therefore Equitable officers decided on a palace revolution and attempted to mutualize the company. This action would transfer control from the stockholders (i.e., Hyde) to the policyholders (who in reality would have no say about whether the officers fired Hyde). The revolutionaries brought in the best hired guns money could buy: William Hornblower (Cleveland U.S. Sup Ct nominee, law associate of Harding State), Bainbridge Colby (Wilson State) and Hughes (Harding State). Three insurgent directors then threw down the gauntlet. They were Cornelius Bliss (McKinley Interior), H. C. Frick (associate of Harding Treasury), and the father of Averell Harriman (Truman Commerce, Carter SALT II treaty spokesperson). Hyde responded by selling his shares to Thomas Fortune Ryan (who was an associate of TR's brother-in-law). Hyde's lawyer Elihu Root (McKinley War, TR State) was generally considered the brains behind Ryan. Root picked up a $25,000 fee for handling the stock sale.

The revolutionaries were angered by this turn of events, as they had eliminated Hyde but had lost control of the company to Ryan. The rebels were particularly outraged that Hyde sold the stock to Ryan for $2,500,000—H.C. Frick had offered Hyde twice that amount. As a further wrinkle, Ryan's lawyer was Hughes's old partner Cravath. Possibly the suspicion of commercial treason inspired the decision to bring in the New York legislature to do some bloodletting. Hughes was appointed to head a New York legislature investigation of insurance companies in the state.

The investigation went further than some participants may have wished, leaving carcasses strewn about the entire insurance industry. Item: Equitable's director Cornelius Bliss (McKinley Interior) was revealed as a bagman for about $50,000 of New York Life money that went to President Theodore Roosevelt's 1904 campaign ($1,400,000 in 2019 buying power). Equitable and Mutual of New York gave similar sums. Item: Equitable director Harriman was exposed as using the New York legislature to foil a fellow revolutionary who had been Hughes's law client in the palace revolt. Item: Equitable director Jacob Schiff (Kuhn, Loeb bank) was exposed selling about $50,000,000 of securities to Equitable. State law required his dismissal for this conduct. Item: Nationwide political operations of Equitable, Mutual, and New York Life were revealed, including a "House of Mirth" for entertaining New York legislators.

Much public indignation resulted. Princeton president Woodrow Wilson (who later became law partner of the revolutionaries' hired gun Colby) forced two Equitable directors to resign from the Princeton board of trustees. The life insurance industry needed a quick salvage job. Former President Cleveland became chairman of the Association of Presidents of Life Insurance Companies. His prestige as the life insurance industry's public relations spokesman did much to restore public confidence. Thomas Fortune Ryan turned over control of his Equitable shares to three men: Former President Cleveland (who had ties with J.P. Morgan and Whitney (Cleveland Navy) and therefore to Ryan and Root), George Westinghouse (whose right hand man was the uncle of Ryan's lawyer Cravath), and New York Supreme Court judge Morgan J. O'Brien. Cleveland's salary as an Equitable trustee was $12,000 a year. The public was assured that if these three great men now controlled Equitable (albeit on Ryan's behalf), then the company must be operating safely and reliably. When Cleveland died, his trusteeship was offered to Root, who declined. Pail Morton (TR Navy, son of Cleveland Agriculture) served as Equitable's chairman while also a cabinet member. Morton had ties with both sides in the mutualization controversy. He had been vice president of Harriman's Santa Fe railroad, which was directed by Frick.

Paul Morton hired former President Cleveland to referee a premium rebate dispute among Equitable, New York Life, and Mutual Life. Cleveland picked up $12,000 for that task. In 1909 Ryan sold his stock to Kuhn, Loeb's arch rival J.P. Morgan. The DuPonts bought Morgan's shares, and later the Rockefellers acquired control. With aid from the law partner of John Foster Dulles (Eisenhower State) Equitable was eventually made a mutual company, as the revolutionaries had intended.

The Hughes insurance investigation also looked into Mutual Life Insurance Company. Hughes found the company president and his close relatives obtained about $15,000,000 from the company. Root (TR State) was a director while this went on. The Hughes inquiry, as one of Root's biographers delicately phrased it, did "not specifically implicate Root."[85] Henry Stimson's (Taft and Truman War) law firm represented Mutual of New York at this time. In one case Mutual's high bid on a $10,000,000 bond issue of New York, New Haven & Hartford railroad was rejected in favor of a lower bid by J.P. Morgan & Co. Stimson got the railroad to switch to Mutual. He did this by threatening to hold the railroad officers personally liable for damages.

Ca. 1894 future President Wilson got a $7,000 mortgage ($203,000 in 2019 buying power) from Mutual of New York to help finance construction of his house. Few home buyers would think of trying to finance the purchase through an insurance company. Fewer still could actually do it. Wilson's success suggests that he was already close to powerful capitalists twenty years before his election as President. Some years later David Houston (Wilson Treasury) was president of Mutual. Ca. 1930 his salary was $100,000 ($1,600,000 in 2019 buying power). As the Great Depression worsened into 1932, Houston's salary was raised to $125,000 ($2,400,000 in 2019 buying power). John Payne's (Wilson Interior) law firm represented Mutual.

The third great life insurance company to be examined by the Hughes investigation was New York Life. New York Life had already been investigated by the state government in the 1890s. New York Life asked Benjamin Bristow (Grant Treasury) to be a company lawyer in that inquiry. Bristow, who had resigned as a New York Mutual trustee because he was suspicious about that company, declined the retainer.

The 1905 Hughes probe showed that New York Life had not made stock divestments which it had claimed to have made. Hughes proved that New York Life vice president George Perkins (J.P. Morgan partner) had sold $4,000,000 of Morgan bonds to New York Life. Perkins also had New York Life reimburse him about $50,000 for money he had donated to the 1904 Theodore Roosevelt campaign.

Conduct of companies investigated by Hughes was probably no more unsavory than what other insurance companies of the era were doing, but the public was startled by Hughes's revelations. Today's more cynical public might be less shocked, and consider companies' behavior a century ago as acceptable conduct today.

Former President Coolidge made public comments disparaging insurance men who urged policyholders to change policies. Generally this "policy churning" practice boosts agent sales commissions and reduces insurance company profits. Although Coolidge didn't name anyone in particular, a St. Louis insurance consultant slapped a $100,000 libel suit on Coolidge and New York Life. Coolidge settled out of court for $2,500 and a letter of apology to the consultant, who then also dropped the suit against New York Life. When attending meetings of the New York Life board of directors Coolidge stayed in suite 801–2-3 of the Vanderbilt hotel for $10 a night.

Chapter 16

"Mellon's Millions"

Although largely unknown to the general public before he entered government service, for years Andrew Mellon (Harding, Coolidge, and Hoover Treasury) had been one of America's wealthiest and most powerful men. He made a fortune from aluminum, banking, coal, and oil.

Aluminum

The mining and manufacturing of this metal is essentially the story of Aluminum Co. of America (Alcoa). Aluminum was once a precious metal used for jewelry. In 1856 it sold for about $500 a pound ($15,000 in 2019 buying power). In 1884 aluminum was used to cap the Washington Monument in the nation's capital. The price then was the same as silver, $16 an ounce ($415 in 2019 buying power). Four years later, however, Charles Hall was producing it at $2 a *pound.* In 1889 sponsors approached Mellon, explaining the metal's industrial possibilities.

Mellon agreed to provide a $250,000 loan, but required financial control and a large share of ownership. Thus the Pittsburgh Reduction Co. was formed, managed by Arthur Vining Davis. Hall pushed aluminum's cost down to $1 a pound. Ca. 1887 Hall had quit the Cowles brothers Electric Smelting & Aluminum Co. Mellon now sued Cowles for infringing Hall's patent. Cowles claimed that Hall was pirating information from Cowles. The case was argued before federal judge (and later President) William Howard Taft. Declaring that Hall was reducing the price and that was good, Taft ruled in favor of Mellon's company. This gave Mellon a monopoly, and the price of aluminum (which had dropped to $0.5 a pound) was raised to $0.8 a pound). Moreover, Mellon's friend U.S. Sen. James Cameron (Grant War, son of Lincoln War) got a $0.15 a pound tariff applied to aluminum imports. Another court ruled in favor of Cowles on another patent, forcing

Mellon's company to pay $4,000,000 for damages and future rights up to 1909.

Ca. 1898 British Aluminum and Mellon's Pittsburgh Reduction organized Aluminum Supply Co. owned 50–50 by the two organizers. Mellon agreed to stay out of the British market, and British Aluminum agreed to buy 3,000,000 pounds of aluminum from Pittsburgh Reduction each year.

Pittsburgh Reduction was renamed Aluminum Co. of America (Alcoa) in 1907. In 1912 a federal judge invalidated a 1908 agreement between Northern Aluminum Ltd. of Canada (subsidiary of Alcoa) and Aluminum A-G dividing up the world market. The 1912 court ruling also voided the Mellon attempt to monopolize bauxite. In 1909 Alcoa had bought all American bauxite producing companies. Thus expiration of aluminum patents in 1906 and 1909 was irrelevant since Mellon could now withhold bauxite from competitors.

In World War I ninety-five percent of Alcoa's sales were for the military. In 1916 the company made a twenty-five percent profit on capital investments—largely from Russian, English, and French orders. The price of aluminum was $0.19 a pound in 1914, $0.26 in 1915, $0.37 in 1916. This rise kept ahead of inflation in those years as measured by the Wholesale Price Index. The price to the U.S. government in World War I was $0.32 a pound. The price of aluminum in 1920 was $0.22 a pound, an even more drastic drop when inflation is taken into account.

Seeking a tax break after World War I, Alcoa told the Treasury Department that the corporation was grossly overexpanded. Alcoa told the Federal Trade Commission however, that facilities were so limited that customers' orders couldn't be filled, meaning Alcoa posed no monopoly threat. Pressed to explain the discrepancy, Alcoa replied that one government bureau should pay no attention to what Mellon's corporation told another bureau.

In 1924 the FTC reported that Alcoa was violating the 1912 court ruling and should be prosecuted.[86] Harlan Stone (Coolidge AG) announced the FTC report was justified and that he was investigating activities of Mellon's company. About two and a half months later Stone was appointed to the U.S. Supreme Court. Suspicious souls suggested that Mellon's cabinet colleague had been kicked upstairs. Stone's cabinet successor John Sargent told a Senate committee that he never heard of Alcoa before coming to Washington, nor had he known of Mellon's connection with the corporation until recently. Sargent dropped the investigation.

In theory Mellon had complied with the law by resigning as an Aloca director when he became Harding's Treasury Secretary. In fact he continued to consult with company executives, and indeed Arthur Vining Davis said that Mellon was expected to rejoin the board when he left the cabinet.

One of President Truman's World War I buddies ran Alcoa's Arkansas mines. He introduced Truman to Alcoa's lobbyist George Romney (Nixon HUD). Romney had attracted the attention of two Alcoa officials while he was dealing with tariff matters on the staff of Sen. David Walsh. Romney was also lobbyist for Aluminum Wares Association. Alcoa initially paid him $3,000 a year in the Great Depression. In 1939 Alcoa was paying Romney $10,000 ($180,000 in 2019 buying power).

In that era Alcoa's relations with workers were troubled. In 1915 workers at the Massena, NY, operation revolted, taking possession of the entire plant. The state militia retook the plant and raided homes of strike leaders, killing one. The plant manager gave each militiaman a set of aluminum cookware. The general manager brought in strikebreakers from Pittsburgh and Canada. American labor refused to work in the plant's hot part, so cheap French-Canadian laborers were imported in violation of contract labor laws.[87] Workers at the New Kensington operation lost a 1916 strike for an eight-hour day and recognition of the American Federation of Labor union. The same year the company's bauxite miners went on strike. Alcoa agreed to a pay raise that boosted the men's pay to $2 a day. The company also agreed not to discriminate against union men. Alcoa, however, did not fulfill their agreement.

In 1917 Mellon's workers went on strike at Aluminum Ore Co. in East St. Louis after the company refused to meet with a worker committee. Mellon agents and others scoured the lower Mississippi River for black strikebreakers, a class of persons who could be ruthlessly exploited without redress. Although only 2,000 men were on strike, 10,000 blacks were imported. Those who were unhired were helpless in East St. Louis. Those hired protested company treatment, saying their pay was less than promised and that they were forced to sleep in railroad boxcars on company grounds. Lots of angry persons were rubbing against one another. An outbreak of violence against black workers on May 28 injured scores, but order was restored. Another eruption started on July 2 when 35,000 armed whites descended on the blacks. There were many shootings, beatings, and hangings. The death toll was twenty-five black, two white. Fire burned 310 black homes and threatened the downtown business section. Congressional testimony said an Aluminum Ore employee secretly obtained U.S. government rifles and ammunition to arm company guards.

In 1932 the East St. Louis Central Trades & Labor Union reported the maximum pay for skilled workers at the Mellon operation was fifty-eight cents an hour. There were no union employees.

Ca. 1924 Alcoa workers near Knoxville reportedly made twenty-five cents an hour. If they worked a fifty-six-hour week they got a two dollar bonus. Sunday work made the week's wages sixteen dollars. In 1932 a

Welfare Council worker at New Kensington complained that the company forced workers, many of whom were in tough financial circumstances, to donate a day's pay for relief efforts.

It's important to occasionally remind ourselves that the wealth of Presidents and cabinet members is not extracted from the earth alone. Nor does the price of goods always indicate their total cost.

Banking

Around the late 1860s the Mellon brothers established a joint stock savings bank in East Liberty, PA. The bank paid twelve percent dividends for five years and was then disbanded. Depositors and stockholders were fully paid.

In 1870 the brothers and their father established T. Mellon & Sons (Pittsburgh). This was a private bank, meaning the books could be hidden from bank examiners. Much of the father's fortune had been built by foreclosing or by purchasing property of debtors who couldn't pay their obligations. The father was mortified when T. Mellon & Sons had to stop payments to depositors in the Panic of 1873. The bank, however, not only weathered the panic but also helped H.C. Frick's coke operation survive the crisis. T. Mellon & Sons bought a majority of the Pittsburgh Petroleum Stock Exchange shares after the Panic of 1893. Members of the Exchange rebelled against Mellon control, walked out, and formed Pittsburgh Stock Exchange. T. Mellon & Sons served big industry and was succeeded by Mellon National Bank in 1902. In World War I reportedly Mellon's Union Trust (founded in 1889), Mellon National, and associated banks made the nation's biggest Liberty and Allied bond purchases.

Mellon National was a banker's bank, with deposits from many institutions. It was run by Mellon, Frick, and various associates and relatives. Mellon National was prepared to buy the insolvent Bank of Pittsburgh in 1931, but Mellon (Hoover Treasury) himself forbade the deal. He felt that if the Bank of Pittsburgh were allowed to fail the depositors would have to shift their money to Mellon National when the smoke cleared, so why should Mellon National spend anything to acquire the deposits? The Bank of Pittsburgh did fail, taking with it scores of smaller banks that had deposited their funds with it. Depositors can often recover their money from a broken bank, but the process takes time. In this instance depositors had to sit through a brutal winter with their money tied up. The public was outraged by Secretary Mellon's conduct. So were businessmen. A few days after the failure the president of McKeesport Tinplate Co. shifted the company's big account from Mellon National. Others followed that example.

Coal

The father of George C. Marshall (Truman State) manufactured brick for coking ovens—Bliss, Marshall & Company. Ca. 1879 the father was president of Persey Mining Co., producing coal. In 1880 he helped organize Fayette Coke & Furnace Co. The father began buying coal lands and in the 1880s was a big western Pennsylvania coke manufacturer. In 1888 the father helped organize Kyle Coke Co. In 1890 he and his associates sold various holdings to Mellon's intimate business associate H.C. Frick. The father probably got about $150,000 in this deal ($4,165,000 in 2019 buying power). He lost it in real estate speculation.

Frick was president and board chairman of H.C. Frick Coke Co., largest coke producer in the world. With Mellon financing Frick cornered the coal market after the Panic of 1873. He upped the price from ninety cents to five dollars a ton. He paid workers in scrip during the Panic of 1873, due to a lack of cash. The scrip was redeemable only at the company store. After the Panic ended Frick nonetheless continued to pay in scrip, an innovation that spread to other coal companies. He was a millionaire by age thirty.

In July 1899 Mellon's Union Trust bank announced a plan to consolidate all coal mines shipping on the Monongahela River. By autumn Monongahela River Consolidated Coal & Coke Co. ("River Coal") had 96 of the 102 operating mines along the river. Mellon decided to merge it with Pittsburgh Coal Co. ("Rail Coal"), a monopoly of mines that shipped by rail. The only bank willing to finance the merger was Mellon's Union Trust.

In 1925 Rail Coal broke its union contract, reduced wages, and established an open shop. Secretary Mellon's brother Richard approved breaking the contract. A strike was called, and Mellon set up a company union. Rail Coal's vice president refused James Davis's (Coolidge Labor) request to meet with strikers. Davis and Mellon were cabinet colleagues. A U.S. Senate committee investigated the strike situation. Mellon's company sent letters to superintendents, telling them to present "safe" employees to the Senate committee. In 1929 company police tortured and murdered a miner. The company police were defended by Mellon lawyers and received light sentences. The company paid the widow $13,500. A shopkeeper whose store housed the workers' relief office also turned up murdered.[88] Mellon's company police were more like a private army, complete with machine guns. The Mellon-influenced governor of Pennsylvania was succeeded by Gifford Pinchot, who revoked the commissions of private armies. Rail Coal and other companies then simply had their agents sworn in as deputy sheriffs.

Oil

The Mellon family was involved with oil pipelines, making a big profit by selling out to Standard Oil. In 1901 a wildcat oil strike was made at the Spindletop salt dome in Texas. Jesse Jones (Hoover Reconstruction Finance Corporation, FDR Commerce) made about $25,000 ($800,000 in 2019 buying power) in one week by fast work with oil leases pertaining to Spindletop. The J.M. Guffey Petroleum Co., was formed, soon renamed Gulf Oil. According to Guffey the company was organized at a meeting at New York's Fifth Avenue Hotel. Those present included Mellon and his intimate business associate H.C. Frick. Mellon said he discussed a bond issue with Edward House (Wilson adviser) and T. Jefferson Coolidge (Old Colony Trust president) at another time. Richard Olney (Cleveland AG), George von L. Meyer (TR PG), and Charles Adams (Hoover Navy) were Old Colony directors. Jesse Jones built Gulf Oil's Houston headquarters building. Gulf directors included Mellon, his brother, his son, and two of his nephews. They began buying leases for many domes on the Gulf coast. In 1904 Gulf Oil was the world's largest independent oil firm. Its general counsel was Thomas Gregory (Wilson AG). Gulf Oil became a holding company for all Mellon oil interests.

In good economic times around the 1920s Gulf paid some Port Arthur refinery workers $0.25 an hour. Company shacks rented for $7 a month—two rooms, kerosene stove, and central wash sheds. A seven-day work week was common. Gulf service station men worked eight to twelve hours a day for $75 a week, plus a small bonus for oil and grease jobs.

In 1931 Gulf halted construction of a $50,000,000 project on Staten Island, aggravating the unemployment situation. This particularly aggravated the chairman of President Hoover's commission on temporary employment, since the chairman knew Gulf had the necessary money set aside. It wouldn't come from current revenue. Mellon's company agreed to resume the project, but later halted it again.

In 1917 Carib Syndicate bought 1,500,000 acres suspected of having oil in the Latin American country of Colombia. Henry Doherty of Cities Service owned seventy-five percent of Carib Syndicate, J.P. Morgan & Co. twenty-five percent. Hayden, Stone & Co. (firm of JFK's father and of Hoover associate William Boyce Thompson) was also involved. In 1926 the Mellons bought Doherty's share. Carib Syndicate stock then went from 4¼ to 14⅞.

Talk of corrupt influence forced changes in the Colombian government. In 1928 the Colombians raised oil royalties that they collected and demanded that Carib Syndicate prove its title to the land it used. American oil interests hired Francis Loomis to lobby both the State Department and President Coolidge. The hiring of Loomis should have sent Colombia a message, as he was a former State Department diplomat who had helped President Theodore Roosevelt carve Panama from Colombia to build the canal. Loomis was joined in lobbying efforts by Allen Dulles (former State Dept. official, future Eisenhower and JFK CIA) whose law partner William Cromwell had mucked about in Panama for years—yet another message.

The Colombians also knew that the lobbying was probably conducted in a friendly atmosphere since Mellon's family then owned seventy-five percent of Carib Syndicate, and President Coolidge's close friend Dwight Morrow was a partner in J.P. Morgan & Co. which then owned the other twenty-five percent. The lobbyists were skillful enough to suggest that Colombian behavior had less to do with anti-colonialism than with British oil interests corrupting the government and using it as a front to drive out the Americans. Something similar had happened in Mexico during the Wilson era. This theory about British influence perhaps perked the interest of Herbert Hoover (Coolidge Commerce) who was ever wary of British Empire skullduggery, and who once had Latin American oil operations of his own.

The Colombians were spunky and refused to alter their behavior toward the American oilmen. The U.S. government then intervened by warning bankers that Colombia bonds were no longer safe. This cut off the dollar supply to Colombia, a financial embargo as serious as a naval blockade (and a foreshadowing of U.S. tactics against Chile during the Nixon administration). By 1930 the Colombians had had enough. The nation's president went to Washington, D.C., and had dinner with Henry Stimson (Hoover State) and Andrew Mellon (Hoover Treasury) to see what could be worked out. Mellon said if the oil situation improved in Colombia, so would its dollar situation. Stimson sent H. Freeman Matthews (assistant chief of State Dept.'s Latin American division) to make sure the oil conditions underwent the specified changes. Mellon's operation was given a fifty-year concession much to the distress of Sinclair. Stimson then sent Matthews to the New York financial community to discuss Colombia's desire for National City Bank money. National City's receptivity might have been influenced by its counsel Garrard Winston (chief aide to Mellon). National City money was sent to Colombia.

Standard Oil Co. has oozed around and through many cabinets. The law partner of William Evarts (A. Johnson AG, Hayes State) was Standard's top attorney. Charles Evans Hughes (Harding & Coolidge State) succeeded Evarts's law partner as Standard's top attorney. President Cleveland was a Standard Oil lawyer, as was Elihu Root (McKinley and TR War). Rockefeller employee John McCloy (FDR Asst. War) was an aide to Root's law partner Henry Stimson (Taft War, Hoover State, FDR and Truman War). James

R. Garfield (TR Interior, son of President Garfield) was on good terms with big Standard lawyers. William Whitney (Cleveland Navy) owned over $7,000,000 of Standard Oil stock. He was a relative of U.S. Sen. Harry Payne (Standard Oil treasurer). Payne's son was John D. Rockefeller's business partner. Before teaming up with Rockefeller the son hired ex-slaves under Army contract for $7 to $8 a month. President Theodore Roosevelt's Rough Rider associate Robert W. Stewart was head of Standard Oil of Indiana. The father-in-law of John Hay (McKinley State) was involved with Standard. John McCone (JFK & LBJ CIA) was a Standard of California director and owned about $1,000,000 of stock. In 1946 Dean Acheson's (Truman State) law firm helped the Standard–affiliated Aramco consortium get tax breaks pushed through Congress. Clark Clifford (LBJ Defense) was a lawyer for Standard of California when he was a Truman adviser. President Kennedy's family owned stock in Standard Oil of New Jersey. Alexander Trowbridge (LBJ Commerce) was an executive of various Standard Oil operations. Nelson Rockefeller (Ford VP) was intimately connected with Standard, as was President Carter's associate David Rockefeller (brother of Ford VP). J.K. Jamieson (Carter associate) was director and executive vice president of Standard Oil of New Jersey. This list of Presidents and cabinet members associated with Standard could be extended, but the point is made.

Teapot Dome

Accounts of Teapot Dome are readily available, so only a few points need to be touched upon here. Treasury Secretary Mellon was no dummy when GOP chairman Will Hays (Harding PG) tried to sell him $50,000 of Liberty Bonds. Supposedly the transaction would help retire debts owed by the Republican Party, but there had to be some reason why Hays was reluctant to simply cash the bonds in a normal manner. Hays was chief counsel for Sinclair Oil Co., and Hays's brother was also a Sinclair attorney. After reflection Mellon refused to take any bonds from Hays but made a $50,000 straight donation to the GOP. Mellon later testified that he realized at the time that the bonds were probably related to corruption regarding the Teapot Dome oil lease, but he felt it was none of his business to say anything.[89] (Teapot Dome was a large oil deposit on land owned by the federal government and much coveted by some oil companies.)

Hays sold $50,000 of bonds to the brother of a top Standard Oil official. Former Rough Rider Robert W. Stewart (head of Standard Oil of Indiana) helped Sinclair set up the company that generated the Liberty Bonds.

Ed Doheny gave $50,000 to President Wilson's 1916 re-election campaign ($1,100,000 in 2019 buying power). Robert W. Stewart's son Robert G.

Stewart was president and son James Stewart was vice president of Doheny's Pan-American Petroleum Transport Co. Franklin Lane (Wilson Interior) was also a vice president of Doheny's Pan-American. In Wilson's cabinet Lane's generosity with California oilmen gave Josephus Daniels (Wilson Navy) the impression that Lane wanted to turn over Navy oil reserves to private operators. Lane approved dubious claims of Honolulu Oil Co. for parts of the Buena Vista Hills Navy oil reserve, but Daniels got President Wilson to override Lane's Buena Vista decision. A February 1920 law partially opened the reserves and gave much discretion to the Interior Secretary. Lane resigned the same month and immediately went to work for Doheny. Reportedly Lane's salary in 1920 was $50,000 ($660,000 in 2019 buying power). Just before getting the Doheny job Lane told friends that his financial situation was critical.

William McAdoo (Wilson Treasury), Lindley Garrison (Wilson War), Thomas Gregory (Wilson AG), and George Creel (Wilson World War I propaganda chief) also worked for Doheny's company. Doheny pad McAdoo $150,000 to handle some Mexican oil matters. Doheny claimed his payments to McAdoo reached a grand total of $250,000. McAdoo, however, denied receiving any money at all from Doheny. McAdoo explained Doheny's money went to McAdoo's law firm, not to McAdoo.

Thomas Gregory's law partner was general counsel of Secretary Mellon's Gulf Oil. Doheny was friends with Albert Fall (Harding Interior) and made a public offer to hire him. McAdoo and Lane were also lawyers for Sinclair. A. Mitchell Palmer (Wilson AG) was lawyer for Fall's intimate friend Edward McLean (*Washington Post* owner) who gave false testimony about Teapot Dome. Paul Cravath (law partner of Harding State) helped Doheny's defense, and the Cravath firm advised Sinclair Consolidated Oil Corp. regarding Harry Sinclair's conduct.

Walter Teagle (Std. of NJ president, Harding "poker cabinet") warned President Harding, as soon as the Teapot Dome leases became known, that the circumstances were suspicious. Standard's attorney Charles Evans Hughes (Harding State) said he was too busy in the State Department to know anything about this. Undersecretary of State William Phillips was just as busy, yet he knew what was going on with Teapot Dome. Moreover, Hughes was attorney for the American Petroleum Institute whose directors included Ed Doheny, Sinclair, and Stewart. Future President Hoover (Harding Commerce) was on good terms with Harry Garfield (close friend of President Wilson, son of Garfield) whose brother James served on Wilson's War Council with Hoover, later headed President Hoover's commission dealing with federal oil lands, kept in touch with Standard Oil attorneys, and blocked any dump–Hoover moves at the 1932 GOP convention. Hoover was in correspondence with Doheny in World War I, was a friend of Doheny's employee Franklin Lane (Wilson Interior), chose Hughes as Chief Justice, Mellon as Treasury Secretary, Patrick Hurley (attorney for Sinclair Consolidated Oil Corp.) as Secretary of War, James Mitchell (lawyer for Sinclair Consolidated Oil Corp.) as Attorney General, Theodore Roosevelt, Jr. (Harding Asst. Navy, Sinclair Oil director, brother of Sinclair employee Archie Roosevelt) as governor of Puerto Rico. When the scandal began to come out, Archie Roosevelt helped Harry Sinclair flee the country. Paul Morton (TR Navy) shared Sinclair's business address of 120 Broadway, as did President Theodore Roosevelt's private secretary William Loeb, Jr. Hoover sold his Langunitos oil operation to Standard of NJ, appointed the brother-in-law of Teagle (Std. of NJ president) to be ambassador to France, and Jesse Jones (FDR Commerce, organizer of a Standard Oil subsidiary) to be Reconstruction Finance Corporation chairman. William Boyce Thompson (Sinclair Oil director, associate of JFK's father) helped get Hoover appointed to President Harding's cabinet and was active in Russia during World War I. Former Rough Rider Albert Fall (Harding Interior) and Harry Sinclair later went to Russia to try to get oil leases—a trip President Harding endorsed, saying to Fall, "I want you to go, and I hope you will make some money." Hoover was involved with Mexican operations of Continental Oil and General Petroleum, was an expert in mineral resources, knowledgeable in finance, kept close tabs on activities in other cabinet departments, and was famed for his private intelligence system that kept watch on the business community.

Mellon knew what was happening and said nothing. Hughes and Hoover were in a position to know, such a good position that they may have deliberately avoided knowledge, if indeed they were ignorant. The three most respected men in the Harding cabinet sat and watched as corruption destroyed what would otherwise have been a competent Presidency.

Albert Fall (Harding Interior) urgently needed money. Although his Tres Rios Cattle & Land Co. was a handsome barony, when he entered the cabinet Fall owed $140,000 ($2,000,000 in 2019 buying power) to M.D. Thatcher Estates Co. Fall leased government oil reserves to Ed Doheny and Harry Sinclair. Sinclair may have had special knowledge about the reserves since during World War I he had served on the oil subcommittee of Committee on Raw Materials, Minerals, and Metals of the Council of National Defense. The oil reserve leases were no secret at the time, and there was no outcry about the known circumstances. Unknown to the public, however, Fall got $100,000 cash the day after Doheny filed his offer for the reserves. Fall also took $233,000 in Liberty Bonds from Harry Sinclair.

These bonds were generated by the Continental Trading Co. of Canada, a firm set up by Sinclair and executives of four other oil companies to milk their stockholders. The company accumulated $2,000,000 which was turned into Liberty Bonds and distributed to the five oilmen. Harry Sinclair donated some of these bonds to the GOP, the bonds Hays (Harding PG) was peddling.

All this raises a question. Why does the Harding administration get exclusive blame for Teapot Dome?

Chapter 17

Calvin Coolidge

President Coolidge (Harding VP) entered the Massachusetts Senate in 1912 as a protégé of an AT&T director and partly owed his rise in the state senate hierarchy to a Kidder, Peabody & Co. lawyer, and to a lawyer for New York, New Haven & Hartford Railroad. These three corporations were all associated with J.P. Morgan. Morgan partners Thomas Cochran and Dwight Morrow both worked hard (and unsuccessfully) to get Coolidge the 1920 Presidential nomination.

Coolidge was glad to be Massachusetts lieutenant governor for the money, a $2,000 salary ($37,000 in 2019 buying power). While governor he declined a $5,000 present. "I can't permit that kind of gift."[90] Coolidge lived in a two-family house in Northampton, MA. He continued to pay the monthly rent of $32 while President. His estate was at least $200,000 when he became President ($3,000,000 in 2019 buying power). He may have saved $50,000 *each year* as President. Rumor says that when his first Presidential paycheck arrived, Coolidge examined it and told the messenger, "Call again." In 1928 his investments were probably $200,000 ($3,000,000 in 2019 buying power) plus a fair amount of Vermont real estate. He lost little in the Great Depression. In 1932 he gave $5,000 ($98,000 in 2019 buying power) to help a former law partner who was in trouble. Coolidge left an estate of $500,000 to $700,000 ($9,700,000 to $13,580,000 in 2019 buying power).

Dawes' Dollars

Highly interested in the possibility of creating a natural gas monopoly, Charles Dawes (Coolidge VP) used money from his bank president uncle and from a business associate to buy LaCrosse (WI) Gas Light Co. in 1894. He and his brothers acquired gas companies in Wisconsin, Iowa, Ohio,

Michigan, Arkansas, Indiana, Louisiana, Alabama, Texas, and New York. Utilities magnate Sam Insull became associated with Dawes in this. From 1907 to 1917 Dawes made profits of about $6,000,000.

Naturally enough Dawes also had ties with the oil industry. One of his brothers was director of Pure Oil Co., and another brother was president. Pure Oil was being accused of price conspiracy in Ohio when Charles Dawes was elected Vice President of the United States. The court action was then quashed, and Pure Oil received a tax refund that had been pending.

President Harding owned stock in Pure Oil Company. Arthur Summerfield (Eisenhower PG) was a Michigan distributer for Pure Oil from 1924 to 1937. Claude Brinegar (Nixon Transportation) managed the merger of Union Oil Co. of California with Pure Oil in 1965. Through mergers Pure Oil became associated with Shell Oil. Luther Hodges (JFK & LBJ Commerce) and two partners were local distributors for Shell. They called themselves Clark Oil Co. and organized 100 gas stations in North Carolina and Virginia. Hodges made $6,000 a year from the operation, which was sold for over $500,000 after he became governor of North Carolina.

When Charles Dawes first arrived in Lincoln, NE (where his relative William Jennings Bryan lived), Dawes invested in local bank stock. This was financed by loans from First National Bank of Marietta where Dawes's uncle was bank president. Dawes had a competitive edge in Lincoln because the loan interest was lower than the stock dividends, putting Dawes in an almost no-lose situation. He became director at several banks and in 1907 was offered (and declined) the presidency of Knickerbocker Trust Co. where New York City's elite socialites gave their business. Knickerbocker closed in the Panic of 1907.

Dawes started his biggest banking operation with money from the son-in-law of George Pullman, on urging from J.P. Morgan's man Charles Schwab (Bethlehem Steel, associate of JFK's father) and George W. Perkins (International Harvester, NY Life). The Dawes operation was called Central Trust Co., and eventually merged with at least a dozen other banks.

In 1912 LaSalle Street Trust & Savings needed $1,250,000 cash to meet bank examiner requirements. Central Trust loaned the cash for a few hours and got it back as soon as the bank examiners were satisfied that LaSalle had the cash. At the time, this type of sharp operation was common among Illinois banks.

In 1931 Central Trust merged with two other financial institutions, forming Central Republic Bank & Trust Co. Central Republic was tied to the Insull utility game. Over forty percent of the bank's total strength was loaned out to Insull utilities. At the time Dawes was Reconstruction Finance Corporation chairman. This federal government agency was begun by President Hoover to save large business corporations and thereby bolster the national economy. While RFC chairman, Dawes remained the biggest stockholder of Central Republic Bank & Trust, and followed its troubles with interest. In June 1932 Dawes resigned from the RFC and hastened to Chicago. There he decided the crisis brought on by the Insull loans could only be solved by liquidating the bank. Other Chicago bankers were dismayed since this would increase panic pressure on them. They insisted that Dawes keep his bank open, but Dawes demanded a $100,000,000 loan to do so ($1,950,000,000 in 2019 buying power). Key figures involved with making this loan included Dawes, President Hoover, Ogden Mills (Hoover Treasury), and RFC member Jesse Jones (FDR Commerce). The loan took eighteen hours to arrange. In the end Dawes got $95,000,000—$5,000,000 from Chicago banks and the rest from RFC. The condition of Dawes's bank was so bad that no such loan could normally be expected. Strong suspicion existed at the time that Dawes had pulled powerful strings to get the money. In August 1944, the loan was all paid back in full, a very unlikely looking prospect in 1932.

In October 1932 money from Bernard Baruch and Owen Young (General Electric) helped form a new Dawes bank, City National Bank & Trust Co., whose directors included Chicago businessmen Frank Knox (FDR Navy) and Robert Wood (Sears Roebuck president).

Stock Market Crash

When Herbert Hoover became President he feared an economic downturn and began disposing of some investments, buying "gilt-edged" instead. When Hoover left the Presidency he was in excellent financial shape.

The great stock market crash was worsened by margin buying. This practice allows people to buy more stock than they otherwise could. In essence, the broker loans the buyer part of the purchase price. In a rising market everything would be fine. In a declining market, however, the broker would demand immediate payment of the margin loan. If the margin buyer couldn't comply, the broker would sell the margin stock to avoid or cut losses of his own. Margin buying was overextended, with big corporations loaning corporation money to brokers to encourage more margin buying, which pushed stock prices up. Since corporation money was tied up in the defaulting margin loans, the crash was even more damaging than one might think.

Then there was the matter of banks and insurance companies depending on stock as a significant liquid asset. As prices declined so did the assets, thereby decreasing the money supply. Businessmen then had trouble getting loans and had to cut back operations. Unemployment reduced deposits and decreased the money supply further. In addition, as declining stock prices reduced bank assets, banks had trouble meeting their own liabilities—such as paying off unemployed depositors who needed to withdraw money so they could eat. Some banks could no longer cover their liabilities and had to close. This encouraged depositors at other banks to withdraw deposits "before it's too late," which caused sounder banks to close. And each closure further decreased the money supply.

In his career as a stock promoter Franklin Roosevelt did his bit to add to the atmosphere that brought on the crash. He was involved with Compo Thrift Bond Corp. Working through banks, the corporation sold its bonds to little investors on an installment plan. When Roosevelt was promoting the company the words "The United States of America" were emblazoned on each bond, perhaps to trick the unsophisticated buyers into thinking they were getting Treasury bonds. FDR said the operation was legitimate, but his long-time business associate Pat Homer stayed clear of Compo and said it was only "catching suckers." FDR also promoted unsafe stocks by offering them to the public as safe. As governor of New York, FDR—and not President Hoover—had authority over the New York Stock Exchange. Roosevelt was unconcerned about stock market conditions as the crash approached, and ignored President Hoover's warnings that reforms were needed to prevent a crash.

President Kennedy's father Joseph specialized in getting options on inactive stocks. A stock option lets a person buy a stock at one specified price for a specified amount of time, regardless of the market price. Stock options are no-risk dream tickets to wealth, the stock market equivalent of betting on yesterday's baseball game. Suppose you have a two-week option to buy XYZ stock at $10 a share. If the market price stays at $10 or lower, you simply refuse to exercise the option and have lost nothing. If the price rises above $10 you exercise the option. The difference between your option price and the higher market price is instant profit. You can't lose, but in order to win big, the market price has to go up while you have the option. Joseph Kennedy found a way to drive prices up. He would continually buy and sell small lots of the stock. People would note the sudden action on this previously inactive stock. With luck, people would suspect that the activity was due to some change for the better in the company. Other persons beside JFK's father would start to buy the company's stock; activity would increase; the price would rise; more people would notice; etc. Joseph Kennedy would then exercise his stock option, immediately sell the stock, and have a no-risk profit.

In the Great Depression Joseph Kennedy was also noted for bear market operations. A "bear market" is when stock prices decline. The traditional way to profit from this is by short selling. Say the price of XYZ stock is going down. You pretend to own 100 shares and sell the imaginary stock to someone, who pays $1000. You promise to deliver the certificates later. This sale is posted on the stock exchange and drives the stock's price down further, say to $900. You then buy the stock at that lower price and deliver it to the buyer. You pocket a profit of $100 on the transaction. In theory you can send the price to zero and make a fortune while wiping out companies, jobs, banks, and depositors. Short selling is one reason the Great Depression lasted so long.

FDR made money from hyperinflation in Germany during the Weimar Republic. This inflation was no accident but was deliberately caused by Germany's wealthy elite in order to escape debts of war contracts. Big operators also used the rapid inflation to acquire property cheaply. A contract might be signed to buy a house for 20,000 marks, but when paid to the seller a few weeks later those 20,000 marks would be worth a fraction of what they were when the bid was accepted. Factories were obtained the same way. Corporations wiped their debts clean and were ready for a fresh start when the inflation was stopped. Thrifty middle class people were wiped out. Via inflation the government deliberately destroyed their savings and pensions to pay rich men's obligations. When those obligations were finally disposed of, the inflation was quickly stopped.

Future President Roosevelt was a founder of United European Investors, Ltd. This was a sophisticated scheme to make money from Weimar inflation. The worse the situation got for the German people, the more money FDR would make. Using German marks investors would buy stock in FDR's company. Apparently these marks might be immediately exchanged for stable currency which was then used to buy real estate, mortgages, and securities. Or the marks might be immediately used for such purchases without exchange to another currency. Either way, the worse the inflation got, the more eager people would be to exchange marks for FDR's stock which kept up with the inflation. This would enable Roosevelt to buy up more German property, which would make his stock more valuable and even more attractive to people holding marks. This would bring in still more marks to FDR, and the cycle could go on and on. The scope of Roosevelt's operations remained small compared to the potential. United European profits, however, were excellent. Investors apparently doubled their money. FDR's profit was about $5,000. His company began in 1922 and was liquidated in 1924—dates exactly matching the German inflation crisis.

In 1927 Franklin Roosevelt became an incorporator and director of International Germanic Trust Co., a holding company that bought German securities. FDR had seventy-five shares of International Germanic. The opening price per share was $170 ($2,500 in 2019 buying power). The price zoomed up in the market and then zoomed down. FDR resigned from the company in 1928, and International Germanic went into receivership soon thereafter. Roosevelt also was an incorporator of Federal International Investment Trust. This dealt in foreign securities.

Anticipating a 1932 Democratic victory and the end of Prohibition Joseph Kennedy helped lead a stock pool in Libby-Owens-Ford during the 1932 Democratic convention. The theory was that demand for bottles would go up. In this pool the actions of Kennedy were legal but unsavory. Just as the questionable details surfaced FDR appointed JFK's father chairman of the Securities & Exchange Commission.

Another stock promoter around FDR was James Forrestal (FDR and Truman Navy, Truman Defense). As a Princeton student Forrestal was in continual financial trouble although his family sent him $6,000 ($153,000 in 2019 buying power). Forrestal sought financial aid from Princeton, claiming his well-off parents couldn't afford the costs. Yet he refused work when it was offered and joined an exclusive eating club. He also bought expensive clothes as a student.

In 1915 a William A. Read & Co. recruiter was searching the Princeton campus for talent. He sought out student newspaper editor Forrestal and urged him to join the banking company. After some initial job switching, Forrestal did. Read died, and his widow sold out to partner Clarence Dillon. Forrestal became the boy wonder of Wall Street, and not all his deals were of unquestionable ethics. He eventually became president of Dillon, Read & Co., and Dillon (JFK Treasury) became board chairman. Peter Flannigan (Nixon aide) was from Dillon, Read. Joseph Cotton (Hoover Undersecretary of State) was a Dillon, Read lawyer. The Shearman & Sterling law firm also represented Dillon, Read plus two of its investment companies—South African Investment Co. and U.S. & Foreign Securities Corp.

U.S. & Foreign Securities Corp. was a holding company formed in 1924 by Dillon, Read. Holding companies simply own stock of other companies. There are two basic kinds of holding companies. One holds stock for the purpose of controlling corporations. The other holds stocks as investments to make money. U.S. & Foreign Securities was an investment holding company. It had stock in just about every major U.S. corporation and had many dealings with foreign industry, transportation, and mineral securities. Dillon, Read was involved with American monopolies in Western Europe, with Royal Dutch–Shell, Siemens, and Amerada Petroleum. Dillon, Read men were on Amerada's board, and the Bank of England owned a substantial percentage of Amerada stock.

In the United States Dillon, Read controlled the Dodge and Chrysler automobile companies and merged them. Via reorganizations Dillon, Read also controlled National Cash Register, Goodyear Tire & Rubber, Union Oil

Co. of California, American & Foreign Power, Seaboard Airline Railroad, and Frisco Railroad.

Forrestal owned 37,000 shares of U.S. & Foreign Securities Corp. In 1929 Forrestal transferred 20,000 shares to a Canadian corporation he had organized, Beekman Co., Ltd. This company's stock was in turn owned by Beekman Corp. of Delaware. Forrestal owned seventy percent of the latter's stock. His wife owned the other thirty percent. Some of the corporation officers were interchangeable. Investigators who peeled back the layers found that the Beekman operation was a slick tax scheme, so slick that it was hard to tell if Forrestal was avoiding or evading taxes. Forrestal made a settlement with Internal Revenue and dissolved both corporations.

Ca. 1947 Forrestal was spending about $60,000 a year ($660,000 in 2019 buying power) and complaining that government salaries were too low.

While a cabinet member, C. Douglas Dillon retained his U.S. & Foreign Securities stock, eight and one half percent of the company's total. Dillon said this was what he "directly" owned. His family owned about thirty-five percent. Dillon turned over many (but not all) of his other stocks to a U.S. & Foreign Securities vice president.

As the stock market frenzy grew in July 1929, J.P. Morgan & Co. offered United Corp. stock to insiders at $75 a share while the market price was $99 a share ($1,475 in 2019 buying power). Takers included William McAdoo (Wilson Treasury) 250 shares, the brother of Andrew Mellon (Harding, Coolidge, & Hoover Treasury) 5,000 shares, and Edgar Rickard (who handled Hoover's personal finances) 400 shares. At the same time J.P. Morgan & Co. offered Standard Brands stock to insiders at $10 a share below market price. Takers included McAdoo 1,000 shares, Mellon's brother 5,000 shares, former President Coolidge 3,000 shares, William Boyce Thompson (associate of Hoover and of JFK's father) 2,500 shares, and William Woodin (FDR Treasury) 1,000 shares. Other persons who participated in such J.P. Morgan & Co. instant profit deals included Gen. John J. Pershing, Charles Lindbergh, Owen Young (GE president), and John Davis (1924 Democratic Presidential nominee).

Hoover's industrious efforts to end the Great Depression are well documented elsewhere, but the influence of his World War I Belgian relief work is worth mention here. The war relief work inherently differed from the Great Depression relief work. In World War I many Europeans could afford to buy food. They were starving due to a failure in food supply, not due to poverty. In World War I Hoover was basically meeting a market demand, supplying food to people who wanted to buy it. Although much food was given away, much was sold to recipients, which in turn helped finance the relief work. The war relief was non-profit, but nonetheless was essentially organized like a standard business operation. In contrast, during the Great Depression the food supply in America was plentiful, but people couldn't afford to buy it. Instead of supplying food, Hoover's task was to raise incomes. Despite his best efforts, Hoover was unable to do this.

FDR

The mother of President Franklin Delano Roosevelt was a millionaire. FDR inherited over $900,000 from her plus $200,000 to $600,000 from his father and stepbrother. The father directed Rockefeller's Consolidation Coal Company, which was tied to J.P. Morgan's Bankers Trust Co. The work of FDR's father led to the founding of Southern Railway System, and he managed Southern Railways Securities Co. FDR's father was president of Louisville RR and New Albany railroad. The father reportedly made $300,000 from railroad activity. The father was involved with James Guthrie's (Pierce Treasury) Louisville & Nashville. FDR's close relative Warren Delano was the brother-in-law of the main owner of Atlantic Coast Line RR, which owned Louisville & Nashville. Delano's son was board chairman of both roads in 1934. "Through him and Mr. Pelley, President of the New Haven, Mr. Curry of the Union Pacific and other relatives, the President [FDR] has his railroad connections."[91]

FDR's brother-in-law worked for Eastern Michigan Railways. William Woodin (FDR Treasury) was president of American Locomotive Co., and Andrew Mellon (Hoover Treasury) was a director. J.P. Morgan and Hayden, Stone (firm of JFK's father) were also involved with American Locomotive Co. Woodin was president of American Car & Foundry Co., biggest company in the business. American Car & Foundry evolved from the iron business of Simon Cameron (Lincoln War).

Inheritance provided Roosevelt with a $5,000 income in law school ($140,000 in 2019 buying power). About this time his wife Eleanor's income from inheritance was $7,500. FDR clerked at the Carter, Ledyard & Milburn law firm, a prominent representative of big corporations and trusts. His $1,500 salary as a state legislator was mere pocket change, though his $25,000 salary as vice president of Fidelity & Deposit Co. of Maryland was a more substantial contribution to Roosevelt's income (roughly $360,000 in 2019 buying power). He entered the Wall Street firm in 1921 and was given a welcoming dinner at Delmonico's attended by Owen D. Young (General Electric president), Adolph Ochs (*New York Times*), Daniel Willard (Pennsylvania RR), and the father of Edward Stettinius (FDR State). FDR got the job in this surety firm through his yachting friend Van Lear Black, president of Fidelity and owner of the *Baltimore Sun*. FDR's office hours were

10:30 to 1:30 *including* lunch. He mainly did the social whirl, to make contacts for the company. FDR bragged about making the firm successful via his political clout with figures in the state and national capitals (he was the 1920 Democratic nominee for Vice President). Roosevelt criticized associates in the firm who didn't attempt to follow his example. In this "work" he was assisted by Louis Howe, assistance which blended business and political contacts. In afternoons Roosevelt tended his private law practice. As part of his work with Fidelity, Roosevelt tried to use his influence with his old boss Josephus Daniels (Wilson Navy) to get the Navy Department to help New England Oil Corporation. During the World War FDR had gotten Daniels to give Navy support to an oil refinery project in which Roosevelt had invested. Pat Homer and perhaps Louis Howe were also involved. The refinery turned out to be a waste of the Navy's money. Homer and Roosevelt were later involved in Wyoming oil exploration but found only sulfur. FDR had bought 2,000 shares in the Wyoming operation and lost all the money he had invested.

Roosevelt was active in other businesses during the 1920s, in addition to the stock market operations noted earlier. Roosevelt, Louis Howe, and Pat Homer bought a lobster plant in Rockland, ME. FDR had majority control of the company—Witham Brothers, Inc. The plan was to buy lobsters and hold them until the price rose. The lobsters were indeed purchased, but the price never rose. The plant managers became angry with the owners and quit. FDR lost $26,000.

Roosevelt and Henry Morgenthau, Jr., (FDR Treasury) were directors of Photomaton, Inc. in 1927. FDR bought 500 shares at $3 a share (paid $44 a share in 2019 buying power). This was an automatic photo machine company. Pop in a quarter and out popped a picture—no need to go to a high-priced human photographer. In December 1928 FDR sold his 500 shares for $17 a share. He got out in time. Photomaton was in receivership ca. 1930. Roosevelt and Morgenthau's father were directors of Sanitary Postage Co., a postage stamp vending machine firm. Morgenthau, Jr. (FDR Treasury), may have been involved. A story appeared in the *New York World* explaining that stamps bought at the post office could have germs, but Sanitary Postage Co. sold germ-free stamps. In 1928 this company merged with four other vending machine companies to form Consolidated Automatic Merchandising Corporation—Camco. FDR was a Camco director, and Morgenthau, Jr. (FDR Treasury) was involved. The plan was to end the need for thousands of clerks across the USA (and thereby end their jobs) by selling all sorts of small merchandise automatically to customers. The wages formerly paid to ex-clerks could then be added to merchants' profits. Camco directors predicted 2000%, even 3000%, profit on their stock by 1933. Lead slugs and fist slugs (to balky machines) turned the operation into a money-loser from the start. Camco also learned that human customers preferred dealing with human clerks. FDR abandoned Camco, and it went into receivership in 1933 with over a $3,000,000 loss ($58,200,000 in 2019 buying power). Note that both Camco and Photomaton were designed to make money for FDR by throwing people out of work.

In the early 1920s Roosevelt was involved with Twin Coast Navigation, a proposed merger of several small lines to get ships from the still operative World War I Emergency Fleet Corp. The idea was to send freight from the East Coast to the West Coast via the Panama Canal. FDR was in contact with Kermit Roosevelt (son of TR) on this plan, and had a letter published in the *New York Times* complaining that the Emergency Fleet Corp. was wasting tax money by failing to sell ships at whatever price they would fetch. FDR needed ships at bargain prices to make the scheme work. He also needed to wrest business from competitors who were experienced. Unlike Compo Thrift Bond Corp., Twin Coast Navigation needed sophisticated and well-heeled investors. Yet their very sophistication made them unlikely prospects. FDR gave it the old college try nonetheless, with pleasant luncheons and teas at which he told the prospects, "I should gladly do this underwriting myself if I did not have so many unusual demands to meet just now." The scheme failed.

Roosevelt, Owen Young (GE president), Mellon's (Hoover Treasury) brother, Marshall Field, and the son of Adlai Stevenson (Cleveland VP) set up General Air to run a New York to Chicago dirigible line (using nonflammable helium floatation). In 1921 FDR said, "Wait until my dirigibles are running and then you will be able to take a form of transportation which is absolutely safe."[92] The project flopped.

In 1918 FDR's gross income was just under $25,000 ($387,000 in 2019 buying power) and rose to just under $54,000 by 1926 ($777,000 in 2019 buying power). From 1918 to 1926 Roosevelt's net income *after expenses* each year never exceeded $7,300. He was usually in the red, outspending his gross income of $54,000 by $20,000 in 1926.

About this time he began the expensive Warm Springs hospital project. Ca. 1927 Roosevelt bought a summer hotel called the Merriwether Inn for $195,000, planning to convert it into a polio hospital. FDR named the operation the Georgia Warm Springs Foundation. Just how much of FDR's money went into this is unclear. He claimed it was a lot of his fortune (which at this time was over $375,000 in stocks and bonds alone), but Warm Springs money may have included sums from investors. For sure, however, Roosevelt was liable for the large debts that the Georgia Warm Springs Foundation was running up. FDR agreed to accept the 1928 Democratic nomination for New York governor only after General Motors executive John J. Raskob promised to clear up the deficit. William Woodin

(FDR Treasury) was put in charge of shaking money from fat cats, who put in $150,000 ($2,250,000 in 2019 buying power). Raskob put in another $100,000, and FDR thereby got the needed $250,000. Roosevelt denied that Raskob paid him to run for governor, which was technically correct. Raskob paid the Georgia Warm Springs Foundation, not Roosevelt personally. Ca. 1930 the Foundation insured FDR's life for $560,000 ($8,960,000 in 2019 buying power). The premium was $25,000 the first year, *decreasing* afterward. If FDR died, money for the Foundation might dry up. So with the Foundation as beneficiary, the policy eased concern about that. (And the Foundation did get the $560,000 when FDR died.)

Ca. early 1941 FDR asked Jesse Jones (FDR Commerce, Hoover RFC chairman) to see about the Reconstruction Finance Corporation buying the Empire State Building for federal office use. Jones was well acquainted with the economics of New York City real estate, having built a hotel, hospital, and skyscrapers in NYC. The hotel was the sixteen-story Mayfair House, built ca. 1912 at 65th and Park Avenue, across the street from FDR's townhouse. Jones quickly showed that erecting a new building for federal offices would be cheaper than buying the Empire State Building. FDR then put the screws on Jones, Director of the Budget Harold Smith, and the Bureau of Public Buildings—with no success. Jones said of Roosevelt: "Of all the requests he made of me this was the one he was persistent about."[93]

Al Smith (1928 Democratic Presidential nominee) was president of the Empire State Building Corp. FDR told Jones that Smith was broke, which Jones knew was untrue. Smith was getting $50,000 salary as corporation president ($825,000 in 2019 buying power) and would get a $500,000 commission for selling the structure ($8,250,000 in 2019 buying power). FDR insisted he was only trying to help his old friend Al, who happened to be one of FDR's deadliest enemies in 1941. More likely FDR was trying to help his old friend John J. Raskob who was heavily involved in the building, to repay the favor of Raskob helping to cover the Warm Springs Foundation debt and thereby making FDR's 1928 gubernatorial candidacy possible. Smith's own motive in trying to sell the building was to help Raskob.

The Reconstruction Finance Corp. loaned $10,000,000 to an insurance company that Basil O'Connor's (FDR law partner) law firm had helped reorganize. O'Connor's fee was $200,000, which RFC chairman Jones (FDR Commerce) balked at paying. FDR told Jones to let O'Connor have a big fee, perhaps $150,000, but Jones still said no. O'Connor went to court and eventually got $ 135,000. The Roosevelt & O'Connor firm's office was next-door to Fidelity & Deposit Co. of Maryland, the surety firm FDR had worked for.

Despite the continual drain caused by the Warm Springs project, Roosevelt's stock and bond holdings increased from $270,000 in 1918 ($4,185,000 in 2019 buying power) to almost $380,000 in 1927 ($5,624,000 in 2019 buying power). FDR and Eleanor probably made $125,000 in his first year as President ($2,425,000 in 2019 buying power), $175,000 to $200,000 the next year. Much of this was from Eleanor's radio, newspaper, book, and magazine work. She got at least $1,200,000 total from 1933 to 1940. Harry Hopkins's (FDR Commerce) son worked for an ad agency which placed Eleanor as a shill for Pan-American Coffee Bureau, an organization backed by eight Latin American nations. She got $1,000 a week. In a six-month period ca. 1934, Eleanor received over $36,000 for a radio program ($684,000 in 2019 buying power). This may have been her fifteen-minute show sponsored by Selby Shoe Co., which said it was donating her salary to a charity of her choice. The assertion that much of her income went to charity is, however, open to challenge. In some cases Eleanor charged $1,000 to $4,000 for each commercial sales pitch she made. She made at least 150 or so, for a money total of about $450,000. She was paid $4,000 to make two broadcasts on the importance of candy to the war effort. The candy industry wanted to prevent its products being classified as non-essential. "Non-essential" would mean a loss of profits due to lower priority in raw materials, shipping, and other factors. Henry Wallace (FDR VP) also broadcast for the candy industry, but for free. Eleanor was a radio huckster for Beauty Rest Mattresses, a toilet preparation, and the products of Manhattan Soap Co. (Sweetheart Soap). In 1938 Jack Garner (FDR VP) declined $1,500 a week for a fifteen-minute weekly radio broadcast ($27,000 in 2019 buying power). Garner felt the broadcasts would be exploiting the Vice Presidency rather than exploit his talents. From 1933 to 1940 Eleanor got $75,000 annually (roughly $1,425,000 in 2019 buying power) for lectures. While First Lady, Eleanor also accepted expensive gifts such as a $10,000 mink coat from Canadian fur breeders and gold jewelry from foreign governments.

Eleanor also ran Val-Kill Industries furniture factory between Poughkeepsie and Hyde Park, NY. "Kill" is an old term for brook. The factory-made reproductions of antiques. "It is a lucky bride who finds herself the owner of three or four pieces of furniture bearing the Val-Kill mark. She has the nucleus of a collection to be handed down to future generations and prized as the old pieces of the seventeenth century are prized by their owners today."[94]

While President, FDR had Postmaster General Jim Farley turn over several sheets of postage stamps before perforations were applied. As a stamp collector Roosevelt knew these would be worth a fortune. This was proven when Farley (who apparently knew little about stamp collecting) released a few more sheets to other persons. One sheet popped up in Virginia with a price tag of $20,000 ($380,000 in 2019 buying power). Public outcry forced the Post Office to release imperforate sheets to anyone who wanted them. These destroyed the value of Roosevelt's. Less known is that he quietly looted die proofs dating back to 1896 from the Bureau of Engraving and Printing. Roosevelt simply appropriated this valuable government property for his personal stamp collection. These die proofs were sold for $59,000 after FDR died (about $767,000 in 2019 buying power), the money going to his estate. The entire stamp collection went for $275,000 (about $3,575,000 in 2019 buying power). Much of that represented a premium price that buyers paid for the sentimental value of owning material from Roosevelt's collection. An anonymous sale would have brought less. FDR thereby left a total estate of just under $2,000,000 (about $26,000,000 in 2019 buying power).

FDR, incidentally, wasn't the only government official to profit from stamp treasures held by the Post Office Department. From 1903 to 1905 73 handsome albums containing about 140 die proofs each were passed out to favored persons. These die proofs ranged back to the first stamp issue in 1847. They were given free to President Theodore Roosevelt, Elihu Root (TR State), Philander Knox (TR AG), George Cortelyou (TR Treasury), and others. Charles Curtis (Hoover VP) got a set of 1898 Trans-Mississippi die proofs. Coolidge as President got forty die proofs. Mrs. Coolidge got three sets of some die proofs, Mrs. Harding one set. The Post Office also distributed freebies to many Congressmen, including Trans-Mississippi and Pan American Exposition die proofs and Pan American Exposition stamp inverts. Such gifts are roughly equivalent to the Treasury Department passing out souvenir $1,000 bills for free. The Post Office was well aware of these gifts' value, and no doubt had its motives for this generosity. There is a difference, of course, between accepting such gifts from a government agency and looting the Post Office archives as FDR did.

When President Franklin Roosevelt was elected, his children were adults and became involved in many business activities during the White House years. Rather than go down the rabbit hole of that topic, one example will be given here to illustrate. In 1939 a New York Congressman contacted the general counsel of the A&P grocery store corporation. The Congressman said that at the request of President Roosevelt he was trying to raise $200,000 for FDR's son Elliott ($3,650,000 in 2019 buying power). The Congressman asked the A&P lawyer to arrange a meeting between young Roosevelt and A&P president John Hartford. At the meeting Elliott told Hartford that the money was to buy a Texas radio station. Hartford was uneasy. Why would the President's son be seeking $200,000 from a grocery executive instead of a bank, especially an executive whose corporation had two or three Federal Trade Commission and federal anti-trust suits coming up against it. To quell Hartford's uneasiness, Elliott phoned the White House, got Dad on the line, and handed the phone to Hartford.

The President of the United States said he hoped Hartford could help young Roosevelt's business deal. The A&P president thereupon loaned Elliott $200,000. Time passed, and the war came. On December 14, 1941—one week after Pearl Harbor—FDR met at the White House with Fort Worth, Texas, oilmen Charles Roser and Sid Richardson (associate of Nixon Treasury). To nosy reporters such a meeting would seem commendable, as oil supplies were a vital military necessity. The meeting, however, related to Elliott's financial situation. Why would independent Texas oil operators be helping Elliott? Perhaps there was a connection with Elliott's official appointment as the President's counselor on independent oil operator matters. Elliott apparently had already gotten a $40,000 loan (which he repaid) from a man interested in a "hot oil" criminal case. (In this context "hot oil" refers to petroleum production that violates state or federal regulations.) Calling a time out from war matters, FDR now phoned Jesse Jones (FDR Commerce) and asked him to meet with Roser and Richardson to help out Elliott. Jones was a big Houston real estate operator and banker, so the three Texans surely all knew one another. The two oilmen informed Jones that Elliott had several big loans outstanding from his radio enterprises: $200,000 from John Hartford (A&P), $50,000 from David G. Baird (NY insurance man), and $25,000 from Charles Harwood (FDR's Virgin Islands governor). In 1942 Jones asked Hartford to accept $4,000 as full payment of the loan and return the radio stock given as collateral by Elliott, which Jones described as worthless. Hartford agreed, transforming the $200,000 loan into a $196,000 gift. Jones gave the "worthless" stock, which was actually worth about $1,000,000, to FDR ($15,150,000 in 2019 buying power). The President turned it over to Elliott's divorced second wife. Jones was a savvy businessman who headed the RFC before becoming Secretary of Commerce. Yet he claimed not to know of the federal legal actions pending against A&P. Jones got Baird to settle the $50,000 loan for $750, but Harwood refused outright. Harwood was peeved, saying he had bought a federal judgeship with the loan but only got appointed as governor of the Virgin Islands.

Ca. 1938 FDR conceived the Franklin D. Roosevelt Memorial Library. His law partner Basil O'Connor, Wall Street operator Ben Smith, movie magnate Joseph Schenck, and others helped raise money from Democratic sources to erect the building. Then Roosevelt deeded sixteen acres of Hyde Park to the U.S. government, with the National Archives furnishing upkeep of the now tax exempt property. In 1943 FDR donated the entire Hyde Park estate to the federal government, although members of his family retained the right to use the property as they wished. (Tax exempt status of the federally owned estate may not have been total—some state taxes may have been paid.)

FDR was fussy about his neighbors, but satisfied with Henry Morgenthau's (FDR and Truman Treasury) purchase in 1913 of several hundred aces in the Hyde Park vicinity. Roosevelt was appalled, however, when he learned in the 1940s that Father Divine, a controversial leader in the U.S. black community, planned to buy an estate next to Hyde Park. FDR asked Claude Wickard (FDR Agriculture) to have the Agriculture Department buy the estate sought by Father Divine and use it for agricultural experiments. Wickard demurred. Roosevelt then wanted the government-run Reconstruction Finance Corporation to buy the estate. RFC chairman Jesse Jones (FDR Commerce) moved indirectly, having the Prudence Company (which was in debt to the RFC) buy the estate, to hold, and sell at a profit later, thereby satisfying both FDR and some of the Prudence Company's debts.

Atomic Energy

The federal government's secret Manhattan Project to produce atomic bombs was one of the Roosevelt administration's most important accomplishments. In the 1930s Lewis Strauss (Hoover Pvt. secretary, Eisenhower Commerce) was in contact with Westinghouse Co., General Motors, General Electric, and the Rockefellers to get private financing of atomic energy research proposed by Arno Brasch and Leo Szilard. Ca. 1937 Westinghouse said it would build a nuclear accelerator, and in 1940 the Rockefeller Foundation provided most of the money for Ernest Lawrence's cyclotron. In 1938 Strauss used former President Hoover to arrange a meeting with Robert Millikan, Nobel laureate in physics at California Institute of Technology. Hoover had easy access to Millikan since both were trustees of the Huntington Library near Cal Tech. Strauss thereby put Millikan in contact with Brasch. Strauss kept in touch with Szilard in 1939, the year Szilard convinced Albert Einstein to approach President Roosevelt for government funding. Legend says that Roosevelt heeded Einstein's warning about an atomic bomb and started the Manhattan Project. Einstein, however, believed an atomic bomb was impossible. The letter to Roosevelt was written by Szilard, and Einstein agreed to sign, despite skepticism on the "scare warnings" because he respected Szilard's knowledge of how to shake money from fat cats. The letter's point was for scientists to get research money. Einstein's letter caused little stir. Its result was a $6,000 project to examine uses of fission as an industrial energy source. Those potential uses, of course, were the reason corporations were sponsoring the nation's atomic research.

In 1940 Vannevar Bush became head of the federal group looking into fission. Bush had worked on a submarine detector during World War I, work sponsored by a J.P. Morgan company. Bush was a postwar consultant to that company. His college roommate was Laurence K. Marshall, who started Raytheon Corp. (in which the son of Hoover Navy and the brother of LBJ AG were executives). Bush, too, was skeptical about an atomic bomb, but in 1941 agreed to further study. In 1942 Bush decided that the evidence justified the Manhattan Project, and got FDR's approval. Henry Stimson (Taft War, Hoover State, FDR and Truman War) turned to George Harrison for help in this project. Ca. 1931 Harrison was a key figure in World War I debt arrangements via his position with the New York Federal Reserve Board. This service had earned Stimson's gratitude. The choice of a banker to deal with atomic physics may seem odd, but for years Stimson's physicist cousin Alfred L. Loomis had been vice president of the Bonbright & Co. investment banking firm. Thus the occupations aren't incompatible. Indeed the "Einstein" letter was delivered to FDR by New York banker Alexander Sachs, who was an associate of William Stephenson ("the man called Intrepid"). Lewis Strauss, who became chairman of the Atomic Energy Commission, was a partner in the Kuhn, Loeb & Co. investment banking firm. Later AEC chairmen included banker John McCone (JFK and LBJ CIA). Harold Brown (Carter Defense) was a director of Schroder Bank, as was McCone's predecessor Allen Dulles (brother of Eisenhower State).

Chapter 18

Harry Truman

In 1916 future President Truman invested in the oil business—$5,000 cash ($110,000 in 2019 buying power) and $5,000 in notes signed by his mother. He thereby gained one-third interest in Atlas-Okla Oil Lands Syndicate and in Morgan & Co. Oil Investments Corp. Morgan was Daniel H. Morgan, one of Truman's two partners in the venture. The other partner was Jerry Culbertson. Oilman Harry Truman liked to take people out to eat in Kansas City at the time. He was "surrounded with ... salesmen, lease men, lease owners, scouts, and what-have-you."[95] Favorite cafes were Johnston's (three blocks from Democrat chieftain Tom Pendergast's saloon) and Valerius's (who had three downtown night cafes, one being two blocks from Tom Pendergast's political headquarters—the Jefferson Hotel). In March 1917 Atlas-Okla Oil Lands Syndicate was reorganized into Morgan Oil & Refining Co. The partners found only dry holes, and then the civilian manpower shortage of World War I forced the company to relinquish its leases. The firm was dissolved in 1919, but Truman lost no money. The company's profits had returned everything he put in.

Truman nominated Indiana oilman Edwin Pauley as Assistant Secretary of the Navy. Pauley had helped lead the dump Wallace forces in 1944 (at the Democratic National Convention many Democrats opposed renominating Henry Wallace for another term as Vice President under FDR). Truman owed his ally Pauley a big favor. Truman seemed to plan on Pauley succeeding Forrestal (FDR & Truman Navy). Harold Ickes (FDR and Truman Interior) claimed that on the FDR funeral train Pauley told him that the Democrats could get several hundred thousand dollars from oilmen if the federal government wouldn't prosecute a lawsuit on oil tidelands ownership. Pauley denied the Ickes story. Former Assistant Attorney General Norman Littell, however, said that Pauley told him oilmen expected something in return for a donation. At any rate, Ickes decided if Truman wanted men like Pauley then Truman didn't want Ickes. Ickes resigned. Truman withdrew Pauley's nomination. In 1950 Pauley unsuccessfully tried to buy into the McCutcheon Drilling Co. of Gaines County, TX, which involved persons associated with Truman.

One of the more important business relationships in history was between Truman and Eddie Jacobson. They knew each other before World War I when Truman was a bank clerk flush enough to own an automobile. Truman and Jacobson served together in the 129th Field Artillery. In Europe they saw how big money could be made off small capital. They made $2,600 off a dance (about $40,300 in 2019 buying power), and their canteen operation paid dividends of 666 percent, leaving a profit of $15,000 (about $232,500 in 2019 buying power). After the war Truman had $15,000 to $20,000 he wanted to invest ($200,000 to $270,000 in 2019 buying power), plus proceeds from selling equipment and livestock from the family farm. (How many returning doughboys had that kind of spare cash?) Truman and Jacobson combined their savings, and with help from loans opened a haberdashery in downtown Kansas City, MO, ca. 1919. They started with $35,000 of menswear merchandise ($472,000 in 2019 buying power) and had hired help.

The first year they did well. The second year started well, but an embezzler and economic policies of Andrew Mellon (Harding Treasurer) hurt the two partners. In 1922 the store folded, leaving Truman with a grudge against the Republicans, whose policies he blamed for the recession that closed his business. He figured his losses at $28,000 ($420,000 in 2019 buying power). Truman eventually paid off his creditors. In addition Truman and Jacobson owed $2,500 to Twelfth Street Bank and over $5,000 to Security State Bank. Jacobson went bankrupt in 1925, but Truman continued working to pay off the banks. The Twelfth Street Bank loan was finally paid off in 1934. Summing it up, Truman stated, "This was a hard experience for me."[96]

Truman and Jacobson remained warm friends, visiting at the White House. Truman did not seem to distinguish the differences among "Jew," "Zionist," "Israelite," and "Israeli," and thereby gave an opening to arguments from Jacobson, who was dedicated to forming the state of Israel. The two men engaged in heated discussion of a type that only a dear friend would dare have with the President of the United States. Jacobson prodded, provoked, and soothed Truman as the occasion warranted. At first the President had no intense interest in Middle East affairs, being swayed by day-to-day events and personalities. Eventually Truman was persuaded to support formation of Israel. The state of Israel owes its origin to many things, not the least of which was a Kansas City haberdashery.

For years, the Truman family had been interested in Jackson County Democrat politics. Future President Truman made $6,000 a year as county executive. He needed still more money in 1926 due to the haberdashery's debts. Truman wanted the $25,000 annual income that the county collector got in salary and fees, but county Democrat chieftain Tom Pendergast refused to support him for that job.

Ca. 1925 Truman sold memberships in the Kansas City Automobile Club. "I got a percentage of the initiation fees. As I remember it, we got about fourteen or fifteen dollars a head of which the salesman got five dollars. I made five or six thousand dollars."

In 1926 Truman, his old Army associate Spencer Salisbury, and others, bought control of Citizens Security Bank in the Kansas City suburb of Englewood. Truman and his associates soon realized the bank was shaky and got out. After they left the bank failed. In 1924 Truman organized Community Savings & Loan Association (sometimes called Community Building and Loan). Salisbury was also involved, and Truman was the institution's president in 1930. He and Salisbury had a falling out, and Truman got a federal investigation of Community which resulted in a prison term for Salisbury.[97] The institution was liquidated, and all depositors got back slightly more than what they had on deposit.

Eisenhower

In late 1939 future President Eisenhower was working in the Philippines, where he was peeved at his boss Gen. Douglas MacArthur and wanted to leave. Eisenhower felt he needed to stay, however, because of the extra money he was getting from the Philippine government. As a five-star general Eisenhower made about $20,000 a year ($288,000 in 2019 buying power). He made $25,000 a year as president of Columbia University ($275,000 in 2019 buying power) and $100,000 as President of the United States (about $950,000 in 2019 buying power). His annual pension as ex–President was $25,000 plus up to $50,000 in expenses. He also got $19,000 a year pension as General of the Army. Eisenhower accepted many gifts for his Gettysburg farm while President, perhaps totaling $300,000. Normally material goods aren't income, so these were tax-free. They included several hundred trees, many bushes, animals, farm implements, house furniture, and appliances. The farm itself was leased to three wealthy oilmen: W.G. "Billy" Byars (independent Texas operator), W. Alton Jones (Cities Service president), and George E. Allen (Eisenhower partner in a downtown Washington, D.C., restaurant). While Eisenhower was President all farm expenses were paid by the three with checks on an account at the Gettysburg National Bank. The group lost $500,000, and Allen claimed a tax deduction on his loss. Eisenhower left a net estate of about $2,730,000 ($18,565,000 in 2019 buying power).

Tidelands Oil

Independent oilman Sid Richardson and Eisenhower were already friends when the United States was attacked at Pearl Harbor. In 1952 Richardson and George Allen flew to Europe where Eisenhower was Supreme Commander of NATO and urged Eisenhower to run for President. Richardson promised to help the campaign if Eisenhower would help him get oil tidelands from the federal government. President Eisenhower did this. Robert Anderson (Eisenhower Treasury) was president of Texas Mid-Continent Oil & Gas Association and member of Independent Petroleum Association of America. Reportedly Anderson was involved with Sid Richardson. For sure John Connally (Nixon Treasury) was. Connally was Richardson's attorney and was involved with many of Richardson's operations, including oil and gas, a gasoline extraction plant, an oilfield servicing company, and underground storage of liquid hydrocarbons. Richardson was a heavy stockholder in Transport Co. of Texas. Edgar Linkenhoger (LBJ friend) was president. In 1961 before Connally became JFK's Secretary of the Navy, the firm got a handsome Navy contract. In his nomination hearings Connally emphasized that his oil experience would help the Navy get the best oil deals possible. He made no big effort, however, to change the Navy contract with Transport Co. of Texas as costs grew and grew.

Dixon-Yates Contract

During the Eisenhower administration the Atomic Energy Commission needed more electricity. Rather than expand the Tennessee Valley Authority a government contract went to Mississippi Valley Generating Co. to build and run a coal-fired steam plant for the AEC. The private company was formed by the president of Middle South Utilities, Inc. (Edgar Dixon) and by the board chairman of Southern Company (Eugene Yates). Eisenhower's close friend Bobby Jones was a Southern Co. director. The Dixon–Yates contract was negotiated secretly by AEC chairman Lewis Strauss (Hoover Pvt. secretary and Eisenhower Commerce) and top Budget Bureau officials. The Budget Bureau Director invited a vice president of First Boston Corp. investment bank to assist. Somehow First Boston then wound up financing the multimillion-dollar contract. The government seemed uneasy about anyone learning of the First Boston official's role in the contract negotiations. First Boston's law firm was Sullivan & Cromwell, the Dulles brothers' (Eisenhower State and CIA) old firm. John Foster Dulles (Eisenhower State) and First Boston chairman George Woods were top officers of the Rockefeller Foundation. Woods arranged the First Boston man's participation in Dixon–Yates and was appointed president of the World Bank by President Kennedy.

Hanna Mining

Mark Hanna (McKinley adviser) had coal and iron operations headquartered in Cleveland, OH. He mined both of these minerals and smelted iron. The company routed transportation of coal, iron ore, and pig iron on the Great Lakes. George Humphrey (Eisenhower Treasury) was board chairman of M.A. Hanna Co. The company's lawyers included the Cravath firm and Jones, Day, Cockley & Reavis which James Lynn (Nixon HUD) belonged to.

In 1943 Hanna obtained mineral rights in an Oregon nickel area. George Humphrey offered to cooperate with the government in developing it during the Korean War. Hanna was to provide $4,000,000 to set up mining and smelting, with the government guaranteeing to pay six dollars a ton. The U.S. was also to give outright $22,000,000 to Hanna Smelting Co. If at any time the Hanna Smelting contract was canceled, the U.S. was to reimburse Hanna Mining Co. for all capital invested in the mine and for profits Hanna would have made in nickel sales. Plus Hanna Smelting wouldn't have to pay back money advanced by the government on Hanna's behalf. After George Humphrey's nomination as Treasury Secretary he worked diligently to have the contract signed by the departing Truman administration. Indeed the U.S. signed four days before Eisenhower became President. This contract to supply nickel to the government wasn't advertised, nor were there any competitors.

The General Accounting Office said Hanna made a 457% profit on nickel contracts from 1954 to 1961. Throughout Humphrey's cabinet tenure he held Hanna stock, worth millions. Cyrus Eaton was a business rival of Humphrey, a rival who directed several steel corporations that banked with Lewis Strauss (Eisenhower Commerce). Eaton founded Cliffs Corp., which merged with Samuel Tilden's (1876 Democratic Presidential nominee) Iron Cliffs Co. to form Cleveland–Cliffs Iron Co. Eaton charged that Humphrey was using his cabinet job to make money. Humphrey and Eisenhower responded indignantly. Later a decision was made to liquidate M.A. Hanna Co., with its assets to be acquired by Hanna Mining Co. and Consolidation Coal Co.

Humphrey was also president and director of Iron Ore Co. of Canada. He explained, "Well, it is just a little complicated—the underlying leases are owned by some Canadian companies. The company that is developing a portion of this ore, which is that part which is now under development and for which the railroad is being built is the Iron Ore Co. of Canada. The Hanna Co. in one way or another had approximately a quarter interest ... in the Iron Ore Co. of Canada." Humphrey listed other companies with an interest in Iron Ore Co. of Canada: Republic Steel, National Steel, Youngstown Sheet & Tube, Armco Steel, and Wheeling Steel, and the Canadian companies Conger Consolidated Gold Mines, the Labrador Mining & Exploration Co., and the Quebec–North Shore Exploration Co. Humphrey said that Bethlehem Steel wasn't an owner but purchased "a substantial tonnage of ore." Bethlehem "controls 1,500,000 tons a year for twenty-five years."[98] Iron Ore of Canada was part owner of a steamship company. Construction of the St. Lawrence Seaway would be a boon to Humphrey's Hanna Co, and to avoid conflict of interest Humphrey pledged to refrain from public advocacy of the Seaway. He said he would limit his advocacy to such occasions as cabinet meetings.

Humphrey owned stock in National Steel Corp., Pittsburgh Consolidation Coal Co., Industrial Rayon Corp., Standard Oil of New Jersey, Phelps Dodge Corp., Seaboard Oil Co., and Dures Plastics & Chemicals. M.A. Hanna Co. owned lesser amounts of stock in still other corporations. This common practice links together many diverse corporations. Keep in mind also that directors of various corporations are often the same persons. These business men and women are more knowledgeable about corporation activities than an outsider might realize. They are also more responsible for corporation activities than they might sometimes like to admit.

Chapter 19

General Motors

The father of Edward Stettinius (FDR and Truman State) was a J.P. Morgan partner and a General Motors director. The father owned $172,000 of GM stock. Stettinius himself was assistant to GM vice president John L. Pratt, who was a neighbor of Lewis Strauss (Hoover Pvt. secretary, Eisenhower Commerce) and later assistant to GM president Alfred Sloan. Stettinius was later a GM vice president. William Woodin (FDR Treasury) was a GM director, as was General Electric president Owen Young. For legal matters GM used a member of the Dulles (Eisenhower and JFK CIA) law firm. Other lawyers helping GM included, Griffin Bell (Carter AG), Theodore Sorensen (Carter CIA nominee), Lloyd Cutler (Carter associate), and Gerard Smith (Carter associate). Clark Clifford (Truman adviser, LBJ Defense) was attorney for the DuPont interest in GM.

In 1923, while Wilson (Eisenhower Defense) was still a Delco Remy executive, he joined seventy-five GM executives in buying a large bloc of stock in General Motors Shares, Inc. This was a holding company having GM shares, an investment trust. By 1929 these insiders had manipulated matters so that their holdings were worth fifty times the original investment. The personal fortunes of Sloan, Pratt, and Charles F. Kettering (World War I airplane controversy) grew from this.

Charles Wilson directed the National Bank of Detroit. "In the tough days of 1933 when the banks were all closed and things were awfully tough.... I scratched up $100,000 and plunked it in—and not many Michiganders did"[99] ($1,940,000 in 2019 buying power). Wilson owned 15,000 shares of this bank, and his wife owned 1,200 shares.

In 1933 Wilson ran General Motors in Detroit. GM's finance committee chairman phoned from New York at 4:00 p.m. one day to ask if GM workers would riot at the plant if the banks didn't open the next day. Wilson didn't know. The finance committee chairman said to post guards if needed. Wilson said he thought that was unnecessary. The banks started to close, and GM was unable to pay workers (having no cash on hand). Wilson prepared a statement to workers, but at the last minute all was okay because Kroger Grocery Co. asked GM to take several million dollars in cash (from panic food buying) off Kroger's hands. So, thanks to Kroger, GM had money to pay workers. This is yet another example of how diverse corporations cooperate with one another.

When Eisenhower nominated Wilson for Defense Secretary he had over 21,000 shares of GM Shares, Inc. and over 18,000 shares of GM common stock. One share of GM Shares, Inc. equaled two shares of GM common stock. The Senate insisted that Wilson sell his stock. Wilson balked. He noted that he owned less than one twentieth of one percent of GM. But that small percentage had a value of $2,500,000 ($23,750,000 in 2019 buying power). His wife had another $700,000 of GM stock ($6,650,000 in 2019 buying power). Moreover, GM had agreed to give him several hundred more shares each year while he was Defense Secretary, plus a cash bonus of about $700,000 over the next four years, plus continuing Wilson's life insurance, plus a pension of $3,333.33 a month in addition to everything else. Wilson said, "That is treating me only like General Motors treats anyone else that retires under the same conditions."[100] To collect all this, however, he had to agree to do nothing against the best interests of GM. Wilson confirmed that he planned to be involved with the Defense Department's GM contracts. Wilson said he didn't understand how anyone could see a conflict of interest in the situation. When pressed on the point he uttered his famous declaration that a conflict of interest was impossible because what was good for GM was good for the country. The GM board of directors ruled that nothing Wilson did as Defense Secretary would be considered as against the best interests of GM, and eventually Wilson sold his stock, feeling that left no ambiguity about a conflict of interest.

Wilson's Defense Dept. assistant Roger Kyes (Eisenhower Deputy Defense) was a GM vice president and general manager of the GMC truck and coach division. He owned about 2,900 shares of GM common stock. While a member of the subcabinet he would receive hundreds of common shares from GM over the next few years, along with a cash bonus of over $460,000 ($4,370,000 buying power in 2019). Kyes confirmed that he wouldn't hesitate to deal with the Defense Department's GM contracts, and he agreed to dispose of his stock.

John Connor (LBJ Commerce) was a GM director. During the Johnson administration GM sales were two percent of the USA's 1965 Gross National Product, and that same year nearly two percent of the federal government's tax receipts came from GM. Its 1964 net revenue exceeded the GNP of all but nine non-Communist countries, making GM one of the most powerful economic forces in the world.

World War I Strikes Again

In World War II Charles Wilson (Eisenhower Defense) was vice chairman of the War Production Board and headed the new Aircraft Production Board. Harold Talbott (Eisenhower Air Force) was the old Aircraft Production Division Director. This was the same Talbott who was investigated for airplane scandals in World War I, as related earlier in this book. He resigned from the World War II aircraft board in late 1942 after both the Army and Navy opposed Talbott's appointment to Charles Wilson's War Production Board operation. Regarding that Army and Navy opposition Talbott testified in 1953, "I know nothing of that."

Talbott took office as Secretary of the Air Force under Charles Wilson. Reports surfaced of Talbott's business dealings while Secretary. A Senate committee decided to investigate, with Robert Kennedy (JFK and LBJ AG) as chief counsel heading the probe. Talbott had reluctantly disposed of stock in some corporations with Defense Dept. business but was permitted to keep his partnership in Mulligan & Co. "I gave up a great deal of income to come down here. Therefore, I was very anxious to retain my interest in Mulligan & Co., on account of the income which I felt I needed."[101] Talbott's salary from Mulligan & Co. was $25,000 ($237,500 on 2019 buying power) plus a 50–50 split of profits with the firm's only other partner—a handy supplement to Talbott's government salary of $30,000. Talbott's share of profits came to $132,000 in his two years as Secretary of the Air Force ($1,255,000 in 2019 buying power). Mulligan & Co. dealt exclusively with clerical efficiency studies. Talbott's function in Mulligan & Co. was to solicit business from his many contacts. He was the key figure in getting contracts with AVCO Manufacturing Corp. (which depended on the Defense Dept. for half its business), Baldwin–Lima–Hamilton–Corp. (directed by Talbott and Arthur Summerfield, Eisenhower Postmaster General), Olin Industries, Greyhound Corp. (in which Defense Secretary Wilson's wife owned stock), and Owens–Illinois Glass Co. Other clients included Armco Steel, Armour & Co., Air Reduction, Bankers Trust, Brooklyn Union Gas, Chemical National Bank, Continental Can Co., Monsanto, RCA, Republic Steel, Standard of Ohio, Union Carbide, and the U.S. Army. Talbott's use of Air Force stationary to solicit prospective clients from the military industry, with the letters marked "CONFIDENTAL," drew particular criticism. Talbott denied any wrongdoing, resigned, and was given a big sendoff (including two medals) by Secretary Wilson.

J.P. Stevens

The father of Robert Stevens (Eisenhower Army) founded J.P. Stevens & Co. In 1952 about thirty percent of the firm's business was from government contracts, $113,000,000 ($1,073,500,000 in 2019 buying power). Robert Stevens was board chairman when nominated as Secretary of the Army by Eisenhower, owning 42,500 shares of common stock worth $34 each ($13,727,000 in 2019 buying power). This was about one percent of the company stock. Stevens, his wife, and children together had 75,000 shares. His mother had 206,000 shares in trust for her, of which one-third would go to Robert Stevens. Other family members had still more stock. John W. Davis (1924 Democratic Presidential nominee) advised Stevens to sever himself from all dealings with the company as Secretary of the Army. Yet Senator Symington (Truman RFC) pointed out that even deciding how many persons were needed in the armed forces would affect J.P. Stevens Co. business, due to uniform sales. Robert Stevens was very reluctant to sell his stock, which yielded $84,000 a year in dividends. Morgan Guaranty Trust Co., Morgan Stanley, and Harriman Ripley handled J.P. Stevens finances. Robert Stevens directed Morgan Guaranty Trust Co., and Thomas Gates (Eisenhower Defense) was a top Morgan Guaranty executive. J.P. Stevens was noted for its anti-labor policies. Clark Clifford (Truman adviser, LBJ Defense, Carter OMB lawyer) was attorney for J.P. Stevens in a National Labor Relations Board case accusing the company of suppressing the Textile Workers Union. The company lost.[102]

Cuba

At the time of the Spanish-American War U.S. citizens owned at least $50,000,000 of property in Cuba (about $1,500,000,000 in 2019 buying power), and U.S.–Cuban commerce was about $100,000,000 a year ($3,000,000,000 in 2019 buying power). William Whitney (Cleveland Navy), two of his brothers-in-law, and William Woodin (FDR Treasury) directed Cuba Railroad Co. In the 1880s Carnegie Steel Co. and Bethlehem Iron Works had Cuban mines for the armor plate industry. Later U.S. Steel had Cuban holdings. Pennsylvania RR used some Cuban ore. North American Trust Co. reorganized in 1901 as Banco Nacional de Cuba with John Carlisle (Cleveland Treasury) as director. J.P. Morgan interests were part owners of Banco Nacional de Cuba. Morgan was the Cuban government's U.S. banker. J.P. Morgan & Co. made various Cuban loans over the years, as did Chase National Bank. National City Bank was active in Consolidated Railroads of Cuba, which was directed by William Woodin (FDR Treasury). United Railways was closely linked to the London branch of Germany's Schroder bank, a bank whose American branch was directed by Allen Dulles (Eisenhower and JFK CIA). The Schroder bank channeled most English money that went into Cuba after the Spanish-American War.

Minas de Matahambre, S.A. was a Cuban subsidiary of American Metal Co. American Metal was actually a German-owned copper operation directed by men from International Nickel and the Dulles (Eisenhower State) law firm. The Dulles law firm was also heavily involved with International Nickel. New York & Cuba Mill Steamship Co. was reorganized by the Dulles firm. A subsidiary of Electric Bond & Share Co. was active in Cuba. In 1920 International Telephone & Telegraph planned to make Havana the center of ITT's Latin American communications system. A Rockefeller syndicate (family of Ford VP) controlled Air Reduction Co., which manufactured acetylene in Cuba, and also controlled Cuba Distilling Co.

Sugar has been king in Cuba. Probably 200 Bostonians had Cuban sugar operations in 1885, with E. Atins & Co. the most important. Richard Olney (Cleveland State) paid close attention to Edward Atkins. The company was absorbed into American Sugar Refining Co. which monopolized U.S. purchases of Cuban sugar. National City Bank of New York controlled the Cuban sugar industry as a result of the Spanish-American War. American Sugar Refining head H.O. Havemeyer seemed to favor outright U.S. annexation of Cuba in 1899. Russell Leffingwell (Wilson Assistant Treasury, J.P. Morgan partner) was a member of the Cravath law firm and was in charge of the firm's involvement with Cuban sugar. Dwight Davis (Coolidge War) married the widow of a Cuba Cane Sugar Corp. director, a company organized in 1915 by the Dulles (Eisenhower State) law firm. Cuba Cane Sugar controlled one seventh of all Cuban production in 1915. As noted earlier, the Schroder bank was linked to Dulles (Eisenhower & JFK CIA). Top Schroder officials directed Francisco Sugar. The Dulles law firm represented Francisco Sugar, which lost 158,000 acres to the Fidel Castro regime. One Schroder director and his relatives were involved with other sugar companies which lost over 200,000 acres to Castro. A Dulles law partner was president of Cuban Atlantic Sugar Co. Another Dulles partner was lawyer for the Aldana, Ceballos, and Czarnikow Rionda sugar operations. Chase National Bank, Guaranty Trust, J&W Seligman, and Hayden, Stone (firm of JFK's father) were closely identified with Cuba Cane Products Co. Hayden, Stone was involved with other Cuban business, such as International Cement Corp. which owned Cuba' s sole cement factory.

Corporations using large quantities of sugar also had Cuban interests. Amos Hershey owned a Cuban mill, as did the Hires beverage company. In the 1920s Coca-Cola also planned to cut the middleman from Cuban sugar purchases. In that decade Coke was even manufactured in Havana. James Farley (FDR PG) was a member of the Cuba Chamber of Commerce, perhaps due to his involvement with Coke.

The Dulles brothers and JFK's father may have had particular interest in Cuba's business climate. To these men the success of Castro would be appalling. Although for decades the U.S. government was unfriendly toward Castro, the stridency of that opposition evaporated when the Kennedy administration ended. Did the change reflect the departure of government figures who may have had a financial stake in pre–Castro Cuba?

Chapter 20

JFK

John F. Kennedy had a $500,000 a year income ($4,200,000 in 2019 buying power) from family trust funds while he was President. His brother-in-law Sargent Shriver (1972 Democratic nominee for VP) was a trustee in charge of these funds. Robert Kennedy's (JFK and LBJ AG) father-in-law was a millionaire. Both John and Robert were notorious for a lack of pocket cash which forced companions to pay their cab fares or restaurant tabs. The two brothers tended to never reimburse those persons. Nelson Rockefeller (Ford VP) had the same trait.

Motion Pictures

Normally we think of movies as an entertainment medium, but their value to American capitalists goes beyond box office receipts. American movies are shown around the world and create desire for American goods that are portrayed on the screen. This is why American television programs in the mid-twentieth century traditionally portrayed characters living on the borderline between middle and upper class. Viewers were supposed to get the idea that this was the normal way to live. Thus viewers would work harder at their jobs to get more money (overtime is cheaper for an employer than hiring new personnel). With that money the viewers would buy more goods, creating more profits and more demand for raw materials from around the world. The motion picture industry eventually merged with television, with movie studios making many of the programs broadcast in America and around the world.

Will Hays (Harding PG) made contacts in the movie industry via 1920 campaign newsreels. After the election he turned down a job offer from one movie company. Hays quit the cabinet, however, for a $150,000 a year job ($2,250,000 in 2019 buying power) overseeing the entire movie industry as president of Motion Picture Producers & Distributors of America, Inc.

President Kennedy's father entered the movie business in 1919. During the 1920s the father was president and board chairman of Film Booking Office of America, a movie production company. Although the elder Kennedy had some involvement with Walt Disney, for the most part Kennedy had the FBO grind out trashy low budget pictures. In 1927 Kennedy met the challenge of sound by selling much of FBO to David Sarnoff. Sarnoff, who had worked for John Wanamaker's (B. Harrison PG) New York radio station, was the organizer of Radio Corp. of America. FBO now had access to RCA's Photophone sound system. The next year Kennedy permitted the Keith-Albee-Orpheum vaudeville company to buy into FBO. Soon thereafter Kennedy wound up as KAO's board chairman. He then made a pile of money with stock sales and consulting fees when he and RCA merged FBO and KAO into a new corporation called Radio–Keith–Orpheum (RKO).

Kennedy also became chairman of Pathé Pictures, planning to merge it with RKO. Talk about the merger boosted the price of Pathé stock. RKO began buying Pathé stock, and continued buying at a high price until RKO had control of Pathé. This depleted RKO's finances badly, and Pathé (now controlled by RKO) agreed to sell its physical assets to RKO for much less than their appraised value. This made Pathé stock tumble. Despite this bargain acquisition RKO was forced to refinance. Regular stockholders in RKO and Pathé lost their shirts in the merger. All that money had to go somewhere, however, and insiders around Kennedy were discovered to have made millions on the merger. (Kennedy later commented that corporations in the 1920s were run for the benefit of management, not stockholders.)

Lehman Brothers, J.P. Morgan, and Goldman, Sachs & Co. were also involved with RKO. RCA eventually sold control of RKO to Atlas Corp. investment trust and Lehman Brothers. Radio City held a minority interest in RKO, adding to the Rockefeller involvement. The reclusive billionaire Howard Hughes eventually owned RKO. The Cravath law firm represented RKO and Paramount. Paramount was financed by Kuhn, Loeb (bank of Lewis Strauss, who was Eisenhower's Commerce Secretary). JFK's father was a Paramount consultant in 1936, and his Hayden, Stone & Co. Bank was involved with Warner Brothers.

Real Estate

Luther Hodges (JFK and LBJ Commerce, father of Carter Deputy Commerce) was vice president of Marshall Field & Company. Ca. 1930

Field spent $28,000,000 (approximately $448,000,000 in 2091 buying power) to build Chicago's Merchandise Mart. The Mart did poorly, in part due to the Great Depression. At the end of World War II Field was thirsty for cash. Although Field claimed the Mart was then worth $21,000,000 ($980,000,000 in 2019 buying power), it was sold to President Kennedy's father for $13,000,000. The father, however, only paid $500,000. The rest of the price was supplied by Equitable Life Assurance Society as a mortgage loan. Kennedy's father boosted his equity by $4,000,000 when he refinanced the purchase with Prudential Insurance Co. of America for $17,000,000 in 1949 ($187,000,000 in 2019 buying power). Sargent Shriver (1972 Democratic vice presidential nominee, brother-in-law of JFK) ran the Mart for the Kennedy family in the 1940s and 1950s. The Mart building was valued at $75,000,000 in 1963 ($622,500,000 in 2019 buying power) and was then producing $13,000,000 a year in rents. In 1977 the building was valued at $150,000,000, producing $20,000,000 in rental income. Ca. 1976 the Joseph P. Kennedy, Jr. Foundation had a $16,700,000 mortgage on the Mart.

In the 1950s a U.S. Senate Committee investigating organized crime became suspicious of an office building. The committee's chief counsel Robert Kennedy (JFK and LBJ AG) issued a subpoena to discover whether the building was owned by criminal elements. When the subpoena was served on the building superintendent he said, "I take my orders from the father, not the boys." The structure was one of an undisclosed number owned by the Kennedy family, an ownership so confidential that even the innermost family members were kept ignorant of details.

Textiles

Luther Hodges (JFK and LBJ Commerce, father of Carter Deputy Commerce) had thirty years or more experience in textiles before joining the cabinet. As a child he worked sixty hours a week as an office boy for a Marshall Field & Co. plant in Spray, NC. The pay was five cents an hour. Hodges attended a company school. After graduating from college he became secretary to the general manager of the eight Marshall Field mills in the Leaksville–Spray area. This was in 1919, for a $1,000 salary ($13,550 in 2019 buying power). The next year Hodges became a personnel manager. In 1927 he was manager of a blanket mill. In 1938 Hodges became general manager of all Marshall Field mills—there were twenty-nine in America and abroad. Hodges became vice president of Marshall Field in 1943. The next year he headed the Office of Price Administration's textile division (which set the price of goods during the wartime emergency). In 1950 Hodges was making $75,000 a year as a Marshall Field executive ($768,750 in 2019 buying power). Ca. 1961 Hodges had a $500,000 "nest egg" ($4,250,000 in 2019 buying power)

Insurance Again

As noted above, Prudential Insurance funded the Merchandise Mart purchase for JFK's father. Prudential vice president J. Edward day became President Kennedy's Postmaster General. Day had also been Illinois state commissioner of insurance. John A. Hartford (A&P grocery head who had bankrolled FDR's son) was a Prudential director. The insurance company's chief counsel was the Shearman & Sterling firm, in which William Rockefeller was a partner.

John Connally (JFK Navy, Nixon Treasury) directed Insurance Securities, Inc. and owned 26,000 shares of common stock. This was a mutual trust fund management company operating solely in California, with only insurance stock in its portfolio. Connally paid $5 a share for this unlisted stock which had no par value and no ready market. He said, "I don't know what it is worth."

Chapter 21

Aviation

John McCone (JFK and LBJ CIA) was a Los Angeles millionaire and therefore probably knew his successor William Raborn (LBJ CIA) who was vice president of General Tire & Rubber Co.'s subsidiary Aerojet General Corp. of Los Angeles. Harold Brown (Carter Defense) was counsel for Aerojet General.

In World War II future President Nixon (Eisenhower VP) negotiated Navy contracts with Bell and with Glenn Martin aviation companies. Roswell Gilpatric (JFK Deputy Defense) assigned the X-22 VTOL plane contract to Bell Aerosystems Development Co., a subdivision of Bell Aerospace. This was after Gilpatric had been advised by Harold Brown (Carter Defense) that Douglas Aircraft had a better and cheaper design. Frederick Korth was a Bell Aerospace Corp. director. Korth was also Bell's banker—president of Continental National Bank of Ft. Worth, TX. Korth promoted business for Continental on Navy stationery. Bell Aersopace was a division of Textron, headed by G. William Miller (Carter Treasury) who was a member of Gilpatric's law firm.

Boeing director William Batten was credited with putting Juanita Krebs (Carter Commerce) on the J.C. Penney board. Boeing wanted the TFX plane contract and would seem to have had an edge in the competition since the Defense Dept.'s technical experts favored Boeing's design over that of General Dynamics. The experts felt pressured to change their opinions and to favor General Dynamics. One protested to Director of Research & Engineering Harold Brown (Carter Defense). The pressure was coming from one of Vice President Lyndon Johnson's men who worked under Cyrus Vance (Carter State). Johnson's desires gave powerful support to General Dynamics. For one thing, Boeing's plants were in the states of Washington and Kansas, small electoral vote states which had gone for Nixon in 1960. General Dynamics plants were in the big electoral vote states of New York and Texas which had gone for Johnson in 1960. (They went for

JFK, too, but LBJ probably took the results more personally.) So giving the TFX contract to General Dynamics could also give business, unions, and voters a message. LBJ appeared at the General Dynamics Ft. Worth factory amid cheers and signs crediting the contract to him.

Ft. Worth was the home of Frederick Korth's (JFK Navy) Continental National Bank, where General Dynamics had a corporate account. Continental participated in a $200,000,000 bail out of General Dynamics arranged by Chase Manhattan Bank in 1962. While Navy Secretary, Korth retained $160,000 of Continental stock. Safety of the Continental loan, and the value of the stock, depended on what business General Dynamics could get. Continental told Secretary Korth of its wish for General Dynamics to get the TFX plane contract. In TFX negotiations Korth officially met with Boeing representatives twice, with General Dynamics sixteen times.

As mentioned earlier, Roswell Gilpatric (JFK Deputy Defense) helped Korth's Bell Aerospace Corp. in the X-22 VTOL plane contract. Gilpatric also helped General Dynamics get the TFX contract. He was a General Dynamics lawyer and attended eighteen General Dynamics board meetings from 1958, when Pace (Truman Army) was General Dynamics president, through 1960. Gilpatric informally advised on the choice of General Dynamics's chief executive officer in 1961 and 1962. Although a member of the Cravath law firm, for a time Gilpatric worked out of an office in the General Dynamics headquarters building. When he joined the subcabinet Gilpatric turned the General Dynamics legal work over to the Cravath firm's senior partner. While in the subcabinet Gilpatric received $20,000 a year from the Cravath firm (about $168,000 in 2019 buying power), and he later rejoined the firm full time. After General Dynamics got the TFX contract the Cravath firm's senior partner quickly became a General Dynamics director. President Carter's associate Packard (Nixon Deputy Defense) was a General Dynamics director.

Automobiles

William Whitney (Cleveland Navy) and others controlled an automobile manufacturer called Columbia & Electric Vehicle Co. He and others also controlled Pope Manufacturing Co., an electric auto concern. Whitney was executive committee chairman of Columbia Automobile Co. and was involved with Electric Storage Battery Co. of Philadelphia (Exide). Electric Storage Battery Co. was the biggest storage battery manufacturer in the world, with its batteries used in several industries besides automobiles. Whitney secretly had Metropolitan Street Ry. Co. buy over $1,000,000 of Electric Storage Battery stock.

Whitney was a key figure in Association of American Licensed Automobile Manufacturers. This was an attempt to control patents for the entire industry—a monopoly by license and lawsuit rather than by manufacturing plants and financial maneuvers. Henry Ford balked at this, and Whitney's operation tried to ruin Ford by threatening his *customers* with patent infringement suits. Ford was almost unknown at the time but got help from one of the biggest names in American merchandising—John Wanamaker (B. Harrison PG). Wanamaker guaranteed to protect Ford's customers from lawsuits, and this protective action busted Whitney's attempt at monopoly. Wanamaker became Ford's New York agent.

Ford owned iron mines, steel mills, coking coal operations, and limestone deposits—partially illustrating the sweep of the automobile industry across others. The son-in-law of Charles Evans Hughes (Harding State) was vice president and general counsel of Ford Motor Co. The Dulles (Eisenhower State and grandson of B. Harrison State) law firm assisted Ford Motor Co. stock transactions of the Ford Foundation. John J. McCloy (FDR Assistant War) was foundation chairman. Persons from Chase National Bank, First National City Bank, and Morgan Guaranty Trust were key figures in the foundation. Goldman, Sachs helped finance installment buying for Ford car purchasers, and at that time the head of Goldman, Sachs was a Ford Motor Co. director.

In 1940 Robert McNamara (JFK and LBJ Defense) left a job at Price, Waterhouse & Co. accountants to teach at Harvard. There he gave a group of Army officers special management training in statistical control, whereby Army Air Force manpower and materiel requirements could be closely estimated a year in advance. McNamara himself then joined the group as a captain. After the war, this group of officers decided to sell themselves, as a unit, to some corporation looking for management expertise. Ford took them. McNamara was second in command of the team, with a $12,000 salary. Eventually McNamara became president of Ford. When McNamara was appointed as Secretary of Defense his pay as Ford's president was about $500,000 a year ($4,300,000 in 2019 buying power), and five of the original group of Army officers were still top Ford executives. Before joining the cabinet McNamara had the right to exercise a stock option for 10,000 shares at $47 per share. Since the current share price then was $69 this meant a tidy profit. McNamara said, however, that he wouldn't exercise the option. He would still continue to receive money from Ford as a cabinet member, from $170,000 in 1961 ($1,445,000 in 2019 buying power) to $24,500 in 1966 ($190,000 in 2019 buying power). These were payments for past services. The U.S. Senate did make McNamara sell all his Ford stock and refrain from buying stock in any company doing business with the Defense Department. Robert Kennedy (JFK and LBJ AG, brother of JFK) informed McNamara that he could technically abide by the Senate's requirement and yet still keep the Ford stock within McNamara's family. McNamara, however, preferred a straightforward sale that met the spirit as well as the letter of the requirement. The stock went for $1,500,000 in December 1960 ($12,900,000 in 2019 buying power). McNamara figured he would lose $3,000,000 over his first three or four years as Secretary of Defense.

Marine Industry Again

The father of President Kennedy was chairman of the U.S. Maritime Commission in 1937. In 1939 John McCone (JFK and LBJ CIA) and the "Six Companies" consortium (which built Hoover Dam) formed Seattle–Tacoma Shipbuilding Corp. The corporation produced merchant ships for the U.S. Maritime Commission and the British government. In World War II McCone helped establish and was president of California Shipbuilding Corp.—which was incorporated in Delaware but operated in Los Angeles, CA. Reports vary on the corporation's financing and profitability. McCone's own statements suggest that California Shipbuilding started with $100,000 subscribed in capital stock and $700,000 in subordinated stockholder loans (subordinated to all other obligations of the corporation). "About a year later," McCone stated, "when the Todd Shipyards Corp. retired, we declared a dividend of $1 million, 50% of which was paid in cash to the retiring stockholder, who owned 50% of the stock, incidentally." A questioner asked, "In other words, he got $500,000 for his initial investment of $50,000?" McCone replied, "That is correct," and went on to say, "Then the other 50% was paid in the form of a stock dividend, thereby increasing the stock from $100,000 to $600,000."[103] Eventually capitalization was raised to $3,300,000 plus bank credits of $4,000,000. Reportedly California Shipbuilding Corp. got a $44,000,000 profit while using $25,000,000 of U.S. government–furnished facilities. McCone disagreed, saying the profit was good but not that good. California Shipbuilding produced 475 ships and employed 45,000 workers.

McCone was also involved with Pacific Tankers, Inc., which operated a big fleet of Pacific Navy oil tankers in cooperation with Standard Oil of California. McCone was a Standard of California director and owned about $1,000,000 of stock. McCone was director of Marinship Corp. and Oregon Shipbuilding Corp. He owned Joshua Hendy Corp., a marine shipping corporation which McCone described as his primary personal business when he was nominated as CIA director. Joshua Hendy Corp. moved bulk cargos (oil, iron ore). Formerly the company was named Joshua Hendy Iron Works. At that time it made heavy equipment for ships.. McCone became company president and switched the company to transporting ore from South America and oil throughout the Pacific. In 1945 McCone established Pacific Far East Line for trade with Japan, China, and the Philippines. Joshua Hendy Co. did business with Standard Oil of New Jersey, Standard Oil of California, Union Oil, Dow Chemical, and Kaiser Aluminum. Those firms which did business with McCone's company also commonly did business with the Atomic Energy Commission when McCone was AEC chairman. Six weeks before McCone became AEC chairman the Commerce Department awarded the *Savannah* nuclear powered merchant vessel contract to States Marine Line in which McCone and business associates were involved. Sequoia Corp. was owned 50–50 by Kaiser Aluminum and Trans-World Carriers. Trans-World Carriers was owned 50% by Global Bulk (100% owned by States Marine), 25% by Joshua Hendy (100% owned by McCone), and 25% by San Marino Corp. of Panama (85% owned by McCone). McCone acknowledged that these marine corporations tended to blend together. States Marine had joint arrangements with Joshua Hendy Steamship line and affiliates. States Marine and San Marino Corp. had a working relationship with Naviors ships, a United States Steel subsidiary.

Rockefeller Foundation

Rockefeller Foundation trustees included Ray Wilbur (Hoover Interior, brother of Coolidge Navy), Robert Lovett (Truman Defense), Clifford Hardin (Nixon Agriculture), and Robert Roosa (Carter associate). President Carter's associate Lane Kirkland was a director of the foundation's Appalachian Regional Planning Commission, which Joseph Califano (Carter HEW) was also involved with. Rockefeller Foundation chairmen included John Foster Dulles (Eisenhower State, brother of JFK CIA) and Cyrus Vance (Carter State). Through the influence of Dulles, Dean Rusk (JFK and LBJ State) was made foundation president. Rusk received what was called severance pay from the foundation while he was in the cabinet. The experience of a "little magazine" produced an example of foundation thinking. The magazine needed money desperately and turned to the Rockefeller Foundation. The foundation responded that it was concerned about the effect on American democracy if such little magazines died. Therefore the Rockefeller Foundation would commission a study on the topic. The magazine in question managed to struggle along without Rockefeller Foundation money for four years while the foundation studied the impact on American democracy. Eventually the foundation granted some money to the magazine. "'Do you think it would make them [the little magazines] soft,' President Rusk once asked a visitor, 'if they knew where their next subsidy was coming from?' The visitor said he didn't. Dean Rusk looked thoughtful."[104] When asked about the burden of turning down most of the pleas for help Rusk responded, "You just have to get toughened to it."[105]

Chapter 22

LBJ

President Lyndon Johnson (JFK VP) was poor in his young manhood. In 1928 he was making $128 a month as a schoolteacher. He became private secretary to U.S. Rep. Richard Kleberg, whose mother was Alice Gertrudis King of King Ranch fame. The King family liked Johnson, and later his brother was Kleberg's secretary. Such connections did no harm to Johnson's political career in Texas. The Great Depression caused him no financial difficulty, but his entry into Congress was costly. Johnson managed to borrow $10,000 from his father-in-law to finance the first election campaign (about $180,000 in 2019 buying power). As a member of Congress LBJ paid off this loan at $500 a month. Since his salary was $833 a month this made things financially tight. In that pre-plastic bottle era, Johnson's wife was reduced to picking up empty glass bottles in the street and taking them to a grocery store to collect bottle deposits. Contrary to later popular impression, the wife wasn't particularly wealthy. By 1942 the extent of her inheritance was $21,000. Aunt Effie Taylor picked up many of the young couple's bills in Washington, and the aunt also made the down payment on their first house. Things changed by the time Johnson LBJ became Vice President. As VP he bought a Washington house. Johnson said he spent $300,000 on remodeling it ($2,500,000 in 2019 buying power), plus another $100,000 a year beyond the Vice-Presidential salary of $35,000 and expense account of $10,000. He had no financial difficulty in doing this. He was probably the richest President until the twenty-first century, surpassing JFK who himself had over $10,000,000 ($84,000,000 in 2019 buying power). Ostensibly President Johnson's business affairs were handled by trustees who kept him uninformed about their activity. Businessmen reported, however, that the big change after JFK's murder was that instead of dealing directly with the Vice President they now dealt directly with the President. Johnson's wealth in 1964 was around $14,000,000 ($114,800,000 in 2019 buying power).

Johnson's career owed much to oil, real estate, and broadcasting.

Brown & Root

In 1962 Brown & Root (a Texas contractor enterprise) got the Project Mohole contract, a federally funded drilling experiment which could yield valuable information to the oil industry. Brown & Root got the contract even though the company was not the first choice of the National Science Foundation. Also in 1962 Brown & Root had $21,000,000 of business in South Vietnam. In a few years more the Vietnam total was well over $1 billon. To account for such good fortune one is drawn to the firm's long-standing intimacy with Lyndon Johnson. Even in his days as a U.S. Representative, Johnson was already doing Brown & Root favors in return for use of their private airplane, free office space in Austin's Brown Building, and earnest help at election time. Such cooperation may have been typical for that era, but an Internal Revenue Bureau investigation began. In 1944 LBJ and Brown & Root attorney Alvin J. Wirtz (FDR Undersecretary of Interior) met with President Roosevelt, who squelched the investigation at LBJ's request.[106]

Real Estate

Lyndon Johnson's real estate deals, like all his business interests, were complex. While he was a member of Congress during World War II, his wife and father-in-law owned land near Karnack, TX. The federal government decided to build an ordnance plant there, on that very spot. On July 27, 1942, Johnson and his wife gave up all their interests in the property. LBJ's father-in-law and mother-in-law then sold the land to the federal government nine days later for $70,000 ($1,050,000 in 2019 buying power). Moreover, the plant was built just a few hundred yards from the in-laws' general store (conveniently located for trade from plant workers).

While serving as Kennedy's vice President, LBJ added to his wife's 3,800 acres of Alabama pine lands. Also while Vice President, LBJ added 12,000 acres to his ranch lands at a price of $1,500,000 ($12,600,000 in 2019 buying power). Johnson bought another 4,000 acres in his first year as President, with an option for 6,000 more. U.S. government dams helped raise the value of some holdings. As Vice President, Johnson and business associate A.W. Moursand bought 4,718 acres from Texas Christian University, where Frederick Korth (JFK Navy) was a trustee. The price was $500,000—$200,000 down and a ten year note due in 1971 for $300,000 at five percent interest. LBJ and Moursand then sold 242.7 acres of this land to Comanche Cattle Corp. for $326,660. Moursand ran Comanche Cattle Corp. for LBJ and himself. LBJ and Moursand then peddled about 100 lots at $6,000 to $7,000 each. LBJ got the Texas Highway Dept. to build a $275,000 bridge across the Llano River to improve access to and value of the land.

Broadcasting

In January 1939 James G. Ulmer, who already ran at least six Texas radio stations via Texas Broadcasting Co., got a Federal Communications Commission permit to build KTBC in Austin. One story says Ulmer agreed to sell KTBC to J.M. West for $125,000 ($2,285,000 in 2019 buying power). The European war broke out during negotiations, and Ulmer reduced the price to $87,000 to overcome West's war jitters. Another version says that Ulmer sold KTBC to Robert Anderson (Eisenhower Treasury) and two other men, and that they sold KTBC to the West family for $87,500. At some point Anderson was definitely involved with KTBC, and either way the West family got it—almost. The day the West family signed the purchase contract was the same day that FDR appointed James Lawrence Fly FCC chairman. Fly was from Dallas and was a vigorous New Dealer. The elder West and his lawyer Dan Moody were vigorous critics of FDR and his Texas protégé Lyndon Johnson. The various opposing gentlemen were itching to do dirt to one another. The FCC began dragging approval of the sale, but West was confident about the course of justice and offered Ulmer $750,000 for the other stations ($13,500,000 in 2019 buying power). In February 1940, the FCC revoked the licenses of all Ulmer's stations. This was an incredible action, as the FCC almost never yanks a commercial station broadcasting license, let alone a whole string of them. This was a financial blow to Ulmer. Being no dummy, Ulmer surely knew what was going on and indeed contacted LBJ's friend Alvin J. Wirtz (FDR Undersecretary of Interior). This was the same Wirtz who four years later would help LBJ convince FDR to squelch an Internal Revenue investigation of LBJ's political finances. Wirtz agreed to be Ulmer's lawyer and handle FCC approval of the sale of KTBC to the West family. Wirtz, however, did nothing for Ulmer. West died in 1942, and Ulmer's financial situation was now critical. LBJ demanded that Wirtz get KTBC for Johnson. After some wheelin' and dealin', LBJ's wife got KTBC for about $16,500. Wirtz grossly exaggerated her business experience to the FCC and said her net worth was $65,000 (about $1,170,000 in 2019 buying power). LBJ's wife told more than one story on how she got the $16,500—once saying it was a bank loan, once saying it was from a settlement of her mother's estate. The FCC approved the sale to LBJ's wife in twenty-three days, after holding up the sale to West nearly four years. Texas Broadcasting Co. was renamed LBJ Co. Publicly Johnson claimed to have no involvement with KTBC, saying it was all his wife's operation. For tax purposes, however, he claimed part ownership. In fact he was the boss.

LBJ was determined to keep KTBC non-union. In 1945 he even posted men with guns, including the brother of John Connally (JFK Navy, Nixon Treasury), to discourage labor union organizers at KTBC. Later U.S. Senator Johnson voted for the anti-union Taft–Hartley bill and for override of the veto.

With the help of John Connally and Connally's brother, Johnson got FCC approval for starting KVET in Austin. Ostensibly this was a 1,000-watt station organized by ten World War II veterans to compete with KTBC, with John Connally as president and general manager. Documents submitted to the FCC were designed to hide LBJ's involvement. (In that era the owner of a radio station was forbidden to hold any interest in a competing station in the same town.) KVET was nonetheless a Johnson operation, working from a building owned by Johnson and even using KTBC employees. The FCC gave KVET very favorable consideration then and afterward. The Civil Aeronautics Administration was also friendly (important due to regulations on tower height). Johnson's White House aide Walter Jenkins was a KVET stockholder.

In 1948 the FCC imposed a freeze on new television station licenses. The freeze ended in 1952. By that time LBJ was on the Senate committee which handled FCC matters. Moreover, the nephew of Johnson's Texas friend Sam Rayburn (Speaker of the U.S. House of Representatives) was an FCC commissioner. LBJ's wife quickly got the only VHF allocation in Austin. (At that time there were two kinds of broadcast television transmitters, VHF for channels 2–13 and UHF for channels 14–83.) No one else had been able to get an Austin VHF permit. In 1952 Johnson pressured the FCC to give him the license for KWTX-TV (VHF) in Waco, TX. At the same time his wife had applied for KANG-TV (UHF) in Waco. The LBJ Co. acquired KANG and put the competitive screws to KWTX, which had gone to another applicant. To better appreciate what happened, one should realize that almost no TV sets could receive UHF signals in 1952. Johnson's KANG should have been a hopeless money loser, as no advertiser would buy commercials on a station that no one would watch. Thus Johnson's KANG should have been quickly snuffed out by VHF competitor KWTX. Instead things worked out the other way around. CBS suddenly canceled plans to make KWTX an affiliate and switched to Johnson's KANG. ABC did the same. This ruined KWTX's viewership, making the station far less attractive to advertisers. The network affiliations also motivated people to install UHF adapters on their TV sets, increasing KANG's viewership and its attractiveness to advertisers. Since, at that time, commercial networks had a "firm rule" against having UHF affiliates, clearly the networks were cooperating with U.S. Senator Johnson, whose Senate committee dealt with FCC. The FCC then hurt KWTX with a transmitter ruling that favored LBJ. KWTX officials knew what was happening and asked the FCC and the Justice Department to take action against Johnson. Nothing happened. An LBJ representative then informed KWTX that Johnson would ruin them. A KWTX representative met with Johnson personally and asked for surrender terms. LBJ demanded controlling interest in KWTX and a large share of its radio operation in Waco. In return he would give them the TV network affiliations. Note that LBJ knew he could order around CBS and ABC with impunity. KWTX agreed. LBJ then shut down KANG, boosting KWTX's viewership and advertising revenues.

KWTX later bought 75% of a Sherman, TX, television operation, 78.9% of Victoria Broadcasters (Victoria, TX, radio), and 50% of Brasos Broadcasting Co. (Bryan, TX, television). The FCC then permitted the Bryan station to switch from educational to commercial, contrary to the FCC's "firm rule" against such a change.

The man who owned KRGV–TV (Weslaco, TX) needed money. The FCC granted permission for the owner to get a loan from Lyndon Johnson in return for fifty percent of KRGV's stock. LBJ Co. soon accomplished a complete takeover and paid the former owner as a consultant for $25,000 a year for five years. Possibly this was a tax dodge. Instead of paying taxes on $125,000 of capital investment, LBJ Co. could write off $125,000 as a business expense.

Johnson was also heavily involved with Texoma Broadcasting in Ardmore, OK. While Johnson was Vice President, his KTBC got a special FCC exemption to move the transmitter to increase the potential viewership by 65,000 persons. This made KTBC even more attractive to advertisers. As President, Johnson also gained control of KLFY–TV in Lafayette, LA.

When Johnson became President, LBJ Co. was renamed Texas Broadcasting Co., apparently to reduce notice of his involvement. Around Christmas of 1963 the new President was having earnest foreign policy discussions with Germany's Chancellor Erhard at the LBJ Ranch. At the same time LBJ was talking with cable television executives at the ranch. This involved Capital Cable, a subsidiary of Midwest Video of Little Rock, AR. The president of Midwest Video was the senior member of U.S. Sen. John McClellan's law firm. McClellan was chairman of the Senate Operations Committee and chairman of its permanent Subcommittee on Investigations. Thus McClellan was a key figure in how deeply the Senate would investigate the scandalous activities of LBJ's intimate associate Bobby Baker. The end result, with a favorable FCC ruling which stymied competitors, was that LBJ got a multimillion-dollar deal at little expense to himself. President Johnson later lied about his interactions with Capital Cable, possibly due to his customary secretiveness about business dealings. LBJ also got the Austin city council's permit to be the city's cable television operator.

In Johnson's lifetime cable television was in its infancy, but LBJ had already sniffed its potential and positioned himself to profit from it.

Johnson was intently involved with LBJ Co.'s profit-sharing plan. Ostensibly this was a fund to help employees. Yet it had the appearance of a different purpose—a means for LBJ Co. to acquire bank stock, mining property, oil and gas operations, and to provide outsiders with loans. In 1963 dozens of Johnson's employees resorted to court action to try to find out what had happened to $50,000 to $75,000 of the profit-sharing plan's funds.

LBJ's Johnson Foundation was established in 1956, ostensibly to donate to worthy causes. Despite this alleged purpose the foundation accumulated eleven times as much money in 1963 than was given away.

To most Americans of the twentieth century television was synonymous with the three commercial networks NBC, CBS, and ABC. As Assistant Secretary of the Navy in 1919 future President Franklin Roosevelt halted General Electric's sale of technology to Britain's Marconi operation. This led to formation of Radio Corporation of America that year, created by General Electric and controlled by GE and Westinghouse. United Fruit and General Motors were also involved with RCA. Indeed, ca. 1930 RCA, GE, and Westinghouse owned forty-nine percent of General Motors Radio Corporation. RCA was an international trust planning to merge with International Telephone and Telegraph (ITT). RCA controlled RKO (motion picture company of JFK's father) and National Broadcasting Company. NBC directors included Newton Baker (Wilson War) and Lewis Strauss (Hoover Pvt. secretary and Eisenhower Commerce). Jane Pfeiffer (Carter Arms Control and Disarmament Agency adviser) was NBC's chairman. Lawyers for NBC's parent corporation RCA included John Griggs (McKinley AG) and Joseph Cotton (Hoover Undersecretary of State). RCA directors included John Griggs (McKinley AG), Newton Baker (Wilson War), Paul Cravath (law partner of Harding State), Charles Dawes (Coolidge VP), and Lewis Strauss (Hoover Pvt. secretary, Eisenhower Commerce). Ca. 1935 President Kennedy's father had a key role in financing RCA. Clark Clifford (Truman adviser, LBJ Defense) had some sort of relationship with RCA. Felix Rohatyn of Lazard Fréres Wall Street investment bankers (whose senior partner was a top Kennedy family financial adviser) was an RCA director, as was his fellow Lazard Fréres partner Donald Petrie. Petrie was also chairman of ITT's executive committee.

Chase Manhattan controlled blocs of ITT, ABC, NBC, and CBS stock.

Even though Chase Manhattan didn't own the stock, but rather managed it for owners, the bank could vote it. This showed it's unnecessary to own stock in a corporation in order to control it.

Ca. 1936 CBS was controlled by the brother of GE's head (a CBS connection with NBC via RCA), representatives of Lehman Brothers (in which FDR's lieutenant governor Herbert Lehman—a relative of RCA's David Sarnoff—was partner and which purchased control of RCA's subsidiary RKO movies), representatives of Brown Brothers. Harriman & Co. (associated with Truman Commerce), and others. Robert Lovett (Truman Defense) and Roswell Gilpatric (JFK Deputy Defense) were CBS directors. President Carter's associate Arthur Taylor was president of CBS, Inc. Ca. 1965 CBS News President Richard Salant worked with Zbigniew Brzezinski (Carter National Security Adviser) on CIA propaganda broadcasts to Red China.

Chapter 23

Richard Nixon

President Nixon's (Eisenhower VP) family was financially comfortable until two of his brothers died of illness. The medical bills devastated the family. Nixon took work as a farm laborer, janitor, and carnival pitchman to help out. Nixon later prospered as a lawyer in Whittier, CA.

Some of future President Nixon's law clients were orange wholesalers. Ca. 1938 they talked him into joining a $10,000 frozen orange juice venture (about $180,000 in 2019 buying power). Two big distributers were willing to take all of Citra-Frost corporation's output, but the technical problem of preserving juice after freezing was insurmountable. This was why Citra-Frost failed, although some participants preferred to blame Nixon's business shortcomings.

During World War II Nixon decided to learn poker, becoming so good that he won perhaps $3,500, enough money to start his political career. Pots ran over $1,000 a game. President Eisenhower was an excellent card player—so good that he quit playing with his subordinates, feeling it unethical to win so much from them. He made an exception for Nixon, inviting the Vice President for a weekend in the country. The letter of invitation gave Nixon directions on how to drive himself there, closing with an instruction to show the letter to the guard at the gate, so the guard would know Nixon was really the Vice President and allow him to pass. A weekend of indignities climaxed with a rigged card game in which Eisenhower and some buddies fleeced Nixon.

In 1946 Nixon's estate included $10,000 in government bonds ($120,000 in 2019 buying power), $14,000 life insurance, $3,000 in savings, and a used Ford. Millionaire Californians picked up $16,000 to $17,000 of Nixon's expenses from 1950 to 1952. None of that money went to Nixon personally. This was the famous "Nixon fund," not necessarily unusual in that era. Adlai Stevenson (1952 and 1956 Democratic Presidential nominee) also had such a fund, run more loosely than Nixon's.

As a Wall Street lawyer in the 1960s Nixon owned the entire fifth floor of a 5th Avenue apartment building overlooking Central Park. He bought it for $135,000 and paid $10,000 a year maintenance. Nelson Rockefeller (Ford VP) was a neighbor. Nixon's estate in the mid–1960s was $500,000.

Nixon said he sold all his stock and owned only real estate as President. In 1968 Nixon had $350,000 of stock in the Florida resort Fisher Island on Biscayne Bay ($2,525,000 in 2019 buying power). In February 1969 Bebe Rebezo (Nixon associate) sold Nixon's stock for a $180,000 profit ($1,225,000 in 2019 buying power). In 1969, with help from businessman Robert Abplanalp and from the brother-in-law of H.R. Haldeman (Nixon adviser) Nixon bought an estate in San Clemente, CA, for $1,500,000 ($10,200,000 in 2019 buying power). Nixon paid $200,000 down. The next year Abplanalp created C. & G. Investment Co. that paid Nixon $1,250,000 for vacant land on the estate. That left him owing only $50,000 on the mansion and surrounding acreage. Nixon's close friend C.G. (Bebe) Rebezo was a partner in C. & G. Investment Co. The auditing firm Nixon used for San Clemente estate matters evolved from a firm whose top officers violated federal law but were pardoned by Nixon. By August 1973 Nixon had used about $2,500,000 of taxpayers' money to upgrade the estate. He said that after he was dead and no longer needed the estate, the federal government could have it. His implication was that spending federal money on the estate was therefore okay. In 1979 Nixon sold the estate to "California businessmen" for an undisclosed sum. Nixon then tried to buy a $925,000 Fifth Avenue condominium in New York, but gave up after objections from neighborhood residents. He then paid $750,000 for a twelve-room house on East 65th Street, next-door to David Rockefeller (Carter associate, brother of Ford VP) and adjoining the residence of Arthur Schlesinger, Jr. (JFK adviser).

Chile

The Nixon administration's hostility toward the election of Salvador Allende in Chile is well known, but United States involvement in Chile long predates Nixon. U.S. engineers were already active there ca. 1855, building railroads, bridges, mines, smelters, gristmills, public buildings, warehouses, among other things. George Boutwell (Grant State) and John Foster (B. Harrison State, relative of Eisenhower CIA) were lawyers for the Chilean government in the 1890s when the United States was considering military intervention there. John Schofield (A. Johnson War) might well have been commanded to lead such an attack. He recalled

> I was asked to make an estimate of the military force which would be necessary to occupy and hold a vital point in Chilean territory until the demands of the United States were complied with. It was assumed, of course, that the navy could easily do all the rest. Pending the consideration of this subject, so disagreeable to me, I had a dream which I repeated at the time to a few intimate friends. I saw in the public street a man holding a mangy-looking dog by the neck, and beating him with a great club, while a crowd of people assembled to witness the "sport." Some one asked the man why he was beating the poor dog. He replied: "Oh just to make him yelp." But the dog did not "yelp." He bore his cruel punishment without a whine. Then he was transformed into a splendid animal, one of the noblest of his species, and the entire crowd of bystanders, with one accord, rushed in and compelled the man to desist from beating him.[107]

U.S. copper interests entered Chile as the twentieth century began, in the form of Braden Copper Company, Kennecott, and Anaconda. J.P. Morgan, Andrew Mellon's (Hoover Treasury) associate H.C. Frick, and Ogden Mills (Hoover Treasury) formed the Cerro Copper company.

Edward Korry (U.S. ambassador to Chile in the Lyndon Johnson and Richard Nixon administrations) testified that the U.S. government and multinational corporations cooperated in secret activities there. Korry said Robert Kennedy (JFK and LBJ AG) oversaw a special White House group coordinating covert political planning regarding Chile with a Latin American business group established by President Carter's associate David Rockefeller (brother of Ford VP). In 1963 President Kennedy specifically asked David Rockefeller to establish the business group. According to Korry, Robert Kennedy okayed global corporations' use of bribery, funding of Chilean political parties, and similar practices to prevent Salvador Allende from becoming president of Chile. In August 1971 John Connally (JFK Navy, Nixon Treasury) took charge of anti–Allende operations, which increased as Allende's government began nationalizing American businesses operating in Chile. Nationalization (as opposed to confiscation) meant that the American owners received financial compensation from the Allende government. Moreover, a federal agency insured the American companies against nationalization, and claims were paid off. Any loss wasn't absorbed by the companies or their stockholders. Global corporations hamstringing the Allende regime weren't protecting their assets, but merely having revenge. At an October 1971 meeting with executives from global corporations William Rogers (Eisenhower AG, Nixon State) explained, "The Nixon Administration is a business Administration. Its mission is to protect business." With American approval the Chilean military overthrew Allende in a coup.

China Again

In 1970 David Rockefeller's (Carter associate, brother of Ford VP) Chase Manhattan Bank established facilities in New York to deal with Red

China. He also set up Chase Pacific Trade Advisors, Inc. to handle negotiations between U.S. corporations and the Red Chinese government. These moves seemed daring, as there were no foreseeable business transactions between the United States and Red China. It was almost as if Rockefeller were aware that his family's adviser Henry Kissinger (Nixon and Ford State) was conducting secret negotiations with the Chinese Reds which would lead to large business agreements. Chase Pacific Trade Advisors was the first U.S. corporation allowed to operate in Red China. National Council for U.S.–China trade, established by Rockefeller, was already financing projects in Red China (via Chase Manhattan) for the Chinese government. U.S. textile firms were especially interested in having production facilities moved to Red China, a "workers' paradise" far from OSHA, where textile laborers in sweatshops received pay of about a dollar a day. Similar conditions in Taiwan may have had much to do with U.S. support of the Nationalist government. Note that as the labor supply grew tight in Taiwan, forcing wages up, the United States government suddenly became interested in normalizing relations with the government controlling access to Red China's cheap labor.

Gerald Ford

President Ford's (Nixon VP) father and another man started Ford Paint & Vanish Company in 1929. The elder Ford's business got through the Great Depression okay. The family sold out eventually. Future President Ford got about $13,000 from sale of stock in August 1969 ($88,400 in 2019 buying power). In 1974 Ford still owned about $9,000 in debenture bonds ($45,000 in 2019 buying power). His brother remained company president under the new owners. Ca. 1940 future President Ford was a successful male model, with his own agency in New York. Ca. 1968 Ford briefly directed Old Kent Bank & Trust Company (Grand Rapids, MI) which paid a $1,000 annual salary. Ford bought 100 shares at about $31 a share, got a five-share dividend, sold all, and broke even. In 1973 Ford's net worth was just over $250,000 ($1,250,000 in 2019 buying power). This included houses in Virginia, Michigan, and Colorado.

Chapter 24

Jimmy Carter

President Jimmy Carter's family was affluent. One Carter associate called him the richest kid in town. Jimmy's father Earl was a sharecropper landlord. In the 1920s 200 blacks worked on Carter farms. Jimmy's father got heavy labor from sharecroppers year round, dawn to sundown, with short rest periods to let mules recuperate. Men received $1.00 to $1.25 a day. Women were paid less, children less yet. The father had a general store patronized mainly by his black sharecroppers. Years later the Carter peanut warehouse was known to pay less than minimum wage, and the Carter worm farm dispensed with hourly wages completely. The worm farm used mainly (if not exclusively) black workers and paid them thirty-five cents per 1,000 worms dug. In 1976 one worker with fifteen years' experience became proficient enough to get 5,000 worms an hour and earned about $60 a week.

When still a child Carter bought five "houses" and from 1937 to 1949 rented out two of them for $5 a month, two for $2 a month, and one for $2.50 a month. These "houses" were shacks for black sharecroppers. Carter eventually sold them to the tenants. A survey of Carter's later sharecropper housing found it typical for the genre. One shack had no toilet and no running water. Water dripped through the roof; broken windows were unrepaired; exterior walls were rotting. Jimmy Carter said such buildings "are better houses than the one I grew up in.... I got a lot of requests around the state from people who would like to live in the tenant houses on my farm." Both those assertions were incorrect. President Carter often spoke movingly of his "hard times" on a rural Georgia farm in the Great Depression. In such reminiscences he omitted mention of his family's house servants and private tennis court. The Carters had running water while other town residents had to use a communal well. During the Great Depression, the Carters had motor vehicles, phonograph records, and books. They built a house next to their man-made fishing pond, a house equipped with kitchen appliances and with other amenities such as a jukebox. "We weren't rich," Jimmy Carter's mother said, "but we weren't poor. We lived very, very well in terms of having what we needed—and a little bit more. You take the radio, for instance, and the car. They cost a lot of money for those days, but Earl thought they were important for us to have and so he just bought them. It was always that way for us." The Carters put in electricity as soon as it was available for their house and were the first family in town to own a television set. Carter's uncle said that Earl (Jimmy's father) was almost a millionaire. President Carter himself was a millionaire, and other family members were financially comfortable. For instance one sister and brother-in-law had a town home, vacation cabin, and vacation home in Europe. The Carter family's influence in their region was demonstrated not only by involvement in town, county, and state government (including the long-held family seat in the Georgia senate), but by Carter's appointment to Annapolis during World War II—no small accomplishment.

Coca-Cola

In the early days of the twentieth century a Secretary of Agriculture hindered a lawsuit claiming the Coca-Cola company violated the Pure Food & Drug Act by adding caffeine to the beverage. He first ordered the suit dropped, but retreated under a newspaper editor's pressure. Then the suit was transferred from Washington, D.C., to Chattanooga. Presence of a Coke factory there promoted a trial climate more favorable to Coke, due to the corporation's economic impact on Chattanooga. Coke won the case there, but in 1916 lost in the U.S. Supreme Court, where Justice Hughes (who was the Republican Presidential nominee running against Woodrow Wilson that year) ruled that Coca-Cola had indeed violated the Pure Food & Drug Act by adding caffeine.

Top Coke executive Robert Woodruff supported Newton Baker (Wilson War) for the 1932 Democratic Presidential nomination won by Franklin Roosevelt. Jim Farley (FDR PG) was board chairman of Coca-Cola Export Corporation, president of Boston Coca-Cola Bottling Company, director of Western Coca-Cola Bottling Company, and director of Coca-Cola Bottling Company of Canada, Ltd. President Eisenhower was friends with a top Coke executive by 1950 and hunted on the executive's estate. As President, Ike publicly refused to drink Pepsi and insisted on Coke.

Coca-Cola's international Headquarters was in Atlanta, GA, and President Carter had connections with Coke. His associate Paul Austin was board chairman. Charles Duncan (Carter Energy, Deputy Defense) was president of Coke, and its former Chairman Robert Woodruff said Duncan himself was the most important acquisition when Duncan Coffee Company merged with Coca-Cola. (Woodruff and Austin also directed Morgan Guaranty Trust.) Coke executives and a Coke political committee helped fund Carter's campaigns for governor and President. Governor Carter made heavy use of Coke facilities around the world—Coke made many of his international travel arrangements, and scheduled meetings between the governor and foreign heads of state. Coke also provided company jets and limousines for the governor's travels around the United States. Such trips were vital for Carter, helping him to enter international leadership circles. Coke chairman Austin shook loose New York City money for Carter's 1976 Presidential campaign. Coke's New York ad man did Carter's 1976 campaign television commercials. The law partner of Coca-Cola attorney Joseph Califano (Carter HEW) was John Connally's (Nixon Treasury) lawyer. Carter replaced Pepsi with Coke as the official White House Cola. (Perhaps Pepsi's status was a holdover from the Nixon presidency. Lawyer Nixon represented Pepsi, and Sen. Joseph McCarthy did some work for Pepsi-Cola.)

Austin apparently became a behind-the scenes envoy of the President around the world. For instance in 1977 Austin went to see Carter after making a trip to Cuba, where Austin held discussions with Fidel Castro. (Coke had a multimillion-dollar grievance against Cuba over the nationalization of Coke properties in 1961.) President Carter made a point of holding sugar prices down—a successful policy worth millions of dollars to Coke. Indeed, Sen. Russell Long labeled this sugar policy the "Coca-Cola program." A lawsuit was filed challenging the legality of this sugar policy. The White House removed about twenty relevant documents from regular files, for possible invocation of "executive privilege" (a custom that the President can withhold documents from Congress and the courts). The White House took the only set of these documents. No copies existed. Three months later the Justice Department, headed by Coke lawyer Griffen Bell (Carter AG) told the plaintiffs that the White House had lost the documents. This carelessness may have saved Coke millions.

The President's 1979 vacation on the Mississippi riverboat *Delta Queen* caused an upsurge in travelers using the boat, making the *Delta Queen* appear profitable for the first time since 1976 when Coca-Cola Bottling Company of New York bought the boat.

Coke president Charles Duncan (Carter Energy, Deputy Defense) had no expertise in defense when he came to the Pentagon. Coke lawyer Charles Kirbo explained that Carter wanted to have a "good businessman" in the Defense Department. Duncan was permitted to keep over $13,000,000 in Coke stock ($52,000,000 in 2019 buying power) even though the Defense Department did business with that firm. This was contrary to usual practice.

When an African leader appealed to the Pentagon for arms to repel invaders, the request was turned down. Instead the Pentagon sent $60,000 of Coca-Cola.

Aviation Again

In 1968 an Air Force cost analyst revealed that Lockheed aviation company had received $2 billion more than a contract had called for. (Ironically, this contract, for the C–5A airplane, may have had contributed to Lockheed's financial problems which necessitated the controversial $2 billion U.S. government loan to the company.) President Johnson's Secretary of the Air Force, Harold Brown, then withheld complete figures from General Accounting Office investigators, to imply falsely that the Air Force analyst had exaggerated $2 billion figure. The cost analyst eventually forced the complete and correct figures into the open. Brown then spiked the cost analyst's career, resulting in lengthy litigation that eventually struck down Brown's actions against the analyst. While running for President, Carter said this affair exemplified the harassment of honest government employees and claimed he would never tolerate such conditions if he were President. Carter then appointed Brown as Defense Secretary.

Carter had long time ties with Lockheed. In 1971 he rode a company airplane to Washington, D.C., where he was met by a Coke limousine. Governor Carter named a Lockheed official to run Georgia's trade office in Brussels. In 1972 Lockheed furnished the airplane Carter used for a three-week tour of Latin America, where he made more international contacts in his quest for the Presidency. Afterward Carter wrote to a Lockheed vice president, "One of the finest experiences of my life was being with you on the trip to Central and South America.... The opportunity to learn more about Lockheed was extremely important to me." Carter went on to say he had been promoting Lockheed's C–130 Hercules airplane among "the State Department, Defense Department, and the Congress, and will continue to do so.... Our government and its agencies should marshal efforts to help all of our friends throughout the world to buy and use this plane .... I want to help in an active way to do so.... Your friend, Jimmy."

In 1974 G. William Miller's (Carter Treasury) Textron corporation unsuccessfully sought to get forty-five percent of Lockheed Aircraft's stock. Bell Helicopter was a subsidiary of Textron. In 1971 Bell sold two copters to Ghana via Bell's Nigerian sales agent Tropical Aircraft Sales, Inc. Although the price was $1,600,000, the Ghanaian government sent Bell $1,900,000. Bell, in turn, then sent $300,000 to Africair, Inc. Africair was heavily involved with the CIA and was the parent corporation of Tropical Aircraft

Sales. This $300,000 went to a Tropical account in a Miami, FL, bank and was later found in the possession Ghanaian military officers.

Lockheed ran Saudi Arabia's air force. Lockheed Missile vice president Stanley Weiss became Deputy Assistant Secretary of Energy, serving under Coke president Duncan (Carter Energy, Deputy Defense). Donald Rumsfeld (Ford Defense) directed Bendix Corporation, which supervised Saudi Arabia's armed forces. Michael Blumenthal (Carter Treasury) was president of Bendix International, driven to and from work by a chauffeur. At his nomination hearings Blumenthal said he would exercise stock options granted to him in 1971 and 1973. Then the stock would go into a blind trust of Morgan Guaranty Trust Company. Blumenthal said he would transfer all his stock holdings to the trust by October 1977. The trust was to be sure that no holdings in Blumenthal's portfolio would be over twenty-five percent of any corporation's stock. Blumenthal stated he believed in "the most broadly based participation in the free enterprise system." He told of a Bendix employee stock ownership plan which qualified employees could join, with Bendix matching some employee contributions fifty-fifty. About seventeen percent of Bendix stock was owned by the plan, making it the corporation's largest stockholder. Blumenthal said his employees thus owned the biggest block of stock. He didn't say whether employees *controlled* that block, or whether management representatives voted the block.

Banks Yet Again

Carter incurred troublesome debt from his 1966 gubernatorial campaign. He tried various alternatives to clear this obligation, and eventually turned to banker Bert Lance (Carter OMB). Lance's complex activities and their relationship to Carter were eventually publicized, but those dealings' complexity—compounded by conflicting stories—left many persons baffled. Telling the full story would require a book of its own, so let us simply touch upon one aspect, involving Saudi Arabia.

In some Arab societies it's customary to approach a leader through his friends or relatives. Gifts can be construed as a legitimate way to gain influence, with nothing untoward about it.

At the end of 1977 Ghaith Pharson agreed to buy National Bank of Georgia stock owned by Bert Lance. Pharson's father was a top adviser to King Khalid. In early January 1978 President Carter traveled to Saudi Arabia where he agreed to support sale of F–15 jet fighters to the royal government. The next day Lance got a $3,500,000 loan ($13,000,000 in 2019 buying power) from the Bank of Credit & Commerce International

(London). The loan had no written terms, not even a written agreement calling for repayment. The day after Lance got this loan, Pharson paid Lance $2,400,000 for the NBG stock. This was about twice the market value of the stock. This purchase gave Saudi Arabia control of the National Bank of Georgia.

At this time, the Carter peanut warehouse was still in debt to NBG. Carter officials announced that sixty F–15s should be sold to the Saudis. Over the next two months negotiations between the Carter warehouse and the Saudis' NBG resulted in an easing of loan repayment terms. The Senate approved sale of the F–15s. The $600,000 Carter debt was transferred from NBG to Trust Co. Bank of Georgia.

Lumber Again

International Paper Company was set up in 1898 to monopolize the U.S. paper business. Ca. 1948 it was the world's largest paper manufacturer. In 1948 International Paper decided to construct a new plant. When the Korean War began, International Paper applied for a tax exemption on sixty-five percent of the plant's cost as a defense expenditure, even though the decision to build it, and the start of construction, predated the Korean War, even predated the Communist takeover of China. The government granted International's request, saving the corporation $12,000,000.

C. Douglas Dillon (JFK Treasury) retained his International Paper stock while a cabinet member. International Paper directors over the years included President Carter's associate Arthur Taylor. Chase Manhattan Bank, run by Carter's associate David Rockefeller (brother of Ford VP), controlled much International Paper stock. Scott Paper Company directors included Thomas Gates (Eisenhower Defense), Robert McNamara (JFK & LBJ Defense), Frederick Dent (Ford Commerce), Patricia Harris (Carter HUD), and William Scranton (Carter Oversight Board).

The National Forest Products Association (a federation of twenty-seven production associations and seven corporations) endorsed the cabinet nomination of Robert Bergland (Carter Agriculture) thereby certifying him as a friend of the industry. Carter picked lumber executive Cecil Andrus as Interior Secretary. Jimmy Carter used Brunswick Pulp & Paper Company's deluxe hunting lodge several times while governor of Georgia. Carter wrote to one Brunswick person, "Perhaps of even more importance was getting to know you … and to learn more about Georgia's most important single industry. You are a fine spokesman for Georgia's forests and their potential."

Coal Again

President Carter and Michael Blumenthal (Carter Treasury) both called for government encouragement of the coal industry. Carter was unwilling to speak out on coal miners' behalf, saying they could find other jobs if dissatisfied with coal industry conditions. Patricia Harris (Carter HUD, HEW, HHS) was director of National Bank of Washington, where she was aware of fraud in the United Mine Workers pension fund there.[108] Clark Clifford (Truman adviser, LBJ Defense) was a director, as was pension fund chairman Tony Boyle who was convicted of murder involving a Mine Workers union dispute. Clifford, incidentally, was Bert Lance's (Carter OMB) lawyer during official investigations of National Bank of Georgia affairs. President Carter appointed National Bank of Washington vice president Emmitt Rice to the Federal Reserve Board.

The Carter Administration Summed Up

During Carter's White House tenure, many commentators characterized his policies as ineffective. Instead of helping workers, minorities, women, and other citizens crucial to his election in 1976, Carter's polices repeatedly increased corporation profits at the expense of those citizens. This was held up as evidence of Carter's "incompetence," and of the "drifting malaise" of his administration. Judging from Carter's ties with big business, however, Carter may have been smarter than partisan commentators thought, helping the elites who brought him to the White House.

Epilogue: A Shadow on the Wall

Monetary self-interest has motivated our leaders throughout our nation's brief history. There's nothing wrong with people having self-interest. How else can they stay alive? Citizens have a right, however, to know intimate details of our leaders' business dealings. How else can we know whether our sacrifices are meant to benefit everyone or cynically intended to enrich a selected few. Such a judgment isn't always clear-cut. Private and public interest can coincide, resonating to mutual benefit. We must keep in mind, however, that beneath our leaders' noble calls for sacrifice we can sometimes find gross motives. We needn't be cynical about our leaders' plans, but we should cultivate a vigorous skepticism. There is nothing unpatriotic about this, quite the contrary. Uninformed trust in our leaders brought tragedies such as Vietnam and Watergate. How different our history might have been if citizens had simply demanded answers to a few questions.

Stripping the noble veneer from our history doesn't cheapen it. Underneath the schoolbook veneer is something solid, sturdy, and good. Viewing American history in terms of economic self-interest can be even more satisfying than traditional views. We see that today's leaders aren't necessarily any baser than leaders of yore. In their own day past leaders muddled through, much as people do today. Only in retrospect do many past leaders seem to possess grand visions of American destiny. In Jimmy Carter's autobiography he wrote how amazed he was to discover that leading Presidential candidates were no smarter than he was. Yet this is the way it has always been. Most of our leaders reached the top not by talent but through family connections, luck, or both. Occasionally we are blessed with leaders such as Washington and Lincoln whose personal charisma made them tower over their countrymen. For the most part, however, a million other Americans could handle the Presidency as well as the incumbent does. It has always been thus. Our history isn't a story of supermen. It is a story of what ordinary men and women can accomplish when given the chance.

In the past, businessmen were excellent choices for government leaders. They had years of training in a cutthroat world organized like competing medieval baronies. Such businessmen had a good feel for national security and foreign relations, able to sense danger where less experienced souls saw hands extended in "friendship." This talent served us well. Even notorious scandals of the past, such as Crédit Mobilier and Teapot Dome, fulfilled great public needs. The transcontinental railroad was built. Cheap oil was delivered. Yes, money was stolen from the public. But in return we received something of value.

As the twentieth century progressed, a big change occurred among the businessmen who run our government. Rarely do the builders of business empires appear in government anymore. Instead we have their children and grandchildren, who aren't necessarily incompetent, but neither are they persons of extraordinary talent. Or we have managers of business empires, not the bold individuals who built them, but the persons who maneuvered to the top of a corporation bureaucracy—people who believe that to get along you have to go along. Ruthless milquetoasts. Such persons brought on the Vietnam disaster, America's first bureaucrat war. The bureaucrats bragged about how they ran the war in the same way they ran their corporations.

These people have changed the direction of capitalism. Capitalism and free enterprise swept across the world because people could use it to make money by solving problems. DuPont, McCormick, Harriman, Ford, and Rockefeller made fortunes by providing chemicals, food, transportation, and energy to entire civilizations. These men knew how to provide a service to solve a problem. Their successors may be competent at providing the same service, but too often they have neither the vision nor the courage to continue solving problems. Indeed corporation executives today are trying to make fortunes by aggravating problems. Suppose today's executives had been running the tollgate at a Rocky Mountain pass in the 1850s. As growing traffic made the pass congested, the executives would have responded by increasing the tolls to reduce traffic volume while increasing profits from the tollgate. The alternative of ramming through a railroad would have been attacked as visionary, impractical, and unprofitable. Too risky, too much capital outlay, insufficient technology to construct a mountain railroad, lack of labor ("From where are we going to get workers, China?"), too many laws and subsidies to push through Congress, too many federal departments and local governments to contend with. Today's corporation executives would have been glad to leave the West Coast a virgin wilderness while the rest of the nation foundered for lack of gold, furs, and timber.

This new capitalist philosophy of making money by retaining problems instead of solving them has the smell of death. Take just one example—maintaining sufficient energy for civilization. The most practical solution is to reduce consumption of energy. People might not have to sacrifice anything important. It may be a question of making devices more efficient, and in some cases new energy efficient technology could ease the transition. Indeed restoration of interurban mass transit might even improve quality of life.

Building a new energy-efficient technology could make fortunes for bold capitalists. Instead, our ruthless milquetoasts have decided the solution is to burn more coal and oil. Disregard the question of what happens as coal and oil supplies are depleted even faster. Just consider that this will increase the amount of carbon dioxide in the atmosphere, and that the increase will melt the polar icecaps in the twenty-first century. People who are alive today may be around as New York, Boston, Washington, San Francisco, Miami, Tokyo, London, and even entire countries begin to disappear beneath the waves. What will be the economic impact as all those urban skyscrapers, factories, apartments, and houses are destroyed? What will be the social impact of millions of hungry, unemployed, angry people fleeing the coasts to wander around the nation's interior? Keep in mind that the ruthless milquetoasts know all this and have decided to make money by deliberately throwing the world into chaos thirty years from now. "Après moi, le deluge."

The test of free enterprise today lies not in military confrontation overseas or in treaties signed and ratified. The test is whether capitalism can face problem as it did in the beginning—as opportunities to make money through solutions. If capitalists choose to make money by improving the condition of humans everywhere and the condition of the planet as a whole, then the appeal of totalitarian philosophies will quickly erode. If instead capitalists of today pursue money as an end in itself, their doom is assured. The choice is theirs, but their fate is ours.

What are the uses to which technology is being put? Automation is sold as a means of increasing efficiency, leisure, and profits. What sort of efficiency are we talking about? Suppose a machine can harvest as many vegetables in one day as fifty humans can. Either way the vegetables get harvested. It's not like there is a labor shortage. The humans may even consume less energy than the machine. Does automation provide leisure? True, a laid off worker has all day to scrounge in garbage cans for food and to hustle pennies for rent. But is that sort of life demonstrably superior to an eight-hour workday which provides enough money for decent food, shelter, family life and peace of mind? Automation is more efficient at generating profits for managers and stockholders, but do these profits generate more jobs or go into luxury goods (such as rare paintings for an inflation hedge)? What is the purpose of an economy? To enrich investors? Or supply society's needs? One such need is gainful employment, which becomes rarer as the economy "prospers." More and more the wealth of a few is based on the impoverishment of many. Our economy makes life more and more hopeless for rising numbers of people, particularly urban residents. This bodes ill indeed. This doesn't have to happen. It's a conscious choice of the businessmen who run our government. This minority has chosen to protect its privileges at the expense of others. Should businessmen object if someday the urban ghettos make the same choice and rise up in their fearsome power again?

The ultimate argument in favor of plutocrats' world order is that global corporations promote peace. This argument is only partly true. It's true that no capitalist nation has gone to war against another since corporations became global after World War II. But wars with socialist, neutral, and Islamic nations have been substituted. Tensions grow. Do we feel any safer today than in 1939? And what will happen if someday global corporations decide to attack one another? Will such economic warfare avoid military action? And what of the planned destruction of our environment—our air, water, food supplies, and seacoasts? Won't this kill millions of persons? What profit is a peace that costs our lives?

Democracy is the answer. Why else would plutocrats fear it so? The most implacable enemies of democracy aren't halfway around the world, but halfway across town, sitting in corporation offices. These are the persons who try to make Americans believe that elections are like athletic events; what counts is how many points someone is ahead. Elections, however, are merely rituals of democracy. Like all rituals they can be emptied of meaning and performed by persons who have no concept of the underlying purpose. The essence of democracy comes down to two things.

First, the feelings of all persons are of equal importance. Yes, some individuals are wiser and more talented than others. But their happiness is no more important than the happiness desired by the rest of us. Therefore the only equitable way to decide a course of action is by majority vote. This method may not result in the best course of action, but it will choose the course that a community desires. Freedom includes the right to be wrong.

The other essence of democracy is vigorous public debate about issues. This is something businessmen and politicians fear, as an informed citizenry will generally choose actions that benefit the majority of people—and rich persons are an ever-dwindling minority. The point of elections isn't to choose officeholders per se but to decide the nation's goals and the paths by which those goals are to be reached. More and more of these decisions pass from citizens' hands as they watch thirty-second television commercials extolling candidates' patriotism and family life.

The essence of democracy is evaporating in America. Big changes will be needed to democratize our nation. We are perfectly capable of making such changes peacefully and with goodwill.

Our nation's history is brief. President George Washington and President John Tyler were contemporaries. Tyler's grandson was alive as the twenty-first century began. People around President Benjamin Harrison's uncle had contacts in the cabinets of George Washington and Lyndon Johnson. Is the United States a three-generation aberration of history? Or are we a seed that has taken root, and which will spread offspring around the world? We cannot know yet. The times are perilous, the challenges awesome. Thus has it always been. Past times seem less fearsome in retrospect only because we look back with the knowledge that we survived. Americans of the 1780s were every bit as uncertain and nervous as we are. They survived, and so can we. Survival isn't inevitable, but is possible if we make it our goal. We can do more than survive. We can prosper and build a paradise on Earth. We have the knowledge and capability. All we need is the will.

"Ultimately, it is this affirmation: what we are now is less than the shadow on the wall of what we can be if we trust ourselves."—Bruce Catton, *The War Lords of Washington*

Notes

Spelling and grammar of quotations may be modernized.

1. *Congressional Quarterly* (1976), p. 3325.
2. Ambler, 137–140.
3. Ambler, 148–149.
4. Goebel, 237.
5. Quoted in Randall, 2:13.
6. Cole, 202.
7. Myers, *Court*, 26 n.
8. Myers, *Court*, 257.
9. Quoted in Meigs, 1:194.
10. Quoted in Van Deusen, *Clay*, 156.
11. Quoted in James, 657–58.
12. Quoted in Fowler 19–29.
13. Quoted in Green, 426.
14. Goebel, 376; Seager, 145.
15. Quoted in Meigs 2:79–80.
16. Nevins, *Ordeal* 1:202.
17. Myers, *Court*, 442.
18. Quoted in Lewis 95, 97.
19. Quoted in Merrill, *Sherman*, 87.
20. Quoted in Merrill, *Sherman*, 93.
21. Quoted in Merrill, *Sherman*, 93-94.
22. Quoted in Merrill, *Sherman*, 106, 111.
23. Quoted in Merrill, *Sherman*, 118.
24. Quoted in Merrill, *Sherman*, 110 .
25. Nye quoting Myers *History of the Supreme Court* in *Congressional Record*, Feb. 13, 1930, p. 3555.
26. Quoted in Brigance, 131.
27. Cain, 300.
28. Quoted in Mackenzie, 295.
29. Quoted in Meigs, 1:87–88.
30. Anne Royall, quoted in Inskeep, 94.
31. U.S. v. Gooding, 12 Wheaton, 460–468.
32. Quoted in Merrill, *Sherman*, 135.
33. Quoted in Merrill, Sherman, 106.
34. Quoted in Merrill, *Sherman*, 142.
35. Quoted in Kaplan, 319.
36. Quoted in Morris, 454
37. Quoted in Beldon and Beldon, 37.
38. Richardson, *Chandler*, 69.
39. Quoted in Nevins, *Ordeal*, 8:151.
40. Quoted in Richardson and Farley, 55–56.
41. Brigance, 216.
42. Quoted in Russell, *Blaine*, 296–97.
43. Quoted in Muzzey, 235.
44. Quoted in Pratt, 94.
45. Quoted in Frank, 14.
46. Quoted in Hesseltine, 176–77.
47. Nevins, *Fish*, 662–64.
48. Nevins, *Fish*, 807.
49. Quoted in Wilson 338, 353–54.
50. Nevins, *Fish*, 503–505.
51. Quoted in Myers, *Court*, 539–40.
52. Myers, *Court*, 612–13.
53. Goff, 181.
54. Quoted in Perling, 145.
55. Nevins, *Cleveland*, 622.
56. Goff, 242–43.
57. Hirsch 547–49.
58. *Dictionary of American Biography*, McReynolds entry.
59. Eggert, 27.
60. Quoted in Eggert, 50.
61. Quoted in Eggert, 50.
62. Merrill, *Vilas*, 27–29.
63. Quoted in Sievers, 3:269.

64. North American Commercial Co. v. United States, 171 U.S. 110 (1898).
65. Quoted in Lambert, 31.
66. Quoted in Eggert, 53.
67. Quoted in Burner, 30.
68. Quoted in Clymer, 59, 229 n.68.
69. Baltzell, 364.
70. Baltzell, 365.
71. Quoted in Martin, *Choate*, 2:20–21.
72. Baltzell, 10.
73. Quoted in Balltzell, 149.
74. Quoted in Jessup 1:136.
75. Quoted in Houston 2:180–81.
76. Quoted in O'Connor, 123.
77. Quoted in Roll, 260.
78. Quoted in Pringle, 1:202–203.
79. Zimmerman, 471.
80. Lundberg, 125–26.
81. Quoted in Coletta, 2:263–65.
82. Quoted in Burner, 131.
83. Quoted in Russell, *Shadow*, 321.
84. Russell, *Shadow*, 91.
85. Jessup 1:441.
86. O'Connor, 162.
87. O'Connor, 209–210.
88. Rochester,70; O'Connor, 225.
89. O'Connor, 26–29.
90. Quoted in Fuess, 192–93.
91. Babson, 48.
92. Quoted in Davis, *FDR*, 704–705.
93. Quoted in Timmons, *Jones*, 335–37.
94. Quoted in Babson, 38 n.–41 n.
95. Daniels, 81–82.
96. Truman, 153–156.
97. Daniels, 137.
98. U.S. Senate Finance Committee, 83 Cong., 1 Sess., pp. 12–13, Humphrey nomination.
99. U.S. Senate Armed Services Committee, 83 Cong., 1 Sess., p. 11 of second hearing on Wilson nomination.
100. U.S. Senate Armed Services Committee, 83 Cong., 1 Sess., pp. 8–9, first Wilson nomination hearings.
101. Quoted in Watzman, 60–61.
102. Pearson and Anderson, 312.
103. U.S. Senate Armed Services Committee, 87 Cong. 2 Sess., p. 64, McCone CIA nomination, quoting U.S. House Committee on Merchant Marine and Fisheries, 79 Cong., 2 Sess.
104. Macdonald, 104–105.
105. Quoted in Macdonald 111.
106. Steinberg 21, 63, 84ff, 200, 209, 577.
107. Schofield, 489–90.
108. Peters, 15.

Works Cited

Where a note citation contains sufficient data to identify the source (such as a law case) such data are not repeated in the following list.

Ambler, Charles H. *George Washington and the West.* Chapel Hill: University of North Carolina Press, 1936.

Babson, Roger W. *Washington and the Revolutionists.* Freeport, NY: Books for Libraries Press, 1970. Originally 1934.

Baltzell, Edward Digby. *The Protestant Establishment.* New York: Vintage Books, 1964.

Beldon, Thomas Graham, and Marva Robins Beldon. *So Fell the Angels.* Boston: Little, Brown & Co., 1956.

Brigance, William Norwood. *Jeremiah Sulllivan Black.* Philadelphia: University of Pennsylvania Press, 1934.

Burner, David. *Herbert Hoover: A Public Life.* New York: Alfred A. Knopf, 1979.

Cain, Marvin R. *Lincoln's Attorney General: Edward Bates of Missouri.* Columbia: University of Missouri Press, 1965.

Clymer, Kenton J. *John Hay.* Ann Arbor: University of Michigan Press, 1975.

Cole, Arthur Harrison. *Industrial and Commercial Correspondence of Alexander Hamilton.* Chicago: A.W. Shaw Co., 1928.

Coletta, Paolo E. *William Jennings Bryan.* Lincoln: University of Nebraska Press, 1965–1969.

Congressional Quarterly.

Congressional Record

Daniels, Jonathan. *The Man of Independence.* Philadelphia: Lippincott, 1950.

Dictionary of American Biography.

Eggert, Gerald G. *Richard Olney.* University Park: Pennsylvania State University Press, 1974.

Fowler, Dorothy Garfield. *The Cabinet Politician: The Postmasters General 1829–1909.* New York: Columbia University Press, 1943.

Frank, John P. *Lincoln As a Lawyer.* Urbana: University of Illinois Press, 1961.

Fuess, Claude M. *Calvin Coolidge.* Boston: Little, Brown & Co., 1940.

Goebel, Dorothy Burne. *William Henry Harrison.* Indianapolis: Historical Bureau of the Indiana Library and Historical Department, 1926.

Goff, John S. *Robert Todd Lincoln.* Norman: University of Oklahoma Press, 1969.

Green, James A. *William Henry Harrison.* Richmond, VA: Garrett & Massie, Inc., 1941.

Hesseltine, William B. *U.S. Grant: Politician.* New York: Dodd, Mead & Co., 1935.

Hirsch, Mark D. *William C. Whitney.* New York: Dodd, Mead & Co., 1948.

Houston, David F. *Eight Years with Wilson's Cabinet.* Garden City, NY: Doubleday, Page & Co., 1926.

Inskeep, Steve. *Jacksonland: President Andrew Jackson, Cherokee Chief John Ross, and a Great American Land Grab.* New York: Penguin Press, 2015.

James, Marquis. *The Life of Andrew Jackson.* New York: Bobbs-Merrill Co., 1938. Consisting of *Andrew Jackson: Border Captain* and *Andrew Jackson: Portrait of a President.*

Jessup, Philip C. *Elihu Root.* New York: Dodd, Mead & Co., 1938.

Kaplan, Justin. *Mr. Clemens and Mark Twain.* New York: Pocket Books, 1968.

Lambert, Oscar Doane. *Stephen B. Elkins.* Pittsburgh: University of Pittsburgh, 1955.

Lewis, Lloyd. *Sherman.* New York: Harcourt, Brace & Co., 1958.

Lundberg, Ferdinand. *America's Sixty Families.* New York: Vanguard Press, 1937.

Macdonald, Dwight. *The Ford Foundation.* New York: Reynal & Co., 1956.

Mackenzie, William L. *The Life and Times of Martin Van Buren.* Boston: Cooke & Co., 1846.

Martin, Edward Sanford. *The Life of Joseph H. Choate.* New York: Charles Scribner's Sons, 1920.

Meigs, William M. *The Life of John Caldwell Calhoun.* New York: The Neale Publishing Co., 1917.

Merrill, Horace. *William F. Vilas.* Madison: State Historical Society, 1954.

Merrill, James. *William T. Sherman.* Chicago: Rand McNally & Co., 1971.

Morris, Edmund. *The Rise of Theodore Roosevelt.* New York: Random House, 2001.

Muzzey, David S. *James G. Blaine.* New York: Dodd, Mead & Co., 1934.

Myers, Gustavus, *History of the Supreme Court of the United States.* Chicago: Charles H. Kerr & Co., 1912.

Nevins, Allan. *Grover Cleveland.* New York: Dodd, Mead & Co., 1933.

Nevins, Allan. *Hamilton Fish.* New York: Dodd, Mead & Co., 1937.

Nevins, Allan. *Ordeal of the Union.* New York: Charles Scribner's Sons, 1947–1971.

O'Conner, Harvey. *Mellon's Millions.* New York: John Day Co., 1933.

Pearson, Drew, and Anderson Jack. *The Case Against Congress.* New York: Pocket Books, 1969.

Perling, J.J. *President's Sons.* New York: The Odyssey Press, 1947.

Peters, Charles. "Why Jimmy Carter Doesn't Hire Jimmy Carters." *Washington Monthly,* Feb. 1977.

Pratt, Harry E. *The Personal Finances of Abraham Lincoln.* Springfield, IL: The Abraham Lincoln Association, 1943.

Pringle, Henry F. *Life and Times of William Howard Taft.* New York: Farrar & Rinehart, Inc., 1939.

Randall, Henry S. *The Life of Thomas Jefferson.* New York: Derby & Jackson, 1858.

Richardson, Elmo R., and Farley, Alan W. *John Palmer Usher.* Lawrence: University of Kansas Press, 1960.

Richardson, Leon Burr. *William E. Chandler.* New York: Dodd, Mead & Co., 1940.

Rochester, Anna. *Rulers of America.* New York: International Publishers, 1936.

Roll, Charles. *Colonel Dick Thompson.* Indianapolis: Indiana Historical Bureau, 1948.

Russell, Charles Edward. *Blaine of Maine.* New York: Cosmopolitan Book Corp., 1931.

Russell, Francis. The *Shadow of Blooming Grove.* New York: McGraw-Hill Book Co., 1968.

Schofield, John M. *46 Years in the Army.* New York: The Century Co., 1897.

Seager, Robert, II. *And Tyler Too.* New York: McGraw-Hill Book Co., Inc., 1963.

Sievers, Harry J. *Benjamin Harrison.* Chicago: H. Regnery Co., 1952–1968.

Steinberg, Alfred. *Sam Johnson's Boy.* New York: Macmillan Co., 1968.

Truman, Harry S. *Year of Decisions.* New York: Signet Books, 1965. Originally published 1955.

Van Deusen, Glyndon G. *The Life of Henry Clay.* Boston: Little, Brown & Co., 1957.

Watzman, Sanford. *Conflict of Interest*. Chicago: Cowles Book Co., Inc., 1971.
Wilson, James Harrison. *The Life of John A. Rawlins*. New York: Neale Publishing Co., 1916.
Zimmerman, Warren. *First Great Triumph: How Five Americans Made Their Country a World Power*. New York: Farrar, Straus and Giroux, 2002.

Index

www.ingramcontent.com/pod-product-compliance
Lightning Source LLC
Chambersburg PA
CBHW031125270326
41929CB00011B/1494

* 9 7 8 1 4 7 6 6 8 4 0 8 6 *